D1293988

American
Pluralism
and the
Catholic
Conscience

American
Pluralism
and the
Catholic
Conscience

by Richard J. Regan, S.J.

WITH A FOREWORD BY

John Courtney Murray, S.J.

THE MACMILLAN COMPANY, NEW YORK
COLLIER-MACMILLAN LIMITED, LONDON

IMPRIMI POTEST

Very Rev. John J. McGinty, S.J.

Praep. Prov. Neo Eboracensis
July 5, 1962

NIHIL OBSTAT

Edward A. Cerny, S.S., S.T.D.

Censor Librorum

IMPRIMATUR

✠ Lawrence J. Shehan, D.D.

Archbishop of Baltimore
July 17, 1962

The *nihil obstat* and *imprimatur* are official declarations that a book or pamphlet is free of doctrinal and moral error. No implication is contained therein that those who have granted the *nihil obstat* and *imprimatur* agree with the opinions expressed.

THE MACMILLAN COMPANY, NEW YORK

COLLIER-MACMILLAN CANADA LTD., TORONTO, ONTARIO

DIVISIONS OF THE CROWELL-COLLIER PUBLISHING COMPANY

PRINTED IN THE UNITED STATES OF AMERICA

LIBRARY OF CONGRESS CATALOG CARD NUMBER: 63-13182

Designed by Andrew Zutis

To My Parents

FROM WHOM I FIRST LEARNED TO LOVE
GOD AND COUNTRY

Preface

No author can adequately express his thanks to all to whom he is indebted. The best he can hope to do is to note appreciatively the most prominent of his creditors. I should like first to acknowledge the inspiration which I derived from Fr. John Courtney Murray and Fr. Francis P. Canavan, both of the Society of Jesus. The writings of the former and my conversations with the latter were invaluable. I do not, of course, wish to shift to them the burden of responsibility for the defects of my work, but I do wish to accredit their vital contribution to any merits which the reader may find in the contents of these pages. My debt to Fr. Murray, moreover, is doubled by his favor of contributing a foreword to this book, and I am most grateful to him for his contribution. For their generous help with the manuscript I should also like to thank my fellow Jesuits: Edward W. Brande, Schuyler Brown, Robert E. Carter, Robert S. Curry, Martin J. Foley, John G. Marzolf, and Herbert G. Ryan. Lastly, I wish to express my appreciation to Mrs. Mary B. Rowe for translating my rough copy into a typed manuscript. To these and to all the others who helped so much I sincerely acknowledge my debt. Special appreciation is also extended to the publishers of *The Catholic World* and *The Catholic Lawyer* for their gracious permission to adapt materials on the Sunday laws and the Connecticut birth control ban which first appeared in their pages.

Richard J. Regan, S.J.

Woodstock, Md.
March 7, 1962

Contents

IO.

II.

Foreword

The ensemble of issues that gather round the American constitutional provisions for the free exercise of religion and for separation of church and state do not constitute the most urgent political and legal issues that confront the American people today. Nonetheless these issues have a peculiar interest and significance.

In the first place, they do not arise by accident of historical circumstance. They are endemic in American society in consequence of its religiously pluralistic character, as related to our traditional aspiration for a maximum of social freedom under a system of limited government. Therefore in regard of these issues, which are destined constantly to emerge, we find ourselves in a course of continual constitutional experiment whose end is not, and likely never will be, in sight.

Moreover, these issues arise in an area in which, naturally enough, we have found it most difficult to create and maintain that social consensus—or public philosophy, if you will—which must somehow furnish the footing for reasonable and commonly acceptable public decisions, whether formally legislative and judicial or informally social. All decisions in this area are reached through widespread public controversy; and each decision is normally the starting point of new controversy.

Furthermore, these issues arise because the sensitive nerve of the religious or moral consciousness has been touched. Ordinarily they do not so much arise as explode. They tend to be felt as issues of truth and error, right and wrong—basic issues in which all men feel emotionally engaged, each in his own sense. Therefore when a conflict of positions occurs, it is accompanied by a collision of passions. And this clash is not seldom intensified by incremental considerations of social power and prestige.

In such circumstances it is often not easy even to discern just what the real issue in the particular case is; and it is never easy to resolve the issue, once it is discerned.

Again, as controversy over these issues tests the temper of our citizenry and its capacity for rational argument, so it also puts our democratic polity itself on trial to see whether it can, in accordance with its own nature, do justice, and therefore guarantee freedom, and in further consequence fulfill its highest duty, which is to the public peace.

Here, I think, the major value of the present book begins to appear. With great sureness of insight the author brings into focus, and keeps in focus, the central principle in the whole matter—what he calls the "political nature of the religious settlement embodied in the First Amendment" (page 278). I shall let him state his own understanding of this complex principle and also make his own case for its centrality. It may be sufficient for me to register my own view that, if the understanding were impressed on the public consciousness, and if the case for its centrality were made integral to the public philosophy, the paramount cause of the public peace would be considerably advanced, and its twin supporting pillars—justice and freedom—would be established with new solidity.

A glance at the Table of Contents will reveal that the author has covered the controversial waterfront with all completeness. A study of the book itself will then reveal that the coverage has been critical, based on careful research, done by a mind that understands both the sacred character of basic commitments in matters of religion and morals and also the uses of pragmatism in matter of politics and law.

The purpose of the book is argument. Writing as a Catholic, the author has his presuppositions, as all authors on the subject do. But the argument itself is evenhanded. There are, I suspect, Catholics who will find it so evenhanded that it may seem to them to be improperly weighted. In any case, no *ex parte* case is here presented. The reader whose acquaintance with the subject is slight will find here the data and the reasoning that will assist him in the formation of a view. The tutored reader, and even the expert reader, whose views are formed, may well discover from these pages (as I did) that his views need revision or refinement here and there. The author's wide field of inquiry has already been covered in a vast literature. This fact makes it the more remarkable that in every corner of the field he has made his own personal contribution. The book will be useful to every citizen who takes seriously his prime duty as a citizen, which is to understand, and therefore to be able intelligently to enter the public argument about, a set of issues that vitally concern the public peace.

JOHN COURTNEY MURRAY, S.J.

1

Introduction

When Senator John Kennedy of Massachusetts inaugurated his successful drive for the 1960 presidential nomination and election, he provided a singular demonstration of certain vast changes consummated in the past half-century in the structure of American society. Sixty years ago the image of America was white, Anglo-Saxon, and Protestant. Today the image is neither so white nor so Anglo-Saxon nor so Protestant. Sixty years ago the Catholic, who belonged for the most part to the servant and laboring classes, was not invited to participate in the world of civic or managerial responsibility. Today few areas of leadership remain closed to Catholics. To these changes the success of the Kennedy candidacy attested.

Perhaps the most important factor in the transformation is

1

simply statistical: the numerical increase of Catholics in the United States. A group of Americans which numbers some fifty million active and inactive members may be an object of suspicion, but it cannot be ignored. The presence of so many American Catholics not only has promoted the acceptance of American Catholics but also has stimulated the desire of Protestants to know more about what the Catholic believes.

Other factors which are qualitative rather than quantitative have also operated for the progressive assimilation of American Catholics. Linguistic and cultural differences which had helped to attach to American Catholics the immigrant label have softened. And the relative mobility of American society has enabled Catholics of ability to advance economically and socially. But significantly, even the specifically Catholic in American Catholic life has attracted the attention and admiration of devout Protestants. As contact between Catholics and Protestants led to knowledge, the Protestant discovered and respected the inner spiritual vitality of American Catholic life. At the same time the Protestant noted and approved the Church's fight for social reform, early recognition of the danger of communism, and vigorous combat against the rising tide of secularism. The spiritual crises of the twentieth century have served to unite Protestants and Catholics in rediscovering the community of belief and activity which they had forgotten for so long.

While Catholics were winning greater acceptance in American life, Protestant creed, code, and culture were being subjected to the fashionable attacks of the intellectuals and writers of the twenties. The seamless garb of Protestant respectability was rent, and Protestantism was no longer inviolable. Besides the loss of inviolability Protestantism at the same time experienced the throes of internal crisis. Changes in economic and social structures threatened the life of the loosely organized Protestant churches. Although rural populations moved cityward, urban congregations shrank. Nor did the fundamentalist Protestant find it easy to cope with or adjust to the scientific and philosophical currents of the twentieth century.

As the Catholic was progressively assimilated into the mainstream of American life and the Protestant shed his complacent feeling of superiority, many of the old tensions were dissipated.

A lively and sincere interest in things Catholic has replaced the earlier blanket hostility. But if many of the old tensions have eased, some with new ramifications have remained or have even increased with the waxing of Catholic influence in American life. Prominent among the latter-day problems are the relations between the theology of the Catholic Church and the political basis of the American state. Is the dogmatic intolerance of the Catholic Church compatible with the civil tolerance of the American state? What are the implications of a dogmatically intolerant Church claiming divine authority for a civilly tolerant state proclaiming theological neutrality? From this central problem many specific conflicts of importance derive: controversies on education, on birth control, on censorship, to mention a few.

That the question of Church and state is a source of tension between Catholics and Protestants scarcely needs to be demonstrated. The reaction in some Protestant quarters to the candidacy of John F. Kennedy and the scrutiny to which he found himself subjected on the question amply evidenced the existence and extent of this tension.[1] And the tension is not merely between Catholics and Protestants, for the unchurched and the unbeliever feel an equal or even greater uneasiness over the impact of the Catholic Church on American political life. In fact, for some years there has existed a strange wedding of Protestant and secular extremists in a joint fear of the "political activity" of the "authoritarian" Church of Rome.[2] The former harbor a selected image of the Church culled from the mutual ill will of previous centuries, while the latter suspect any claim to authority over the consciences of citizens by a power external to the state. Others besides the extremists, however, perceive the existence of the tension and of the problem which underlies it.[3] Men of sincerity and sympathy, both Catholic and non-Catholic, are anxious to resolve the problem and ease the tension.

The concrete issue of a Catholic president has already been solved on the practical level, as most political issues ultimately are, *ambulando*. The election of John F. Kennedy to the presidency has not resulted in any encroachment on the religious liberty of non-Catholics. Even on the speculative level the issue of a Catholic president was more a symbol of group identification and social status than a real concern of political theory. As *Amer-*

ica observed in the spring of 1960 and as candidate Kennedy himself emphasized to the Houston ministers in September of that year, the president of the United States takes an oath to uphold the Constitution.[4] In the imaginable but highly unlikely case in which the dictates of a president's conscience—whether formed by him autonomously or under the aegis of an external authority, on his own initiative or in response to the voice of the religious teacher—clashed irreconcilably with his constitutional duties, the president would be obliged to resign his office rather than violate either trust to the public or his integrity of conscience. Above all, faced with such a dilemma, he could not justify, morally or legally, the violation of his sworn oath. To challenge the propriety of a Catholic president is, in effect, to challenge the sincerity with which Catholics as a group treat sworn oaths and to attribute to Catholics as a group the stigma of moral dishonesty. This attribution Catholics rightly regard as a group libel.

But however easily the specific issue of a Catholic president has been eliminated, the over-all problem of the relation of the theology of the Catholic Church to the political basis of the American state cannot be solved so easily. The Constitution, if it is not written in the hearts of citizens, will become an insignificant piece of paper. If the theology of the Catholic Church were truly incompatible with the political processes of the American state, then the Constitution as we know it could not long survive the political ascendancy of a militantly Catholic majority. A strong majority has the power to change the Constitution in various ways, and a Catholic majority could thus put an end to religious liberty in this country. Where the issue of a Catholic president in the context of a non-Catholic majority was symbolic and spurious, Catholic teaching on the relation of the state to the Church, when coupled with the political power possessed by a secure majority, may represent a serious problem for both the Catholic and the non-Catholic, for both the citizen and the political analyst. Of course, such a majority is not at all a real prospect for the present or the foreseeable future, but still the problem is a speculatively genuine source of deep concern to the non-Catholic.

With this general problem of the Catholic Church and American democracy, candidate Kennedy was far from successful at formulating a satisfactory explanation. Of course, he was a candidate for office, not a professional political theorist or theologian. But his expressions at Houston and elsewhere during the campaign did indicate an inadequate understanding of the social dynamism of Christian belief. During the campaign Kennedy consistently maintained that his religious views were "his own private affair," that where he went to church on Sunday made no difference, and that the Church could not tell him how to conduct his office.[5] Here the candidate stretched a good point too far. From the days of the Old Testament prophets even to our day it has always been the role of the Church to preach the imperatives of public as well as private, social as well as individual morality. Precisely at the point where the Church's moral teaching forms the conscience of the individual on matters of social or public concern the Catholic's religious views are no longer merely "his own private affair." An individual Catholic may ignore the Church's teaching on a specific social or public question (segregation, for example), but to do so is to separate himself from the authoritative source of truth, the living Church of Christ. The faithful Catholic, then, is equally responsive to the instruction of the Church on the moral demands of social and public action as to its instruction on the demands of individual and private action. The problem of the Catholic Church and American democracy is not to be resolved by relegating the role of religious influence to matters of private morality. The Church must speak on the moral imperatives of public concerns as well; the Catholic must listen to that voice.

The general problem of the Catholic Church and American democracy exists on two levels: the speculative and the practical. On the speculative level, the question is whether the teaching of the Catholic Church is incompatible with the democratic theory of the American state. Does the dogmatic intolerance of the Church imply the necessity of political intolerance? The answer to this question, as the present work intends to indicate, is in the negative. But the problem of the Church and the American state exists on another level, a practical level, where the question is whether individuals within the Church can abuse their right, responsibility, and duty to instruct the faithful in moral matters by intruding themselves without cause into political decisions and processes. It should be obvious that no Catholic can give any guarantee against the imprudence of fallible individuals. But neither can any non-Catholic, for that matter, guarantee that non-Catholic spokesmen will refrain from intervention without justification into political processes. The finesse and éclat of the Catholic bishops' maneuvers in the politics of Puerto Rico were matched by the undisguised political activity of Dr. Norman Vincent Peale and his associates. Yet the over-all record of both Catholic and non-Catholic spokesmen for non-interference in political affairs is a remarkably happy one. Catholics can give no guarantee against, and have no monopoly in, the vagaries of human folly. We must consign the practical level of the Church-state problem to the control and intelligence of an alert public.

Non-Catholic commentators often insist that the distinctive feature of Catholic belief which makes the Church, unlike other churches, incompatible with democratic processes is the power of the hierarchy not merely to instruct the faithful but specifically to bind their consciences. Now, unquestionably the power of the hierarchy in the exercise of their pastoral office to bind the conscience of the faithful does multiply the potential dimensions of any conflict between the Church and the state. But the locus of ecclesial power should not be mistaken for the causative source of Church-state conflicts.

The responsiveness of the faithful Catholic to his religious teachers is incompatible not with the theory of democratic government but only with the theory of state absolutism. Unless we accept the premise that man's supreme allegiance is to the state—which is political absolutism—then it necessarily follows that the free response of the human conscience to the moral imperatives of man's nature and God's will, as communicated by the Church's teachers, is not an evil to be tolerated but rather an act of virtue to be praised. That the bishops instruct the Catholic conscience does not alter the fundamental fact that it is the integrity of conscience which the Catholic places beyond the authority of the state. This is nothing unique among the churches but is what all men of principle, especially men of religious principle, have preached and practiced throughout the history of Western civilization.

There can be no sound objection within the tradition of reason and faith to the responsiveness of the human conscience to the instruction of the religious teacher. The non-Catholic may legitimately ask, however, what moral imperatives the Catholic conscience responds to and what moral instruction the Catholic religious teachers impart to their flock. If political issues often have moral imperatives, so too do moral imperatives often have political implications. On the speculative level, therefore, the basic question concerning the Church and the state which is the proper concern of non-Catholic citizens and the interest of political analysts is the status and impact of Catholic beliefs on American political institutions.

It may surprise, if not scandalize, the non-Catholic to discover the lack of unanimity in the responses of Catholic theologians to this problem. For a Church claiming divine authority her human spokesmen do not show the concordance which the non-Catholic might expect. On the one side, from the Catholic University of America and the pages of the *American Ecclesiastical Review* have sounded the voices of Fr. Francis J. Connell, Msgr. Joseph C. Fenton, and Msgr. George W. Shea.[6] On the other side, from Woodstock College and the pages of *Theological Studies*, Fr. John Courtney Murray has stirred old water with new spirit.[7] To all of these theologians we shall listen with respect and discrimination, but we must confess in particular our debt to the work of Fr. Murray as a source of inspiration for the present analysis.

At the outset it is necessary to reject an unhappy formula of expression which some non-Catholic commentators, including the Right Reverend James A. Pike, Protestant Episcopal Bishop of California, have recently employed to describe the two streams of Catholic theological thought on the problem of the Church and the state.[8] Bishop Pike has described as "official" the view that the state is obliged under "ideal" conditions to prefer the Catholic religion by public law, and as the "American interpretation" the view that religious freedom and equality are under appropriate circumstances a first-best accommodation of the Church and the state.

It may be admitted that the former view is held by many officials of the Church—for instance, Cardinal Ottaviani—as their private theological opinion, without constituting the view as "official."[9] The term "official" inevitably suggests that the view so described is the authoritative teaching of the universal Church and that the "American interpretation" is somehow in opposition to that teaching. Such a dichotomy does a disservice to those Catholic theologians who hold what Bishop Pike calls the "American interpretation." For if the former view is "official" in the sense of authoritative, then it is the duty of Catholics to give reverential assent to the living voice of the Church. Yet it is precisely the contention of the theologians of the "American interpretation" that the opposite theological view is not "official" at all. Moreover, the thesis that political tolerance under appropriate conditions is a first-best accommodation of the Church and the state is not restricted to American theologians but is a view developed and endorsed by many prominent European theologians.[10] Catholic theological opinion in Europe, as in the United States, is divided on the Church-state question.

In addition to the Catholic attempts to deal with the question, several non-Catholics have approached the problem and proposed solutions. Professor Robert Cross contends that the Catholic Church in America emerged "liberal" into the twentieth century.[11] Professor Cross, however, chose to avoid "recurrence to deductive logic" or, in other words, an analytic approach.[12] Thus he did not ask and he did not answer whether the "liberal" emergence of the Chuch in America was simply the happy product of practical necessity and historical uniqueness. Professor Currin Shields has attempted the frontal approach which Cross avoided, but with something less than complete adequacy or success. Shields indeed demonstrated that the Catholic Church is compatible with democracy as pure process.[13] But his interpretation of democracy as pure process should nurture as much apprehension concerning democracy as non-Catholics may already feel concerning Catholicism. Far more adequate and successful have been the efforts of those non-Catholic commentators who made an investigation of the analysis of Catholic theologians.[14]

How, then, do we intend to approach the problem? We might have chosen to accentuate the historical perspective of the ideological confrontation, but we prefer to initiate the discussion directly in terms of the theological and political problematics. We prefer to reserve to the historians, as far as possible, the thorough consideration of church-state controversies of the past, whether in Europe or in this country. We cannot and shall not, of course, ignore history, especially American history, but our interest in the historical perspective will always be subservient to the purposes of analysis. It is true that the analytic viewpoint exposes us to the risk of empty conceptualization, but this approach can give what a purely historical reconstruction may obscure: the principles of theology and politics requisite to approach a satisfactory solution to the modern American problematic. To be genuinely theological, moreover, the analysis must proceed not as an autonomous operation of pure reason but in full resonance with the teaching authority of the living Church.

The analysis required is both theological and political. It must be theological in order to explicate the moral principles which the Catholic believes are relevant to the American political order, to unravel the implications of the Church's teaching for the American political structure. But as theological analysis is pertinent to an investigation of the Church's impact on American institutions, so, too, political analysis is pertinent to an inquiry into the impact of American democracy on the Church. Just as the non-Catholic questions whether the Church's teaching is compatible with political tolerance, so, too, the Catholic is concerned whether the dynamics of the American accommodation of church and state is compatible with the beliefs and rights of Catholic citizens. The Catholic counters the question of the non-Catholic with one of his own: Does the American formula of "separation of church and state" constitute a politically based "article of peace," or does it incorporate an "article of faith" theologically based on the Protestant or secularist creed? The problem of the Church and the state, it must not be forgotten, is a problem not only for non-Catholic Americans but also for American Catholics. The non-Catholic quite often forgets the Catholic counterpart of his own concern.

It is not difficult to see how necessary is a consideration of particular issues in order to resolve both the apprehensions of non-Catholics concerning the compatibility of the Church's teaching with American political tolerance and those of Catholics concerning the compatibility of the American accommodation of church and state with the beliefs and rights of Catholic citizens. Merely to state general principles without reference to the concrete focal points of tension would be to risk the deception of an illusory harmony. Principles of the political order are designed as norms not of contemplation but of action. Their essence is not their speculative reasonability but their practical wisdom, which is tested by particular applications. Principles are indeed indispensable to the solution of political problems, but it is application that demonstrates their wisdom.

Both non-Catholics and Catholics are concerned more with specific issues than with the general church-state problem, and their concern will not be assuaged without a consideration of the former. What should Catholic and other parents fairly expect of the state with respect to the financial support of church-related schools? What should Catholic and other parents fairly expect of the state with respect to religious instruction in the public schools? What should Catholic and other parents fairly expect of the state with respect to legal enforcement of the Sunday rest? What should Catholics and other citizens fairly expect of the state with respect to the prohibition or promotion of birth control? What should Catholics and other citizens fairly expect of the state with respect to the censorship of socially harmful material?

Fr. Murray, be it observed, has already offered a brilliant analysis of the theology of the Church's confrontation with American democracy. Many Catholic commentators, be it further observed, have already brought historical, political, and constitutional insight to bear on the general theory and on most of the particular problem areas of the American polity's confrontation with religious activity. (Only in the area of a common program of religious instruction in the public schools have Catholic commentators, in our opinion, been woefully deficient in realistic political analysis and in a genuine spirit of sympathy toward the interests of non-Christians, especially of nonbelievers.)

What, then, does the author propose to contribute specifically to the discussion of the Church and the state in America? First of all, probably every commentator is vain enough to think that the content and expression of his critique constitute some advance over preceding attempts. Specifically, the aim of this work is to provide an integral synthesis of theology and politics. There is no lack of theological analysis of the Church's relation to the democratic state nor of political analysis of America's relation to religion. But there does exist a need for a Catholic effort to synthesize the theological and the political into a comprehensive and harmonious whole. Theologians have commented on the theology, historians on the history, lawyers on the law, and political scientists on the politics of the Church and the state. This singleness of purpose is quite proper and even necessary for the limited objectives of specific analyses, but by the same token it is inadequate for the fuller objective of an integral synthesis. American Catholics must be conscious of more than the well-defined edges of separate pieces of the puzzle; the health and vitality of their ideological personality depends on a successful integration of all the component elements into a unified whole. And non-Catholics may be excused from missing the point of disparate analyses if they do not see their inter-relations.

Strange to say, it is apparently ever necessary for a Catholic commentator, whether on theology or on politics, to make clear the personal and interpretative nature of his work, yet there is no basic reason for confusion in this matter. No Catholic theologian on his own authority can speak for the Church; this authoritative role of religious prophecy is the exclusive function of the Church's magisterium, the bishops. He indeed can and should seek to shed a measure of light on and to impart a degree of understanding to the truths of the faith taught by the Church. But this effort at understanding, insofar as it proceeds from the theologian himself, is not the formal and authoritative teaching of the magisterium. Rather it is an explanation whose degree of acceptability depends on its fidelity to the Church's teaching and on the soundness of its basis and development.

Still less is there any reason for confusing the opinion of a Catholic commentator on American institutions and policies with that of all American Catholics. The Catholic commentator here even more decisively speaks for himself rather than for the Church or for his fellow Catholics. Catholic principles, of course, will shape the conscience of the Catholic commentator, but the evaluation and resolution of the concrete problems with which the political order is concerned are necessarily his own. This work, then, though inspired by and responsive to the Church's teaching, is a personal and interpretative effort both in theological and political science. The author hopes, to be sure, that the effort succeeds in articulating a point of view which, at least in its general structure, American Catholics can accept as an adequate expression of their beliefs and attitudes and which American non-Catholics can accept as a fully democratic participation in the life of the American polity.

It will be salutary here to sound a note of self-depreciation concerning the entire problem of the Church and the state. The nature of the Church-state relationship is certainly not the most pressing theological problem of our time. The essential theological problem of our time, as perhaps of any other time, is to articulate in modern idiom the timeless "good news" of the new alliance. The task of the theologian is to shape and develop the instruments by which the Church can penetrate and sanctify contemporary culture and civilization. Within this frame of reference the problem of the Church and the state cannot be said to be the most vital phase of the theological enterprise today, although it does constitute an aspect of the task. Nor does the relationship of the Church to the state constitute the most pressing political problem of our time. Of far more concern to the modern statesman are the preservation of world peace, the defense of liberty, and the promotion of a socially just international economy.

As a theological and political problem, therefore, the relation of the state to the Church and vice versa is to a considerable extent the relic of a nineteenth-century polemic. In fact, the sloganary nature of so much current discussion concerning the Church and the state reveals just how symbolic and ritualistic the problem has become. Those Americans at one extreme who appeal to the "absolute separation of church and state"—which is neither the law nor the fact—are neatly balanced by those at the other extreme who refer to this country as a "Christian nation"—which is neither the law nor, at least today, the fact. Yet there does exist a genuinely speculative problem of the theology and politics of Church-state relations that has wide and important implications for particular areas of American life. The successful resolution of the real and symbolic areas of this problem has the inestimable value of removing an all-too-effective roadblock to the unified civic aspiration and action necessary for the achievement of common goals, which is so essential to the healthy functioning of the polity, especially the democratic polity. It would, moreover, free citizens to devote their undivided energies to the more urgent political problems faced in our day by this country and the world.

Before concluding these introductory remarks, I would like to note one more point. This book has labored to harmonize the political aspirations of Catholics with those of their fellow citizens. But there is a deeper harmony of godly and brotherly love which both Catholics and non-Catholics must achieve. Catholics and non-Catholics must overcome through charity their religious separation from one another. They must move out of isolation into communication, out of estrangement into understanding, and out of hostility into cooperation. This harmony is the unfinished and never finished work to which all men of good will aspire.

NOTES

1. See the statement issued by Dr. Norman Vincent Peale and his associates on September 7, 1960. *The New York Times,* September 8, 1960, p. 25. But especially examine the scrutiny of candidate Kennedy at Houston on September 12, 1960. *The New York Times,* September 14, 1960, p. 32.

2. In recent years responsible Protestants have shied away from any association with the efforts of Protestants and Other Americans United and the works of Paul Blanshard. They recognize in the POAU and Blanshard not only an extreme perspective on Catholi-cism but an immoderate and none-too-latent secularism.

3. See Philip Sharper, ed., *American Catholics: A Protestant-Jewish View* (New York: Sheed & Ward, 1959), for a good sample of the tension to which intelligent non-Catholics bear witness.

4. *America,* April 23, 1960, pp. 94, 96; *The New York Times,* September 13, 1960, p. 22.

5. *Ibid.*

6. Francis J. Connell, C.SS.R., "Christ the King of Civil Rulers," *American Ecclesiastical Review,* Vol. CXIX (1948), pp. 244–253; George W. Shea, "Catholic Doc-

trine and 'The Religion of the State,'" *American Ecclesiastical Review,* Vol. CXXIII (1950), pp. 161–174; Joseph C. Fenton, "The Status of a Controversy," *American Ecclesiastical Review,* Vol. CXXIV (1951), pp. 451–458; Connell, "The Theory of the 'Lay State,'" *American Ecclesiastical Review,* Vol. CXXV (1951), pp. 7–18; Shea, "Catholic Orientations on Church and State," *ibid.,* pp. 405–416; Connell, "Reply to Father Murray," *American Ecclesiastical Review,* Vol. CXXVI (1952), pp. 49–59; Fenton, "Principles Underlying Traditional Church-State Doctrine," *ibid.,* pp. 452–462; and Fenton, "Toleration and the Church-State Controversy," *American Ecclesiastical Review,* Vol. CXXX (1954), pp. 330–343.

7. John Courtney Murray, S.J., "Current Theology: Freedom of Religion," *Theological Studies,* Vol. VI (1945), pp. 85–113; "Freedom of Religion: I. The Ethical Problem," *ibid.,* pp. 229–286; "Governmental Repression of Heresy," *Proceedings of the Third Annual Meeting of the Catholic Theological Society of America,* 1948, pp. 26–101; "St. Robert Bellarmine on the Indirect Power," *Theological Studies,* Vol. IX (1948), pp. 491–535; "Contemporary Orientations of Catholic Thought on Church and State in the Light of History," *Theological Studies,* Vol. X (1949), pp. 177–234; "On Religious Freedom," *ibid.,* pp. 409–432; "The Problem of 'The Religion of the State,'" *American Ecclesiastical Review,* Vol. CXXIV (1951), pp.

327–352; "For the Freedom and Transcendence of the Church," *American Ecclesiastical Review,* Vol. CXXVI (1952), pp. 28–48; and "The Church and Totalitarian Democracy," *Theological Studies,* Vol. XIII (1952), pp. 525–563. The four articles of Fr. Murray on Leo XIII are cited in Chapter III, note 2. "The Problem of 'The Religion of the State'," which also appeared in *Theological Studies,* Vol. XII (1951), pp. 155–178, probably contains the best schema of Fr. Murray's analysis. Fr. Victor R. Yanitelli, S.J., has provided a useful anthology of Fr. Murray's work through 1951: "A Church-State Anthology: The Works of Fr. Murray," *Thought,* Vol. XXVII (1952), pp. 6–42. Fr. Yanitelli and Fr. Gustave Weigel, S.J., have produced two helpful commentaries on the controversy between Fr. Murray and his critics: "Chronicle: A Church-State Controversy," *Thought,* Vol. XXVI (1951), pp. 443–451, and "The Church and the Democratic State," *Thought,* Vol. XXVII (1952), pp. 165–184, respectively.

8. Rt. Rev. James A. Pike, *A Roman Catholic in the White House* (Garden City: Doubleday & Company, Inc., 1960), Chs. III, IV.

9. See Alfredo Cardinal Ottaviani, "Church and State: Some Present Problems," *American Ecclesiastical Review,* Vol. CXXVIII (1953), pp. 321–334.

10. For example, Augustin Léonard, O.P., "Freedom of Faith and Civil Tolerance," in the symposium *Tolerance and the Catholic,* translated from the French

by George Lamb (New York: Sheed & Ward, 1955), pp. 95–136, and Max Pribilla, S.J., "Dogmatische Intoleranz und bürgerliche Toleranz," *Stimmen der Zeit*, Vol. CXLIV (1949), pp. 27–40.

11. Robert D. Cross, *The Emergence of Liberal Catholicism in America* (Cambridge: Harvard University Press, 1958).

12. *Ibid.*, p. vii.

13. Currin V. Shields, *Democracy and Catholicism in America* (New York: McGraw-Hill Book Company, Inc., 1958).

14. For example, John C. Bennett, *Christians and the State* (New York: Charles Scribner's Sons, 1958), and Robert McAfee Brown (and Gustave Weigel, S.J.), *An American Dialogue* (Garden City: Doubleday & Company, Inc., 1960); but the work of Dr. A. F. Carrillo de Albornoz, *Roman Catholicism and Religious Liberty* (Geneva: World Council of Churches, 1959), is unquestionably the most competent presentation of the current status of Catholic theological discussion by a non-Catholic commentator.

2

The Catholic Church
and Political Tolerance:
an Investigation of
Theological Principles

Strict considerations of scientific method might seem to require us to initiate our theological investigation with an examination of the Church's teaching on the proper principles of her relationship to the secular organization of society and subsequently to seek a theological understanding of that teaching. In this case, however, we prefer to invert the more customary procedure for convenience, since it is difficult to appreciate the precise meaning and relevance of the Church's teaching without first grasping the outline and terms of the theological discussion. We shall begin, therefore, with an effort to understand the theological problematic, and in the succeeding chapter we shall return to examine the basic expressions of the Church's teaching on the subject.

16

THE POLITICAL AND ECCLESIAL SOCIETIES

At the outset we should note that when the Catholic theologian speaks of "Church" and "state" he is not speaking primarily of twenty centuries of history but rather of the two societal structures which lie beneath the dust of any past, or the flesh of any present, historical moment. The language, quite natural to him and even necessary, is the language of the schoolmen, the language of Aristotle and St. Thomas. The terms "society," "common good," "authority," "natural," "supernatural," and the like flow freely in his discussions, and if he fails to give some explanation of his terms, those untrained and unfamiliar with them—Catholic and non-Catholic alike—may be forgiven for mistaking the true contours of the analysis.

Any discussion of the problem of Church and state, whether theological or political, presumes the nature of social organization itself. A society, of course, involves more than one person. But a society is also more than a mere group, because the members of a society seek a common goal in union of mind, heart, and action. The members of a society are united, not in each seeking his own individual good, but in all seeking a good precisely as common and shared. All contribute to the achievement, and all share in the enjoyment of the common good. Moreover, a society must select and shape the means required to achieve the common goal. Except in the relatively rare case where the means are uniquely and necessarily related to the goal, a society must employ some principle of authority to make a determination among alternatives. This specification of the means to the end is an essential function of authority. Contrary to the dictates of classical liberal and totalitarian ideologies, authority is not essentially identical with coercion, nor is coercion an essential function of authority.[1] Rather, coercion is substitutional in character and functions as an instrument of authority to ensure the efficacy of the means specified where the members of a society are not perfectly virtuous. Authority, then, is the efficacious direction of the members to the goal of a society.

Some societies are conventional; their goals and structures are specified by the members of the society themselves. The Chamber of Commerce and the League of Women Voters, for example, determine their own goals and write their own by-laws. But, unlike the Chamber of Commerce and the League of Women Voters, the members of a family are not free to specify its goals or basic structure. Rather, the goals and structure of the family are specified by nature itself. Hence the family is a natural society. A conventional society, like the Chamber of Commerce, seeks a restricted human goal, that is, a goal which is particular to some special line of human activity; a natural society, like the family, on the other hand, seeks a specifically human goal, that is, a goal which is radically common to the structure of man.

Now, the family, although perfect by reason of its specifically human goal, is imperfect by reason of its inability to provide satisfactorily the means to achieve this goal. No family has the necessary or sufficient material, intellectual, or moral means to fulfill the goals of human existence. For this reason families must unite to promote conditions that offer to members the opportunity of fulfilling the exigencies of their human existence. A union of families to foster these conditions is a politically organized society, which is perfect both in terms of its specifically human goal and in terms of its capacity to supply the means to attain this goal.[2]

Foremost among the conditions requisite for human development is public tranquillity. This involves not only the security of citizens from foreign aggression or domestic violence but also their freedom to live without fear of unjust or arbitrary action. Beyond peace and freedom, the dynamic and positive finality of a political society requires a public climate favorable to the physical, intellectual, and moral *self*-development of its citizens. As befits human freedom, citizens develop themselves; a political society can offer only the opportunity for such development. Thus, the goals of a political society are summarized in the time-honored and classic philosophic formula: "To promote the public peace and the public prosperity."

But God has initiated for all men a destiny higher than anything to which human nature on its own could aspire or achieve. By an absolutely free act of love and an entirely gratuitous breakthrough into history God chose to invite men to the intimacy of personal union with Him. This union of man with God, imperfect in the present life and perfect in the next, is accomplished through and in His only begotten Son, Jesus Christ. This union, moreover, is not accomplished on the atomistic basis of isolated, individual action; it is accomplished, rather, in the mystical community of all the faithful with Christ which is the Church. The invisible but truly real community of the faithful with Christ is the Church viewed from its innermost essence. Yet the selfsame Church is also a visible community in which the bishops, under the primacy of the Bishop of Rome, authoritatively teach the "good news," communicate the sacramental life, and direct the footsteps of the faithful along the path of union with God. This is the Church viewed from its outer reality. Quite clearly, both the theologian and the political analyst who seek to examine the Church's relation to the state limit their concern with the Church to a consideration of her outer reality as a visible society, that is, as a visible union in mind, heart, and action of all the faithful under the authoritative direction of the hierarchy seeking the common goal of sanctification or union with God.

As societies, then, the body politic and the Church differ fundamentally. The body politic is the union of all citizens, of all those who are seeking to promote the good, common to all, of a full human life; the Church, on the other hand, is the union of all the faithful, of all those who are seeking to promote the goal, common to all, of union with God according to His salvific designs. The body politic is natural and secular both in its goal of the "good life" and in the means of attaining it, both in its institution and in its constitution; the Church, on the other hand, is supernatural and sacral both in its goal of union with God and in the means of attaining that union, both in its institution and in its constitution.

We should first note the distinction of the two societies in terms of their finalities. The body politic's goal of the full human life is natural, or secular, whereas the Church's goal is supernatural, or sacral. This distinction is commonly referred to as a distinction between the "temporal" and the "spiritual." Unfortunately, such an expression of the distinction may be misleading. It will mislead the unwary if the "temporal" is taken in opposition to the "eternal," or if the "spiritual" is taken in opposition to the "material." The truth is that the Church, because of her supernatural goal, is concerned with the sacral and with everything sacral. Hence the Church is concerned with the sacral in the temporal. So, too, the body politic, because of its natural goal, is concerned with the specifically human and with everything specifically human. Hence its goal includes not merely the common conditions that promote man's material well-being but also those that promote man's spiritual self-development, since the human good is both material and spiritual. In view of their finalities, therefore, the distinction between the Church and the body politic is better expressed as a distinction between the order of natural, or secular, society and the order of supernatural, or sacral, society.

Consequent upon this distinction of Church and body politic in terms of their finalities, there is a distinction between them in terms of their derivation of authority. Every society requires efficacious direction toward its designated goal, but the direction imparted to the members of a society does not always come by the same route. The foundation of the Church as a society was accomplished from above downward, from divine constitution, but political society originates from below upward, from human constitution. Before we probe the implications of this distinction for the Church-state question, it will be necessary to introduce the concept of the state as the specific instrument of political society.

THE STATE AND THE CHURCH

The purpose of society, as politically organized, is to protect and perfect itself as a whole. This good is a good of the whole, a good common to all the members of the society, diversified but still unified. Now, the state is not synonymous with political society but rather is the particular subsidiary organization of the body politic whose special purpose looks to the good of the whole society. There is within the body politic a whole range of responsible organizations—familial, economic, scientific, and cultural—with partial tasks respecting the good of the whole society. These organizations indeed protect and advance the good of the whole society, but the state alone has this as its *specific* function. As the rational expression and specific instrument of political society the state is the highest subsidiary of the body politic, but it is a subsidiary which derives its authority from below, from the other subsidiary and responsible organizations of the body politic. Hence the state is limited according to the traditional principle of subsidiarity: the state should do for the citizens only what the citizens through their responsible organizations cannot conveniently do for themselves.

There are, moreover, limits other than those necessarily imposed on the authority of the state by the inferior but responsible organs of the body politic. On the one hand, the state, as a historically conditioned institution, as part and parcel of the historical process, is limited by its own past, present, and future uniqueness. On the other, the state of itself is utterly incompetent with respect to the aspirations of man which transcend the order of justice. Political authority can establish an order of rights and obligations which will have the strength of harmonious organization, but of itself this cannot actuate the higher aspirations of man for love and communion with his fellows, which supplies a third dimension to a genuinely human life. Nor can political authority of itself actuate the highest aspiration of man for the love and communion with God, which is man's supernatural destiny. As the state is without power to legislate for the natural order of human love since its authority is directed solely toward the order of justice, a fortiori the state is without power to legislate for the supernatural order of divine love. Insofar as man's destiny is supernatural, neither individually nor societally may he propose, define, or interpret such an order. The unique authority for the transmission of divine revelation is from above, from Jesus Christ through the bishops under the primacy of the Bishop of Rome. It is the responsibility of all men to hear and to receive the Word when God graciously deigns to reveal Him to them.

To the hierarchical Church belongs the unique task of authoritatively proclaiming and effecting God's salvific designs for men. The role of the people—including their highest instrument, the state—is to establish the order of justice in which the divine plan may be freely fulfilled, to provide the natural conditions in which salvation history may be freely accomplished. According to Fr. Murray, there are three principles which must be verified in every valid Church-state accommodation: First, the Church must be free to teach, sanctify, and rule her members, and, conversely, the members must be free to be taught, sanctified, and ruled. Secondly, between the two orders of ecclesiastical and political authority harmony or concord must prevail. Lastly, the Church and the state must cooperate positively with each other, each according to the principles of its own constitution.[3] These requirements are, of course, necessary implications of the fact that God not only authored man's sacral and secular aspirations but also intended their harmony. As divine grace perfects human nature in the order of the individual, so the Church perfects the body politic in the order of society. As the same concrete man qua individual participates in the orders of divine grace and human nature, so the same concrete men, qua socially organized, belong to Church and body politic.

IS LEGAL ESTABLISHMENT REQUIRED?

The freedom of the Church, the harmony, and the cooperation of the Church and the state are absolutely necessary exigencies of both institutions. The question which theologians have asked in consequence is how legal establishment is related to these exigencies of Church-state accommodation. Is legal establishment a required mode of Church-state accommodation? Is political intolerance a necessary corollary of the dogmatic intolerance of Catholic belief? Or, to insert the question in the democratic context, is political tolerance genuinely compatible with the dogmatic intolerance of Catholic belief?

The classical model of legal establishment is today largely a historical anachronism, but the theologian understands by that term (1) the public profession of Catholicism as the one and only religion of the state, (2) the financial support of the Catholic Church alone, and (3) the use of the coercive power of secular society to prevent the public propagation of non-Catholic religions. The expressed intent of legal establishment is to regulate only the public, social forum, not the private forum of the individual conscience. In theory, legal establishment does not deny the right and duty of the individual to follow the dictates of his conscience even when he is sincerely mistaken. Rather, legal establishment seeks to act in the public area where the individual conscience affects the social order and the social order affects the individual conscience.

No theologian, of course, ever contended that legal establishment is constitutive of, or an absolutely necessary instrument to, the Church's freedom and the mutual harmony and cooperation between Church and state. Were legal establishment so constitutive or so instrumental, then such an accommodation absolutely and without exception would have to be verified in all valid Church-state relationships. No claims of practical necessity would excuse the state from this obligation nor the Church from demanding this status. A view so extreme would run counter to the variety of Church-state arrangements embodied historically over two thousand years and would even deny any role to prudence in human affairs.

But many theologians, though rejecting the contention that legal establishment is an absolutely necessary instrument to the Church's freedom and to concord and cooperation between Church and state, nonetheless consider legal establishment relatively necessary.[4] Thus, they contend, there is an obligation based on the structures and goals of the two societies to adopt the system of establishment although special circumstances may require the substitution of such other means as a guarantee of religious freedom and the equality of all religions before the law. The latter means, however, remain substitutional in character and must be replaced by the required means when conditions permit.

What special circumstances release the state from the obligation of legal establishment? Many American non-Catholic commentators unfamiliar with the language of the Catholic theologian have erroneously concluded that the permissive circumstances are simply those which constitute Catholics a religious and political minority. This interpretation both ignores the repeated denials of the Catholic theologians in question and attributes a self-seeking, insincere opportunism to American Catholics. To evaluate correctly the true character of the circumstances which many Catholic theologians call permissive of religious freedom as a valid mode of Church-state accommodation, we must look to the concrete factors which inspire this form of relationship between the Church and the state.

The Church has always been strongly mindful of the role of tradition not only in her own development but also in the dynamics of secular history. Indeed, as a result of the excesses of the French Revolution the Church throughout the nineteenth century lived in fear of the dangers of abstract political blueprints that ignored all continuum with the past. The Church has always recognized that any given moment of history is truly unique, but that part of its uniqueness is determined by the past from which it issued. This is not to deny the necessity or propriety of political change; a political tradition must be effective as well as established, and the test of any political system is its success. But only an intransigent and foolhardy dreamer would recommend the radical alteration of the basic framework of an established and effective political system. The Church, therefore, is perfectly aware that the tradition of religious freedom in many countries, including the United States, is a genuinely established and effective element in a successfully operating political system which should in no way be altered.

Respect for the established tradition of religious freedom in this country and other countries is no narrow historicism. A tradition worthy of respect must be a rational response to real conditions. And the tradition of religious freedom is uniquely responsive to the present national and international conditions of religious pluralism. Without peaceful and harmonious relations among citizens the further goals of a political society can never be reached. To deny religious freedom in a pluralistic culture is to create classes of citizens on the basis of religion and invite friction between them. Hence the tradition of religious freedom is founded on the rockbed of a political fact of life, religious pluralism.

Not only may political consideration of modern conditions require the policy of religious freedom but also religious consideration of the same conditions may urge this policy. It is a curious historical fact that the Church appears weaker rather than stronger in nations which have enjoyed the "privileges" of legal establishment. Moreover, legal establishment under modern conditions appears to block rather than to facilitate the Church's ability to communicate her message of salvation to the mind and heart of the non-Catholic. Simply as a pragmatic conclusion from modern conditions, therefore, the Church is led to embrace the policy of religious freedom.

For these reasons many Catholic theologians speak of religious freedom under modern conditions as a permissible, perhaps necessary, mode of Church-state accommodation. If they do not accept the policy of religious freedom as a theological right of the autonomous individual to determine for himself the content or conditions of divine revelation, neither do they accept it as an opportunistic device beneficial to a Catholic minority. Rather, they respect the principle of religious freedom on the historical basis of modern tradition, on the political basis of religious pluralism, and on the theological basis of the Church's mission to all men. But these Catholic theologians absolutely refuse to call the modern settlement "ideal." For them, legal establishment remains a necessary means under "ideal" conditions to harmonious Church-state relations. They urge that society, no less than the individual, must praise, reverence, and serve God, and this according to the manner which He prescribes. Since the Catholic Church is the one true Church, the state must under "ideal" conditions profess, protect, and advance the Catholic religion by legal prescription.

Many other theologians, however, follow the lead of Fr. John Courtney Murray[5] and deny that legal establishment is a relatively necessary instrument to ecclesiastical freedom, to concord, or to cooperation between Church and state. They maintain that there are many possible Church-state relationships. Indeed, legal establishment, far from being obligatory as soon as conditions permit, is permissible only when circumstances necessitate. Conceding that the goal of society, no less than that of the individual, is to praise, reverence, and serve God through the mediation of Christ and His Church, these writers distinguish between society and its highest instrument, the state. Society, to be sure, must aim to be integrally and totally Christian, but the state in a democratic society is not suited to the role of professing, protecting, and advancing Christ's dispensation by legal prescription. In a democracy a "union" or "establishment" of the Catholic religion can exist only between the conscience of the people and the Church. If the people be vitally Catholic, then the "rulers" of the democratic society and the Church will be truly united.

DEMOCRACY AND RELIGIOUS EQUALITY

The theologians who agree with Fr. Murray argue that freedom of religious exercise and the equality of all religions before the law is a form of Church-state accommodation at least as "ideal" under proper conditions as legal establishment is under others. The "proper conditions," in their view, are those embodied in modern democratic governments. Perhaps we can explicate why the theory and practice of democracy may be said to require freedom of religious exercise and the equality of all religions before the law.

As process, democracy indicates the mode of policy formation by majority decision. But no student of modern history can fail to grasp that democracy understood simply as the process of government by majority decision can be as destructive of human values as the worst manifestations of paternal government. In view of the purpose of the state as the highest instrument of man in political society, the state cannot by any form of government which it institutionalizes absolutize its role. Democratic government, no more than paternal government, therefore, is a pure process, but it is a process limited by the nature of the human person and the society of which the democratic state is only an instrument.

As process, however, democracy has important corollaries. Institutional formation of policy by majority decision demands equality of citizens and the political rights of free speech, free assembly, and free press. If decisions are to be made by the majority, the voice of each citizen must be equal; if rational decisions are to be made by the majority, the citizens' sources of information must be safeguarded.

Other political consequences follow the choice of the democratic process, but no consequence is more fundamental than the freedom of religious exercise and the equality of all religious before the law. Religion, as the ultimate value to which men commit themselves, determines every other value. If, therefore, citizens were denied by the democratic polity the freedom of commitment to this value, their disaffection from the polity would unbalance their equality with their fellow citizens and diminish their role in the decision-making process. This disaffection may be overlooked by a selective decision-making process but hardly by a decision-making process which requires the active participation of citizens as equals. Democratic equality is not of numbers but of persons, and religious values are paramount to personality. While blemishes of the economic or social order poison the equality of citizens from the surface inward, inequality of citizens at the level of commitment to religious values spoils democratic equality from the core outward.

Two points in this analysis must be underscored. First, freedom of religious exercise, like the freedoms of speech, of the press, and of assembly, is not absolute but related as a means to the end of democratic decision making. When, therefore, speech becomes slander, assembly becomes riot, press becomes libel, or religious exercise becomes cannibalism, the value of these as means in the decision-making process is outweighed by the rights of other individuals or of society. This balance is delicate, but the essence of reason is delicacy. Secondly, freedom of religious exercise, again like the freedoms of speech, of the press, and of assembly, is a political right proper and necessary to democratic government, not a natural right of the autonomous individual to determine for himself the condition and content of divine revelation.

What is natural to man is the right, when conditions permit, to choose democracy as a form of political organization. As individual man is morally obliged to harmonize his being with the divine initiatives of faith and charity, so societal man is obliged to create from below the conditions which harmonize with the organization of the supernatural society from above. If the political right of religious exercise is consonant with the obligation of harmony between the Church and the state as the specific instrument of political society, then it is difficult to see why freedom of religious exercise is not at least as "ideal" a means of Church-state accommodation as its counterpart, legal establishment.

Freedom of religious exercise, however, has not been safe from its friends. Classical liberalism also embraced this freedom, and the embrace was, from the Church's view, a deadly one. In the classical liberal posture, society, atomistic by nature and contractual in origin, was a grudging concession from individuality rather than a perfection of personality. For the liberal, man was an island, and his freedom of religious exercise, like the freedoms of speech, of the press, and of assembly, was a hallmark of his insularity. Thus freedom of religious exercise was not a political right based on the democratic form of government but a "natural right" based on a conception of man as autonomous; not a right related as means to the democratic process but an absolute right with each individual an end to himself.

By autonomizing the individual and the subjective without the complementarity of the social and the objective, liberal theory warped the world of nature. But for the Catholic theologian the worst defect of liberal theory was the fact that it destroyed the world of grace. Both in doctrinal tendency and historical eventuality liberal theory proclaimed the authority of the autonomous individual in religious belief and exercise. To this the Church counterclaimed unique authority from God to preach His revelation and sanctify all men. As the Church rejected the theology of the Reformation, so too she was obliged to reject the philosophy of the Revolution.

Neither historically nor ideologically are liberalism and democracy synonymous. Historically, the classical liberal never quite practiced the equality he might seem logically required to preach. Qualifications on voting, class legislation, and restrictions on religious organizations were characteristic of nineteenth-century liberal regimes. Ideologically, liberalism is more synonymous with anarchy than with democracy. For the liberal, society, whether democratically or paternally organized, opposed the autonomy of the individual. But liberalism did lead or, rather, did give way to modern democracy because the liberal presumed to equate democracy with the absolute autonomy of the individual proper only to anarchy. The results of this equation are still heard in discussions on freedom of speech, press, assembly, religion, and, less distributively but no less vociferously, on freedom of economic enterprise. Yet, although democracy articulates more fully than paternalism the organization of political society from below, it is essential to recall that democracy does not proclaim an absolute autonomy for the individual nor deny the perfective role of society for the human person. Rather, democracy is simply a way of directing the society in and through which the human person is perfected.

Nor is liberalism a bulwark against collectivism. Again, this is both a historical and an ideological paradox. Historically, the reaction to liberalism was fascism and communism. Ideologically, the liberal's autonomous individual became the collectivist's anonymous individual, and the liberal's atomistic society became the collectivist's organistic society. But although liberalism and collectivism are antithetical in their conclusions, they share several common premises. Like the liberal, the collectivist accepts an opposition between society and the individual, but, unlike the liberal, he opts for society. Like the liberal, the collectivist accepts society as the sum of individual power units, but, unlike the liberal, he glories in this superiority of power. If the collectivist is empirical and modest, he speaks of the "greatest good of the greatest number"; if he is romantic and self-determining, he speaks of the *volonté générale;* if idealistic and deterministic, he speaks of the *Volksgeist;* if materialistic and deterministic, he speaks of the dialectic. From a false antecedent, as the modern logicians say, any consequent may follow.

Classical liberalism is synonymous not with democracy but with anarchy, and indeed shares several premises with collectivism. As reason opposes the liberal system in general for absolving the individual and the subjective from the social and the objective, so Catholic theology opposes the liberal freedom of religious exercise in particular for absolving the individual and subjective conscience from the social and objective revelation of Christ. Democracy is inextricably related to social order, not to autonomous individuals, and freedom of religious exercise is inextricably related to democracy, not to anarchy.

The scandal of democracy is the possibility of license permitted by political freedom. As freedom of speech entails the possibility that citizens will speak against the natural good of society, so freedom of religious exercise entails the possibility that citizens will exercise their religious zeal against the supernatural good of society. Concretely this means that freedom of religious exercise entails the possibility that citizens will fail to achieve social conditions open to the divine initiatives of faith and charity. Now, we have previously indicated that the state as the specific instrument of political society is obliged to provide a social forum favorable to the divine salvific initiatives. It therefore seems necessary to choose, as extremists of both sides have always claimed, between democracy and the Church.

But this is scandal only to the weak-spirited. The role and function of a part of society must be scrupulously distinguished from the role and function of the whole society. The body politic would fail to create the social conditions receptive to divine initiative only if the conditions created by the whole body as such failed to promote that reception. Now, in a democratically organized society the Church receives from the whole body the full freedom to preach and fulfill God's salvific designs. This freedom of the Church extends to every member and to every subordinate group that shares in the apostolic mission of Christianizing society. If parts of a democratic society work against this reception of God's revelation, the society as such does not. The democratic society, qua society, does not work against the ontological order either of nature or of supernature.

It may be objected that the body politic permits parts of the society to work against the good of the whole. The key word here is "permits." Because the body politic does not oppose by law and coercion particular actions detrimental to the good of the whole, it does not follow that the body politic promotes those actions. We are dealing here with the political order. When a society determines to direct itself democratically, it accepts certain corollaries, among them the freedom of religious exercise. This freedom is a freedom granted by the body politic because of the chosen method of direction. Unless the body politic assumes the liberal theory that the autonomous individual conscience has an absolute right to specify the content and conditions of divine revelation—which is to establish subjectivism as the religion of the state—the body politic does not endorse false religious activity. The political freedom of religious exercise is consistent with the obligation of political society to promote conditions conducive to the fulfillment of God's salvific designs.

PATERNALISM AND LEGAL ESTABLISHMENT

Democracy, however, is not the only form of government; the body politic may be organized paternally as well as democratically. Overzealous democrats, of course, have attacked the legitimacy of all paternal government, but the postwar enlargement of American political experience has forced a reappraisal of this gratuitous rejection. As democracy is possible only where there is a mature body politic, so immaturity in the body politic may require its paternal organization. In a democratic society "the many" are mature enough to specify and achieve the goals of the society, but in a paternal society the immaturity of the many requires "the few" to specify and direct the body politic toward the social goals which the many would be incapable of determining and achieving for themselves.

The impact of this specific function of paternal government on Church-state relations is transparent: rulers in a monistic, paternal, and Catholic society cannot refuse on principle to profess publicly the Catholic religion as the religion of the state without implying hostility to the Church. In such a society the subjects, who look to their rulers for guidance in all that concerns the highest goals of community aspiration and action, would take the action of the government to imply at least the indifference of the rulers to the truth or relevance of the Catholic religion for society. Moreover, it would be assumed that the government desired to establish a purely individual, invisible, and subjective religion as the supreme social good in preference to the social, visible, and objective claims of the Church, or perhaps even to establish the supremacy of material, natural, and secular values in preference to those which are spiritual, supernatural, and transcendent. In short, the structure of a monistic, paternal, and Catholic society is such that, whether the rulers act or on principle refuse to act, they will establish some value or set of values as ultimate for the society. The rulers therefore cannot refuse on principle to profess publicly the Catholic religion as the religion of the state although they may tolerate all religions as equals for reasons of political necessity.

Moreover, the paternal society differs from the democratic not only in the function of policy when formed but also in the mode by which policy is formed. As process, paternalism indicates the mode of policy formation by decision of the few. To the few is entrusted the direction of the body politic through its specific instrument, the state. The few are the caretakers, the trustees of the body politic. As the father provides for his family, so the few provide for the body politic. In view of the purpose of the state as the highest instrument of man in political society, the state cannot by any form of government which it institutionalizes absolutize its role. Paternal government, like democratic government, is not a pure process but, rather, a process limited by the nature of the human person and the society of which the paternal state is only an instrument. To identify paternal government with totalitarian government, therefore, would be inaccurate and gratuitous. Paternal government, like democratic government, is limited by the order of nature. Nor should paternal government be equated with the "divine right" theory. For the authority of political society, as we have said, derives from below—even when entrusted to the hands of the few. Paternal government does not deny the principle of subsidiarity, but the special character of social conditions requires the direction of the state by the select, and this mode of direction paternalism institutionalizes.

As process, paternalism has important corollaries. Institutional policy formation by the select not only fails to require, but even denies, the equality of citizens and the political rights of free speech, free assembly, and free press. Since decisions are to be made by the select, the voice of each citizen is not equal. From this it follows that free speech, free assembly, and the free press are not required as means for the functioning of the governing process. In fact, because of the immaturity of the body politic the indiscriminate extension of such freedoms would threaten the entire governing process.

Another corollary of the paternal process affects religious exercise. Because its method of policy formation is by decision of the select, paternal government does not require, but even denies, the equality of citizens, and because paternal government does not require equality of citizens, there is not that political necessity for the freedom of religious exercise to which democracy gives rise. In fact, religious pluralism—precisely because of the transcendency of the religious value—might threaten the unity of a paternally organized body politic. An immature society requires paternal government because the many are unable to specify amicably and discriminately the good of the whole body politic. Under such conditions pluralism of culture, especially of religion, accentuates differences, fragments the body politic, and hinders the few from specifying the good of the whole and the many from accepting the specifications. As democracy is not the only form of government, so freedom of religious exercise is not the only form of Church-state accommodation.

Paternal and democratic governments, then, are organizational responses by the body politic to different sets of conditions. In an immature society the many do not possess the knowledge and the stability to determine and pursue the good of the whole body politic. Moreover, the immature society is incapable of coping with pluralism: diversity is identified with political division. In a mature society, on the other hand, many possess both the knowledge and the stability to determine and pursue the good of the whole body politic. The mature, unlike the immature, society is capable of coping with pluralism: diversity is compatible with political unity. In fact, the democratic organization of the mature society requires the freedom to be or to become pluralist.

As the maturity or immaturity of the body politic determines to what extent democracy is possible or necessary, so the pattern of democratic or paternal government determines to what extent the freedom of religious exercise is possible or necessary. Freedom of religious exercise is a consequence not of liberalism but of the democratic organization of the body politic, and the absence of that freedom is the consequence not of Catholic theology but of the paternal organization of the body politic.

RELIGIOUS EQUALITY VERSUS LEGAL ESTABLISHMENT

Is legal establishment a relatively necessary means of Church-state accommodation? We have followed Fr. Murray and answered this question in the negative: the equality of all religions before the law is no second-best accommodation of the democratic state to the Church. We may also ask further whether religious equality and legal establishment are equally valid means of Church-state accommodation, neither being favored by an exigency of nature. This question, too, we answer, with Fr. Murray, in the negative. Legal establishment is entailed by the paternal organization of an immature body politic. But as childhood is a transitory and imperfect stage in the development of the individual, so immaturity is a transitory and imperfect stage in the development of the body politic, and as the parents' authority loses its *raison d'être* with the child's maturity, so the paternal authority of the few loses its *raison d'être* with the maturity of the many. Because paternal government is founded on an essentially transitory and imperfect stage in the development of the body politic, the legal establishment which paternal government may entail is also subject to the same limitations. Hence legal establishment, far from being necessary when circumstances permit, rather is permitted only when circumstances necessitate.

Many theologians do not agree with the conclusions of Fr. Murray's analysis. On the ethical plane they emphasize the duty of the state to worship the Creator. In the context of God's revelation this, they say, means legal establishment under "ideal" conditions. But the state can only "worship the Creator" according to its own proper structure. The state, as the specific instrument of political society, must indeed grant the Church freedom to perform her mission and must work in harmony with her. The body politic, through its specific instrument, must indeed provide social conditions open to the divine salvific initiatives. If the state fulfills these exigencies, it will worship the Creator according to its own proper structure. While the fulfillment of these exigencies is obligatory for the state, the method of fulfillment is dependent on the organization of the body politic. Under paternal government, these exigencies may be fulfilled through legal establishment. Under democratic government, these exigencies are fulfilled through the freedom of religious exercise accorded to the Church. Both legal establishment and its democratic counterpart are corollaries from diverse patterns of organization of the body politic. If these patterns of political organization are intrinsically valid, so too are the accommodations of Church and state which they imply.

Although a pure democracy is not likely to be found outside the small city-state, a representative democracy preserves the essence of the democratic process by providing for periodic review of policy decisions. Even representative democracy, however, is rarely embodied in history without an admixture of paternalism. These factors may make the division between paternal and democratic governments seem sharper in idea than in history. But "mixed" government has felt the pressures of attempting to direct the body politic both paternally and democratically. The mixed government, insofar as it has been mixed, has experienced the tension created by rival modes of societal direction. In modern history this tension has been largely resolved in favor of democracy, leaving the paternal element its traditional form but little of its substance save the power to delay decisions. And as this tension in mixed government has relaxed in favor of democracy, so the corollaries of the democratic process have become exigencies for the body politic.

RELIGIOUS FREEDOM AND THE FREEDOM OF FAITH

We have developed as a political principle Fr. Murray's thesis that religious freedom is an intrinsically valid and even a relatively necessary means of Church-state accommodation. A consideration of the relation of religious freedom to the life of the Church leads to the same conclusion. History demonstrates both the greater vitality of the Church where she has not enjoyed the "privileges" of establishment and the futility of repression of heresy in societies of advanced cultural consciousness. Faith, far from renouncing freedom, as the secularist believes, demands freedom in order to exist. Faith is a gift, but it is a gift that is accepted freely or not at all. Hence it is not surprising that the conditions of religious freedom are more productive of the vitality of the Body of Christ than are the conditions of legal establishment. Nor is it surprising that the repression of heresy, which cannot elicit a single act of Christian faith, has proved a historical failure in the religion-conscious West.

Many theologians, in fact, see in the most unfettered political freedom of religious exercise compatible with the goals of human society an at least relatively necessary condition for the very actuality of genuine Christian faith. Human society, they argue, must respect both the sovereignty of the divine initiative and the freedom of the human intellectual response in the matter of faith. This the Scriptures, the Fathers, and the Church's magisterium have constantly taught. Political freedom of religious exercise, they add, respects the way in which God acts on the human soul and the way in which the human soul arrives freely at the truth of God's salvific designs, while legal establishment introduces a social coercion which respects neither the sovereignty of God's initiative nor the freedom of man's intellect with respect to the acceptance of Christian belief. Hence political freedom of religious exercise is the "ideal" mode of Church-state accommodation, and legal establishment can be justified, if at all, only when political conditions necessitate. This is a theological argument for the propriety, even the necessity, of political freedom of religious exercise which develops exclusively from a consideration of the ontological conditions of the act of faith rather than from a consideration of the political good of human society. We may expect a greater emphasis along these scriptural and patristic lines in the future elaboration of a theology of tolerance, especially in view of the impetus which His Eminence Giacomo Cardinal Lercaro recently gave to the development.[6]

From the viewpoint both of religious and of political principles, then, legal establishment cannot be called a relatively necessary means of Church-state accommodation. In fact, since democracy offers to the mature body politic the optimum mode of self-development and since religious freedom better promotes the vitality of the Church and is itself a real condition of the act of faith, we should rather conclude that religious freedom and not legal establishment is the relatively necessary means of Church-state accommodation.

NOTES

1. For the most thorough analysis of the nature and functions of authority to date see the late Yves R. Simon's *The Philosophy of Democratic Government* (Chicago: University of Chicago Press, 1951), pp. 1–71.

2. No isolated political organization of a restricted geographical area can adequately ensure the peace, freedom, and prosperity of its citizens today. If political organization is to fulfill its function in the modern world, some form of world organization is absolutely necessary.

3. John Courtney Murray, S.J., "The Problem of State Religion,"

Theological Studies, Vol. XII (1951), pp. 156–159.

4. For a survey of the writings of the American theologians of this opinion see *supra,* Chapter I, note 6, pp. 13–14. Also see note 9 of the same chapter for a reference to a translation of the views of Cardinal Ottaviani.

5. A list of Fr. Murray's writings on the theology of Church and state will be found *supra,* Chapter I, note 7, p. 14.

6. Giacomo Cardinal Lercaro, "Religious Tolerance in Catholic Tradition," *Catholic Mind,* Vol. LVIII (1960), pp. 12–24.

3

The Modern
Papacy and Political
Tolerance:
Leo XIII and Pius XII

THE AUTHORITY OF PAPAL TEACHING

If a Protestant is asked why he believes a religious proposition to be true, he will rest his belief on the teaching of the Bible or perhaps on the inner testimony of conscience. But if a Catholic is asked the same question, he will reply that the proposition is true because the Church teaches that it is. In this lies the chief difference between the faith of the Protestant and that of the Catholic. The Catholic looks not to the Bible or to internal testimony but to the Church for the authoritative teaching of God's revelation to man. Specifically, the Catholic looks to the bishops and above all to the Bishop of Rome for authentic religious and moral instruction. The bishops, especially the Bishop of Rome, who alone enjoys the fullness of episcopal power in which all other bishops share, teach the faithful the revelation of Christ. The Catholic therefore listens to the Bishop of Rome as the supreme source of religious teaching and moral guidance. The Bishop of Rome speaks with the fullness of episcopal authority; the bishops speak with the Church's authority; the Church speaks with Christ's authority; and Christ speaks with divine authority.

In every matter of faith and morals, therefore, the Catholic looks to Rome for his ultimate instruction and guidance. Especially should this be true in the intricate and far-reaching question of the Church's dynamic relationship to the specific instrument of political society, the state. It is a question which involves the relation of Christ's unique supernatural organization, the Church, to the highest instrument of man's natural organization, the state; it is a question that concerns the constitution and finality of both organizations, and it is a question that concerns their vital interaction.

Now, when the Pope, speaking in his role of teacher and pastor, and in virtue of his supreme apostolic authority, declares a doctrine concerning faith or morals to be a doctrine of the universal Church, he teaches by way of definition. Because Christ promised to be with the Church all days and to build His Church on the Rock of Peter, the Catholic believes that papal definitions enjoy the divine guarantee of infallibility. In addition to teaching by way of definition or "extraordinary teaching," however, the Pope may, and as a general rule does, teach the faithful without any formal definition. He explains to the faithful the teaching of the Church, defends it from overt or covert attack, and applies it to particular problems of the day. One of the most important ways for the Pope to communicate his "ordinary teaching" is the encyclical letter to the whole Church. Of course, to the extent that encyclical pronouncements state or restate the extraordinary teaching of the Church they are infallible. But what of encyclical pronouncements that are not definitions or restatements of definitions?

The Pope's ordinary teaching may enjoy the guarantee of infallibility not simply because it is expressed in an encyclical but because it expresses a consensus of ecumenical teaching. No doubt a consensus tends to form around papal pronouncements, but, unless and until such a consensus is formed, no infallibility attaches to the papal pronouncement. This is not to say that the teachings of the Pope as found in the encyclicals, unless and until a definition is forthcoming or an ecumenical consensus is in evidence, can be considered to express mere opinions which the Catholic may feel free to hold or not as he sees fit. Although not binding on the Catholic conscience as a matter of faith, the ordinary teachings of the Pope are closely related to the Catholic's faith because they are the expressions of the supreme teaching authority in the Church under the special assistance of the Holy Spirit. To the papal encyclicals, as to the living voice of the Church, the Catholic must give a reverential assent. Pius XII made this point amply clear:

Nor is it to be supposed that a position advanced in an encyclical does not, *ipso facto,* claim assent. In writing them, it is true, the Popes do not exercise their teaching authority to the full. But such statements come under the day-to-day teaching of the Church. . . . And when the Roman Pontiffs go out of their way to pronounce on some subject which has hitherto been controverted, it must be clear to everybody that, in the mind and intention of the Pontiffs concerned, this subject can no longer be regarded as a matter of free debate among theologians.[1]

The encyclical teachings of the Popes, therefore, have a transtemporal significance. But they are also time-conditioned. Though the message is transtemporal, it is also occasioned by, and destined for, a definite moment of time. To understand the papal message properly it is necessary to interpret the utterance in the light of the historical circumstances which prompted it. Apparent discontinuities in papal teachings, especially on the question of Church and state, must take account of the many historical stimuli which evoked the diversity of papal responses.

Another factor that conditions papal teaching is the conceptual and linguistic framework in which the message is structured. To a great extent the Pope must rely for his tools of analysis and expression on the Church's speculative theorists, the theologians, who attempt to synthesize the Church's teaching with the concepts and language of each age. The ideological and cultural currents of each age occasion new dimensions of theological thought and expression hitherto unenvisioned. The result is to make papal teaching dependent to that extent on a particular mode of thinking and speaking. This factor is of particular importance in considering the attitude of the nineteenth-century papacy on relations between the Church and the state.

THE TEACHING OF LEO XIII ON CHURCH AND STATE

The French Revolution was the watershed which separated the old from the modern era of Church-state relations. Over the course of previous centuries, to be sure, the Church had experienced numberless trials and persecutions at the hands of emperors and kings, and on the occasion of some of these she had expressed her views. But with the advent of the Revolution the Church found herself for the first time in the so-called Catholic countries of Latin Europe face to face with a willful group of hostile unbelievers anxious for a thoroughly radical separation of Church and state. Where the Reformation prince had established the Protestant religion the Revolutionary Jacobins determined to establish a militant secularism.

Throughout the nineteenth century and even in the opening decades of the twentieth, the Church struggled with the heirs of the Revolution over the self-styled "separation" of the Church and the state. The most articulate and systematic voice in the struggle was that of Leo XIII. On the relation of the Church to the post-Revolutionary political order Leo not only accurately summarized the tradition of his nineteenth-century predecessors but expressed himself more fully and systematically in encyclical after encyclical than had any pope before him.[2] The Leonine doctrine is fundamental to any theological consideration of the problem of the Church and the state. What Leo said at the end of the nineteenth century is of more than historical interest to the theologian; the theologian seeks not merely to reconstruct the historical significance of a doctrinal pronouncement but to grasp through that context the transcendental teaching of the Church.

The *idée maîtresse* of Leo's political doctrine is the absolute dependence of all creation on the divine power and will. Man, though the crown of creation, remains subordinate to God both as an individual and as socially organized. His being is from God and is a reflection of God. His liberty is from God and, to be true liberty, must conform itself to God's will. An objective order exists to which man in the exercise of true liberty must conform: "the nature of human liberty . . . supposes the necessity of obedience to some supreme and eternal law, which is no other than the authority of God, commanding good and forbidding evil."[3] This eternal law of God is the sole standard and rule of human liberty, "however it be considered, whether in individuals or in society, whether in those who command or in those who obey."[4]

The social organization of men is a natural necessity and not an arbitrary artifact: "Man's natural instinct moves him to live in civil society, for he cannot, if dwelling apart, provide himself with the necessary requirements of life, nor procure the means of developing his mental and moral faculties."[5] But, as no society can hold together without a principle of authority directing all toward the common good, "every body politic must have a ruling authority, and this authority, no less than society itself, has its source in nature, and has, consequently, God for its author."[6] Hence rulers derive their authority to rule from God and must govern their subjects as God governs the world, and their subjects must obey them in all that they command justly.

The Church, on the other hand, has been "established by Jesus Christ Himself" and has for its unique "aim and end the eternal salvation of souls."[7] "Over this mighty multitude God has Himself set rulers with power to govern and He has willed that one should be the head of all. . . ."[8] This society is thus distinguished by its supernatural and spiritual goal from civil society, whose goals are natural and temporal. But as with the body politic, so too with the Church; men must obey those who hold their authority to rule from God Himself.

With respect to the relation between the two societies Pope Leo first recognized and insisted on the independent "excellence and nobleness" of each:

The Almighty, therefore, has given charge of the human race to two powers, the ecclesiastical and the civil, the one being set over divine, and the other human things. Each in its kind is supreme, each has fixed limits within which it is contained, limits which are defined by the nature and special object of the province of each, so that there is, we may say, an orbit traced out within which the action of each is brought into play by its own native right.[9]

At the same time, however, Pope Leo equally recognized and insisted that society, no more than the individual, can be indifferent to the worship of God:

For, men living together in society are under the power of God no less than individuals are, and society, no less than individuals, owes gratitude to God who gave it being and maintains it and whose ever-bounteous goodness enriches it with countless blessings.[10]

Therefore the two societies ought not to stand off from each other by a spurious "separation" which presupposes either that the Church is hostile to civil society or that religion is a purely private, internal, and individual affair with no social dimension. Rather, the Church and civil society, both of whose claims to authority derive from God, should harmonize their activities so that each facilitates the task of the other. The ideal relationship between the two societies is not the greatest distance and separation but the closest harmony and unity. Especially in matters of "mixed jurisdiction" such as education and marriage:

It is in the highest degree consonant to nature, as also to the designs of God, that so far from one of the powers separating itself from the other, or still less coming into conflict with it, complete harmony, such as is suited to the end for which each power exists, should be preserved between them.[11]

From this Leo concluded that the state should establish the Catholic religion as the religion of the state: ". . . the State . . . is clearly bound to act up to the manifold and weighty duties linking it to God, by the public profession of religion."[12] It is the "bounden duty" of rulers "to favor [the Catholic] religion, to protect it, to shield it under the credit and sanction of laws. . . ."[13] But the Church "does not, on that account, condemn those rulers who, for the sake of securing some great good or of hindering some great evil, allow patiently custom or usage to be a kind of sanction for every kind of religion having its place in the State."[14] And the Pope cautioned explicitly against the use of force to coerce adherence to the Catholic religion: "the Church is wont to take earnest heed that no one shall be forced to embrace the Catholic faith against his will. . . ."[15]

Leo's concept of the "ideal" relation of the Church and the state seems quite clear. Tolerance, indeed, is permissible, but "the more a state is driven to tolerate evil, the further is it from perfection."[16] The Church may acquiesce "in certain modern liberties, not because she prefers them in themselves, but because she judges it expedient to permit them. . . ."[17] Were the discussion to end here, Leo's doctrine would seem to fall hard against the Catholic "liberals" who hold legal equality of all religions before the law a fully legitimate, and even preferable, mode of Church-state accommodation. The worst fears of non-Catholics and the strongest claims of Catholic "conservatives" would appear quite justified.

INADEQUATE INTERPRETATIONS

The Catholic liberal, then, seems required to fish or cut bait: either to "interpret" Leo in a way which would have him not mean what he seems to mean or to reject Leo's judgment on the particular issue of Church and state. Clearly, the latter alternative would be a radical one for the Catholic theologian to follow. Though the pope in his ordinary teaching may err in a particular matter, still the Holy Spirit is the animating force in the Church and guides the Church's supreme teacher with provident care. The theologian will explore and exhaust every avenue of explanation rather than suggest papal error. And yet, to "interpret" Leo's teaching is to risk working violence on what seems to require no explanation. The Catholic liberal appears caught between the Scylla of theological temerity and the Charybdis of intellectual dishonesty.

Two types of solution have been tendered either separately or conjunctively in an effort to escape the rigor of Leonine teaching on Church and state. One solution tends to interpret Leo beyond

recognition, and the other veers subtly toward an implicit rejection of Leo's teaching. Both solutions emphasize historical
context as the key to the problem, and in this they contribute
much to an understanding of Leo's doctrine.

The historical context which is so important, of course, is the
context of nineteenth-century liberalism. While preaching a self-
styled "separation" of the Church from the state and a "free
Church in a free state," the Latin liberals of the last century in
actual practice displayed hostility and even violence toward the
Church. In the name of liberty, as Leo pointed out, the liberals
suppressed and despoiled the religious orders, secularized education without respect to the wishes of Catholic parents, and required civil ceremonies for all marriages. Leo wrote the
encyclicals on Church and state precisely to condemn such acts of
aggression against the Church's freedom. The Pope rightly cen-
sured the so-called "separation" which was, in fact, a declaration
of war by the Church's secularist adversaries.

In view of this historical context, may Leo's teaching fairly be
interpreted solely as an expression of opposition to the false
separation of Church and state so characteristic of nineteenth-
century Latin liberals? Was the Leonine doctrine on the political
order simply a negative reaction against the excesses of the
liberals rather than a positive pronouncement of a transcendental
schema? To reply in the affirmative would have the merit of
underlining what was certainly Leo's primary objective in the
encyclicals, but it would fail to account satisfactorily for the quite
positive and universal language which Leo actually employed
and frequently repeated on the "ideal" relations between the
Church and the state. Leo, in our view, spoke clearly and unequivocally not only against the excesses of liberalism, admittedly
his primary objective, but also in favor of an ideal blueprint
which he intended to be accurate and comprehensive. There is
no reason to doubt that Leo meant exactly what he said. To think
otherwise, would be to "interpret" Leo beyond recognition.

Another approach is to suggest that Leo's teaching on Church
and state is so historically conditioned as to have no transcendental significance for ages other than his own. Of course, Leo's
condemnation of philosophical liberalism with its antisocial and
antireligious implications is of lasting doctrinal importance. But
Leo's blueprint of the ideal relationship between Church and

state was simply the product of nineteenth-century historical factors and thus is without import for other ages. The dynamics of history, it is argued, do not permit Leo's schema to be ideal for more than a narrow phylum of past time. Now here, too, there is much merit. The argument rightly stresses the restricted nature and the historical contingency of human utterance. But it so underlines historical context that it may leave little room for, and no explanation of, Leo's doctrinal content. Leo did seem to intend to speak in terms of import for all peoples and for all times. Any successful interpretation of Leo's doctrine on Church and state, in our view, must take Leo at his word and must illumine precisely why and under what conditions Leo judged that legal establishment of the Catholic religion constituted an "ideal."

LEO AND PATERNALISM

We propose to incorporate elements from the preceding approaches but with more attention to the exact terms of Leo's analysis and the precise nature of his argument. We propose to show that Leo's ideal was designed, and accurately designed, for a specific set of political circumstances. If Leo's references to the "body politic" and the "state" are specifically applicable to *paternal* society, then it is an inescapable conclusion that his blueprint on the ideal relationship between the Church and the state was specifically designed to apply to that type of society. If he never expressed the conception of democratic society in the modern context, then it would be foolish and grossly unfair to Leo to suggest that he intended his blueprint as an ideal for that type of society. This is not to belittle Leo's contribution; as we shall indicate, it was Leo's genius to see what so few in the nineteenth century saw—that disestablishment of the Church was necessarily inconsistent with the principles of a paternal organization of society. Nor should he be expected to think and speak about a type of government that was emerging but was not yet a distinct and friendly reality in Europe. The vital point now, however, is to indicate that Leo thought and spoke concerning paternal rather than democratic society.

When Leo referred to the "body politic," the "state," or the "government" in his encyclicals on the political order, he was always careful to draw a sharp distinction between the "rulers," on the one hand, and the "people" or the "subjects," on the other. The Church is solicitous of the "liberty of both rulers and their subjects."[18] The Church cannot be an "object of suspicion to rulers nor of hatred to the people."[19] In fact, "no society can hold together unless someone be over all, directing all to strive earnestly for the common good. . . ."[20] But "they who govern others possess authority solely for the welfare of the state."[21] Those who rule "should rule with even-handed justice, not as masters, but rather as fathers. . . ."[22] They must "rule their people kindly and with almost paternal charity."[23] Subjects, for their part, are bound "to their rulers, not merely by obedience, but by reverence and affection."[24] They should obey their rulers "with reverence and fealty not unlike that which children show their parents."[25]

It is not difficult to see that these references are intended to describe a paternal society and that type of society alone. The rulers constitute a distinct class whose function is to provide for the "people" who are their "subjects." These "rulers" must act as "fathers" of their community, while their "subjects" should respond with the "reverence" which "children show their parents." This description, of course, simply will not fit the modern democracy in which the "rulers" and the "ruled" constitute a single class. In a democracy the "people" rule themselves by the process of majority decision. A democracy may in practice envelop an elected leader with a charismatic aura, but this reverence and affection is a personal phenomenon and not an institution of the political process. The presupposition of a democratically organized society is that the people are not "children," that they do not require a "father" to make their ultimate political decisions for them.

LEO AND DEMOCRACY

Leo was not unacquainted with popular government. In fact, his encyclical comments indicate that he considered the term equivocal enough to describe two diametrically opposed political schemes. The first was that of Rousseau, the second that of Aquinas; the first was championed by the Revolution, the second by the Church.

Leo recognized that the nineteenth-century heirs of the Jacobins had appropriated the term "democracy" to describe a political model of absolute and unlimited popular sovereignty, and for such a model Leo had no words of encouragement. The essential vice of the doctrine of absolute and unlimited popular sovereignty, a doctrine which he saw to be "exceedingly well calculated to flatter and inflame many passions," was that it constituted the people the "spring-head of all rights and of all power" to the derogation of human and divine authority.[26] In one direction, the direction of *laissez faire*, an autonomous and freewheeling "will of the people" could operate to destroy that authority of government necessary to preserve social order. In the other direction, the direction of totalitarianism, the same will could operate to unleash a regime whose excessive authority would crush individual liberty. Leo had the wisdom to realize what Jacobin mysticism always obscured, namely, that majorities do not create basic human rights and duties. Both individuals and society are restrained inexorably by human values and divine commands which they can ignore or disobey only at their own peril. Leo saw clearly that the Jacobins wished to replace God and nature with the "will of the people" as the ultimate source of morality, and that such a "democracy" was a secular religion whose central mystery was to incarnate "all right and all duty . . . in the majority."[27]

But there was another political scheme of popular government which Leo recognized and approved. "The right to rule is not . . . bound up with any special mode of government . . . provided only that it be of a nature to insure the general welfare."[28] Specifically, "it is not of itself wrong to prefer a form of government regulated by the popular class" if only the origin and exercise of its powers are correctly understood.[29] It is not "blameworthy in itself, in any manner, for the people to have a share, greater or less, in the government."[30]

Now, the last-cited statements on the propriety of the "popular class" having a "share . . . in the government" reveal most decisively that the popular participation which Leo endorsed was a variety of the Aristotelian-Thomistic mixed "polity" rather than a variety of the modern type of democracy. The difference is an important one, with far-reaching consequences, for an understanding of Leo's theology of Church and state. The Aristotelian-Thomistic polity in which the people have a share is a form of constitutionalism and within the original logic of parliamentary rule, but it most assuredly is not modern democracy. In the theory of modern democratic government the people do not *share* the decision-making process with others; rather the people *are the ultimate source* of political decisions. The modern democracy does not constitute the people a class on a par with the aristocracy in directing the politically organized society; the modern democracy, rather, institutionalizes the popular will as the radical and ultimate source of decision making. The medieval notion of "polity" of which Pope Leo approved was a shadow but not the substance of the modern concept.

Thus the democracy which won Leo's approval did not incorporate popular rule through majority vote as the ultimate foundation of the political process. Nor did this type of democracy require an equality of citizens to exercise the function of decision making. In fact, since the people shared power with the traditional ruling classes rather than constituted the ultimate voice in the political process, Leo's concept of democracy positively excluded the equality of citizens which is the indispensable condition of modern democratic theory. Leo's democracy, therefore, actually represented another mode of paternal organization. It was not a pure monarchy nor a pure aristocracy, of course. But —and this is the crucial point—neither was it a pure democracy. A society which does not rest its political process without qualification on the principle of majority decisions, whatever the people's share in the government, remains essentially paternal. The concurrence of the traditional classes, if not their initiative, is required for political decision; the few still enjoy the prerogative of prescribing the political good for the many.

Leo's doctrine on Church and state may now be placed in its proper ideological perspective. The state for which Leo outlined the ideal relationship to the Church was a paternal state.[31] Leo recognized that the organization of society might rightfully take different shapes to fit varying indigenous needs. But whatever legitimate shape the organization of society took, Leo presupposed that it would be paternal. The only strictly nonpaternal organization of society which Leo acknowledged as distinctive was the godless and anti-Christian democracy of the Jacobins. There was, of course, no need and no possibility of a satisfactory, much less an ideal, relationship between the Church and such a political organization.

The possibility and implications of a responsible democratic society which was neither paternal nor Jacobin, Leo seems never to have expressly conceived, at least as far as his writings indicate. With the historical context in mind of the times in which Leo lived and reigned, this should not prove at all surprising. The nineteenth century was the century of liberalism and not the century of democracy, although the latter was emerging through the gradual extension of the franchise. During Leo's reign, universal suffrage—the trade-mark of modern democracy—existed in only two European countries, France and Switzerland, both of which were hostile to the Church's freedom.[32] Even in England the Lords were not shorn of their residual power until the resolution of the constitutional crisis of 1910–11, and universal suffrage did not become a reality until 1918.

Parenthetically we should note that there is nothing inconsistent or even strange about the fact that the liberal governments of the nineteenth century were paternal rather than democratic in character. The central doctrine of classical liberalism was not universal suffrage or majority decision but the autonomy of the self-sufficient individual. This doctrine is ultimately more compatible with anarchic than with democratic principles, since democracy is a pattern of genuine social organization. Unlike classical liberalism, democracy does not challenge the objective and perfective, the creative and dynamic nature of social organization itself. What the nineteenth-century liberal really desired was a freedom *from* society and government in which only the fit survived. This was the liberal's vision which he believed the liberal elite would prescribe for the unenlightened. The classical liberal crusaded for a suffrage broad enough to include himself, but he feared that further extension of the franchise to the masses would swell the ranks of his adversaries both on the tradition-bound right and on the radical left. The peasant might support a return to the old order, and the city worker might support radical government intervention in economic affairs. His fears were fully justified; the nineteenth century parties of classical liberalism were doomed everywhere in Europe when modern democracy and universal suffrage became twentieth-century realities.

Leo had an opportunity in 1892 to speak about the Church's relations with a modern democracy when he wrote in an attempt to rally French Catholics to the support of the Republic.[33] In the course of the letter he reaffirmed the validity of different forms of government according to the principles expressed in "preceding Encyclicals."[34] To the difficulty that the Third Republic was animated by anti-Christian sentiments, Leo wisely distinguished "between *constituted power* and *legislation*."[35] Anti-Christian legislation there might be, but the constitution remained a valid form of political organization. Leo closed the letter with a strong admonition to the French against "the principle of the separation of the State and the Church which is equivalent to the separation of human legislation from Christian and divine legislation."[36]

In fact, to wish that the State would separate itself from the Church would be to wish, by a logical sequence, that the Church be reduced to the liberty of living according to the law common to all citizens. . . . It is true that in certain countries this state of affairs exists. . . . But in France . . . the Church should not be placed in the precarious position to which she must submit among other peoples. . . .[37]

In the case of France, Leo had much reason to dislike the political system which in 1880 had banned the Jesuits and secularized education without any concern for the rights of Catholic parents. Yet Leo wrote to French Catholics in 1892 precisely to gain their support for the Republican constitution as a gesture of conciliation. Significantly, though, Leo did not advert to the strictly democratic process of the French polity, nor did he intimate that this fact had any bearing on the issue of Church and state. His "preceding Encyclicals" on the political order had "already exposed" the principles which were to govern the ideal relations between the Church and the state. But the "state" described in

those encyclicals was, as we have indicated, paternal in character. Leo either did not notice the difference between his concept
of the state in the earlier encyclicals and the existing French political structure or, if he did recognize the difference, he did not
realize the implications of the difference for the principles which
govern the relations between Church and state. Profession of the
Catholic religion by public law was no longer permissible or consistent with the new democratic pattern of political organization
in France. Of course, as events of the next decade would prove,
those who sought to "separate" the Catholic Church from the
French state wanted more than the equality of all religious beliefs before the law; they wanted to remove Catholic influence
from the entire social order. Such a self-styled "separation" was,
in fact, the establishment of secularism and a declaration of war
against the Church.

There was, indeed, one democratic society, both nonpaternal
and non-Jacobin, both genuinely democratic and friendly to the
Church's mission—the United States. But of the uniqueness and
ingenuity of the American pattern of political organization and
church-state structure at that stage of world history Leo nowhere
in his encyclicals indicated any recognition, though he did note
that the Catholic Church in America was "free to live and act
without hindrance."[38]

Yet, though all this is true, it would be very erroneous to draw the
conclusion that in America is to be sought the type of the most desirable status of the Church, or that it would be universally lawful
or expedient for State and Church to be, as in America, dissevered
and divorced. . . . [B]ut she would bring forth more abundant fruits
if, in addition to liberty, she enjoyed the favor of the laws and the
patronage of the public authority.[39]

Leo was obviously impressed by the freedom and prosperity
of the Catholic Church in America. But either he did not recognize that the United States was strictly democratic in political
structure, or else he did not discern the strictly political implications of a democratic, nonpaternal pattern of political organization. The "favor of the laws and the patronage of the public
authority," for which Leo expressed a preference over the exist-

ing separation of the Church and state, would be totally inconsistent with the equality of citizenship on which the American
political process rests; the equality of all religions before the law
is a necessary function of political equality. In fact, Leo always
referred to the United States as a "republic" rather than as a
democracy, which no doubt was in sound accord with the language of the Constitution but which passed over in silence the
most relevant political development in the American experiment.

POLITICAL STRUCTURES AND LEO'S THOUGHT

The truth is that Leo was exclusively absorbed with paternal
society and the nature of its relation to the Church. Leo gave no
notice that he perceived the unique character of modern democratic society and the nature of its relation to the Church. The
explanation for Leo's restricted conception of political problems
in general and the Church-state issue in particular lies as much
in the direction of history and psychology as in that of theology
and political philosophy. The overwhelmingly dominant pattern
of political organization in the Europe of Leo's reign was paternal. Democracy was a novel and emerging political concept not
yet free from association with the French Revolution in the
minds of Europeans trained, as Leo was, in the old tradition. He
had been schooled at the Academy of Noble Ecclesiastics, served
as papal governor of the enclave of Benevento and the city of
Perugia during the early period of the Italian revolutionary tur-
moil, and spent the thirty years before his election to the papal
throne as bishop of the latter city throughout the events of the
risorgimento. Leo should not be criticized for failing to penetrate
a novel and even suspect pattern of political organization not yet
fully emerged or, in Europe, free of Jacobin tendencies. Leo must
be judged rather on the acuteness of his analysis of the foundations of paternal society and its relation to the Church, foundations which he understood well.

Leo's contribution to the political theory and the Catholic
theology of Church and state was the insight that no paternal
society could refuse *as a matter of principle* to make public pro-

fession of the Catholic religion through legal establishment without implying hostility to the Church. Leo demonstrated that the structure of a paternal society is such that by commission or by omission it tends to establish some value or set of values as ultimate for the society. The duty of rulers in a paternal society, precisely as paternal, is to specify the good to which the inferior members should direct their will and energies. Since the corresponding duty of their subjects is to look to the rulers for that direction, they will inescapably interpret the absence of public profession as a denial of the unique claims of the Catholic Church. In the context of these mutually exclusive alternatives, therefore, legal establishment of the Catholic religion is obviously the "ideal," although, as Leo pointed out, to secure a "great good" or to hinder a "great evil" rulers may allow "every kind of religion" to have a "place in the state."[40]

Certainly Leo saw nothing in the attitude and actions of the nineteenth-century liberal governments of Latin Europe to mark any diminution in historical fact of the antagonism to the Church which he saw disestablishment to involve in paternal theory. Liberal efforts to "separate" the Church from the state were undisguised maneuvers of paternal inspiration to "free" unenlightened subjects from the bondage of a medieval and anachronistic superstition. The liberals loudly touted separation as a blow against the Church, and, even without any of the further positive restraint on the Church's religious freedom which regularly accompanied the self-styled separation, the act of disestablishment stood revealed in fact as well as in theory for what it really was—an establishment of secularism or at least the enshrinement of religion as a purely subjective and internal matter. Fact as well as theory supported Leo's argument that liberalism could not be yoked to paternalism without implicit hostility to the Church.

In the order of political process, moreover, paternal organization has important conditions which militate against any unrestrained liberty of expression, including liberty of worship and the equality of all religions before the law. The formation, decision, and execution of political policy belongs in a paternal society to the few. Citizens are politically unequal, and the free access of the many to communications media is not required for the functioning of the political process. In fact, due to the immaturity of the many, the indiscriminate extension of these free-doms would threaten the whole organization of a paternal society. Similarly, no exigency based on the equality of citizens requires religious freedom. As in the case of the former freedoms, an injudiciously extended religious freedom would threaten the unity of a paternally organized society.

The many in the immature society, either for lack of knowl-edge or want of stability, are incapable of determining the good of the whole body politic peacefully and prudently. The imma-ture society is incapable of coping with pluralism and diversity. This is why the immature society requires paternal organization. Under these conditions, pluralism of culture, especially of reli-gion as the transcendental value, tends to accentuate differences in the body politic and to thwart the few from the tasks of direct-ing the society and the many from receiving direction. Thus the strictly political implications of the paternal pattern of social or-ganization will minimize the possibility of full-fledged religious liberty.

Leo and his predecessors were well acquainted with the work-ings of paternal government. They consistently recognized the necessity for rulers in a paternal society to specify and support the Catholic religion as the supreme social good, and they con-sistently argued against unrestricted religious liberty as a threat to the very processes of paternal political organization. For this reason Leo and his predecessors regularly linked their censure of unrestricted religious liberty with censure of unrestricted liberty in other areas of expression and communication: speech, press, and teaching.[41] Leo and his predecessors understood very well that all liberties of public expression and communication were closely allied in the operation of the paternal pattern of political organization.

Leo's analysis and blueprint of the Church's ideal relation to the paternal state is inapplicable to the modern democracy. Un-like the paternal polity, the democratically organized society does not aim to prescribe through public law every phase of the com-mon good. The democratic polity does not separate a special class of rulers to supervise the activities of their subjects as a father would his children. Nor are there "subjects" in a democratic pol-ity who look up to their "rulers" for the specification of all major social goals. As a result of this difference in finality, therefore, the absence of legal establishment of the Catholic religion in a democratic state does not imply the establishment of secularism or religious indifferentism. Equality of all religions in the law of a democratic state implies no public profession of an ontological equality of all religions or none in the law of God. Because the democratic state has no finality to make every major prescription of the social good for its citizens—whom democratic theory presumes to be mature enough to act responsibly on their own—the omission of professing the Catholic religion through public law conveys no anti-Catholic ontological or theological presuppositions.

Not only is a democracy under no political exigency to profess and protect the Catholic religion through legal prescription, but a democracy, simply as a political process, is enjoined from such profession and protection. As process, democracy demands the equality of citizens in the ultimate determination of political policy. If decisions are to be made by the majority, the voice of each citizen must have equal weight. Were a democratic polity to deny to some citizens the freedom of religious commitment, the action would make citizens unequal, limit their role in the decision-making process, and disaffect them from the polity. Religion is the ultimate value to which men commit themselves, and it colors their every other value. Inequality here would rot the core of common aspiration and participation in the political process. A paternal polity with its selective pattern of decision-making may overlook the inequality and disaffection of religious minorities, but a democratic polity, which requires an active role for all citizens in the exercise of the decision-making power, can hardly do so. The mature, unlike the immature, society is capable of coping with pluralism because diversity is compatible with political unity.

Leo, of course, did not recognize these strictly political implications of modern democracy. That the patrician Pope missed the significance and underestimated the vitality of democracy should not be at all surprising.[42] Democracy was an emerging but not yet established pattern of government in Europe. But the most important reason why Leo did not discern the political implications of democratic process on the issue of the Church and the state was that the nineteenth-century apostles of separation never argued their case on that basis. Liberals like Cavour and Crispi in Italy and Gambetta and Ferry in France proposed separation of Church and state—accompanied by a program openly pledged to limit the Church's liberty—in the name of an enlightened human secularism or an indifferent religious subjectivism. If Leo never understood the political character of modern democracy, it was because his liberal counterparts never offered or exemplified truly democratic principles.

To recapitulate briefly, Leo summarized the tradition of his papal predecessors of the nineteenth century on the issue of the Church and the state. The state about which Leo thought and spoke was paternal in structure. Consequently, legal establishment represented the ideal relationship between the Catholic Church and such a state. This relationship was ideal for two basic reasons: First, the rulers in a paternal society, qua paternal, must establish by commission or omission the major goals of the society; and, secondly, the paternal political process, as process, cannot sustain the pluralism and diversity which an unrestricted religious liberty would risk. The only nonpaternal pattern of political organization whose existence and uniqueness Leo recognized was the "democracy" of the Revolution, which positively excluded the authority of God and His law in favor of the autonomous will of the people. Neither in theory nor in practice could the Church maintain harmonious and satisfactory relations with the latter. Leo gave no indication that he discerned the existence or political implications of a nonpaternal but responsible type of political organization, modern democracy, which had already developed in the United States and was in Leo's own reign emerging in Europe. Leo's analysis and blueprint for the ideal relationship between the Church and the state is inapplicable, and never was designed to apply, to modern democracies.

THE ADVENT OF PIUS XII

A half-century after the death of Leo, another patrician occupied the throne of St. Peter and spoke as the supreme teacher

of the Church. The times were vastly changed. Classical liberalism, caught in a pincer movement by the rise of mass parties,
was no longer the major threat to the Church. Classical liberalism, as a doctrine essentially geared to government by the
chosen, enlightened few, passed off the main stage of world history with World War I. The new threat to the Church came not
from those who exaggerated the autonomy of the individual but
from those who exalted the cult of the collectivity; the new threat
to the Church came from the totalitarian mass parties of the left
and of the right which had come to power in Russia, Italy, and
Germany. Pius XI died worn out with his struggles against the
dictators shortly before the outbreak of World War II.

The very first encyclical letter of his successor, Pius XII, issued
a scant seven weeks after the German and Russian invasion of
Poland, protested vigorously against "the error of those who im-
piously endeavor to dissociate civil authority from any connection at all with the Divine Being; forgetting that the community
quite as much as the individual depends upon Him as its first
author and supreme governor."[43] Pius XII specifically prayed for
the Church that "those who control the destinies of nations may
give the Church freedom of action. . . ."[44] If the state governs the
commonwealth according to the dictates of natural reason and
the Christian conscience, "it will help the individual human being
to achieve his own perfection in this present world, in all that
concerns his physical, mental, and moral well-being, and so
promote his attainment of his supernatural end."[45]

Where Leo emphasized the genuine authority of the state
against the efforts of the liberals to abdicate it, Pius stressed the
limitations on the state's authority against the attempts of the
dictators to deify it. Where Leo emphasized what the state must
do to protect citizens from the abuse of liberty, Pius stressed
what the state must not do to deprive citizens of liberty. Where
Leo proposed profession of the Catholic religion through legal
establishment, Pius asked only for the freedom of the Church to
carry on her mission. Where Leo emphasized the specification of
religious and moral goods through legal formulae as a matter of
logical necessity, Pius stressed the concrete conditions which help
the individual to achieve his perfection and "*so* promote his attainment of his supernatural end."

PIUS AND DEMOCRACY

Understandably, of course, the Pope's comments in the fall of 1939 were limited to specific principles relevant to the new and tragic disruption of the world order by the totalitarian powers. Five years later, in the sixth and final Christmas message of the war, however, Pius had occasion to speak more hopefully of the future. The Axis dictatorships were doomed, and Pius took the opportunity to recognize the advent of a postwar world order in which democracy would play the key role. The Pope did more than affirm with Leo that the Church does not condemn any form of government in itself; he went far beyond Leo to note that the "democratic form of government is considered by many to-day to be a natural postulate of reason itself."[46] Pius acknowledged that civil liberty and equality on the basis of human freedom and dignity were essential ideals of democracy, and that self-rule and free communication of opinion were "two rights of the citizens which find their expression in a democracy."[47] At the same time Pius was fully aware that "this form of government makes very great demands upon the moral maturity of individual citizens. . . ."[48]

A healthy democracy will not ascribe to the state an "authority beyond limit or restraint and which, despite deceptive appearances to the contrary, will transform even a democratic regime into a system of absolutism pure and simple."[49] The majesty of human law is "beyond appeal only when it conforms, or at least does not conflict, with the absolute order established by the Creator and set in a new light by the revelation of the Gospel."[50] In a future destined to belong to democracy, "an essential part . . . will fall to the lot of the Church. . . ."[51]

It is the Church's mission to proclaim to the world, now demanding more and more perfect forms of democracy, the message than which there can be none more sublime or more necessary: that of the dignity of man, that of his vocation to be a son of God.[52]

Pius did more in this message than acknowledge and tolerate democracy as the only alternative in the modern world to the totalitarian heresies; he clearly revealed that he understood the democratic processes and approved warmly what he understood. Pius frankly faced the fact that democracy today "may be a natural postulate of reason itself," and went significantly far to distinguish "the maturity of individual citizens" as the precise foundation on which reason would naturally postulate democratic government. As long as immature societies remained, of course, paternal political organization would remain. But paternalism was no longer possible when citizens realized their right and ability to govern themselves, and paternalism was no longer justifiable when citizens had the maturity to rule responsibly. Moreover, Pius recognized absolute civic equality, maximum individual liberty, and particularly liberty of expression as political necessities of the democratic process.

That Pius in 1944 should so thoroughly understand the political structure of the democratic process is no more surprising than that Leo a half century earlier should have failed to do so. Both popes were men of their day. Democracy had emerged as the dominant form of government in Europe at the end of World War I and had proved its sustaining power in World War II. In contrast to the totalitarian powers the democracies honored human liberties and the Church's freedom. Pius did not need to be a prophet to see this. Moreover, political analysts had had time since Leo's day to make evident the nature and operations of democratic government. Pius himself had invaluable experience as papal Secretary of State and had traveled widely—even to the United States, where he personally witnessed the responsible workings of the world's first modern democracy.

What Pius had to say about the relation of the democratic state to the Catholic is doubly significant. In the first place, Pius affirmed the liberty of the Church against abuse by the public power. He reminded the democracies that the Church teaches the truth and communicates the grace which implement "that order which is the ultimate foundation and guiding norm for every democracy."[53] The Church's mission is to proclaim to the world the most sublime and the most necessary message of the dignity of man and his vocation to be a son of God. The democracies, therefore, are under a strict obligation to respect the liberty of the Church, and she in turn provides them with the "ultimate foundation." In the second place, Pius' remarks are even more significant because of what they omit. Pius made no reference to the profession of the Catholic religion through legal establishment or to restrictions on the liberty of non-Catholics' religious exercises. This omission, when read in connection with Pius' insight into the democratic principles of liberty and equality, may be taken to imply obliquely that public profession and restricted liberty of worship do not constitute an "ideal" relationship between the Catholic Church and the democratic state.

PIUS AND TOLERANCE

In the years following the restoration of peace Pius spoke on several occasions of the relations between the Church and the state. On October 6, 1946, in an allocution to the Roman Rota, Pius extolled political, civic, and social tolerance in the context of a modern pluralistic society, not merely as permissible but even as "a moral duty":

The increasingly frequent contacts between different religious professions, mingled indiscriminately within the same nation, have caused civil authorities to follow the principles of "tolerance" and "liberty of conscience." In fact, there is a political tolerance, a civil tolerance, a social tolerance, in regard to adherents of other religious beliefs which, in circumstances such as these, is a moral duty for Catholics.[54]

It is hard to see how Pius could have endorsed political tolerance in the context of modern pluralism with any greater clarity, and it is to be regretted that Catholics and non-Catholics alike have not given this important text more careful attention.

On October 29 of the next year, in another allocution to the same body, Pius again remarked on the relation of the Church to the state. This time the Pope cautioned against a misinterpretation of the fact that the sacred and civil societies differ essentially in their respective goals. The difference between the two societies "does not exclude every kind of union between the two. . . . Such a view would . . . leave out of consideration the fact that the

Church and the State both have their origin in God and both are concerned with the same subjects—human beings."[55] Here the Pope wisely noted that the Church and the state must cooperate with each other, that an absolute and hostile separation of the Church and the state is inadmissible within the framework of Christian teaching and social reality. The Church as well as the state is a visible society whose life necessarily manifests a physical and social dimension. The simultaneous interaction of the two societies with respect to the same human beings makes cooperation the only acceptable possibility. As the order of grace perfects rather than destroys the order of nature in the individual, so, too, the ecclesiastical order complements rather than threatens the civil order in the social context. Any attempt to separate the secular so absolutely from the sacred in matters of common concern would establish an unjustifiable hostility between the two and constitute an intolerable breach of the divinely intended harmony.

But undoubtedly the most expansive and authoritative expression of Pius' views on the relations to obtain between the Church and state was provided in an address to the Italian jurists on the place of religion in the emerging world community.[56] Though the main import of the address bore on the role of tolerance within the world community, the Pope's remarks were applicable, and intended to be applicable, *mutatis mutandis*, to the role of tolerance within the national community. What made this address so authoritative on the issue of Church and state was the element of timing. Over the preceding several years an intense discussion which centered on the so-called "new thesis" of Fr. John Courtney Murray had stirred Catholic theological circles, especially in the United States. Events came to something of a head when Cardinal Ottaviani, Pro-Secretary of the Sacred Congregation of the Holy Office, speaking unofficially as a private theologian, voiced strong opposition to the views of Fr. Murray in March, 1953.[57] His comments received wide circulation among Catholics and non-Catholics alike, and there can be little doubt that Pius spoke on the Church-state issue on December 6, 1953, with this background quite prominently in mind.

At the outset Pius sharply distinguished two questions: (1) What is the obligation in conscience toward objective truth? and

(2) What is the obligation of the politically organized society toward religious error? He properly dismissed the first question as one which "can hardly be a matter for discussion."[58] But the second question "can be of extreme importance and urgency."[59] No human authority, or course, can command or authorize what "would be contrary to religious truth or moral good."[60] The more delicate aspect of the second question, however, is whether free exercise of religious belief is permissible where plural religious beliefs exist within one political community. "Could it be that in certain circumstances He [God] would not even communicate the right to impede or repress what is erroneous and false?"[61] Pius answered in the affirmative: to say that "religious and moral error must always be impeded, when it is possible, because toleration of them is itself immoral, is not valid absolutely and unconditionally."[62]

The duty of repressing moral and religious error cannot therefore be an ultimate norm of action. It must be subordinate to *higher and more general* norms, which *in some circumstances* permit, and even perhaps seem to indicate as the better policy, toleration of error in order to promote a *greater good.*[63]

The Church, in contrast to political society, "has the duty" as a matter of absolute obligation, to be sure, "of teaching and educating in all the inflexibility of truth and goodness."[64] But the Church acts with tolerance "for higher and more cogent motives" out of regard "for those who in good conscience . . . are of different opinion."[65] The attitude of the Church is determined, on the one hand, by what is necessary to preserve "the common good of the Church and the State in individual states, and, on the other, the common good of the universal Church, the reign of God over the whole world."[66] No other norms "are valid for the Church except the norms . . . for the Catholic jurist and statesman."[67]

Pius closed his comments with a rejection of a "complete separation of the two powers" of Church and state.[68] This was a reiteration of a theme struck several years before in the 1947 allocution to the Roman Rota. "Complete separation" of the Church and the state from any cooperative interaction in matters of common concern would imply an active hostility to Catholic belief, would not "assure to the Church a stable condition" in the state, and would not "guarantee to her full independence in the fulfillment of her divine mission."[69] Thus the Church cannot approve the complete separation of the two powers, but their co-operation may take place without any proclamation of their "common religious conviction" and within the framework of "simple tolerance" according to the principles already elaborated as "the norms for coexistence of the Church and her faithful with the civil powers and men of another belief."[70]

Pius' able distinction of the unconditional and absolute obligation of all men to acknowledge the objective truth of the Catholic religion from the conditional and relative obligation of the state to establish the Catholic religion is the key to understanding the further development of his views. It was precisely here that Pius offered a clarifying refinement to the whole magisterial discussion of Church and state. From this distinction Pius drew the inevitable conclusion that the political society may be under an obligation, under certain conditions, *not* to establish the Catholic religion or to restrict the freedom of non-Catholic worship. There are "higher and more general norms" which not only permit but may even require political tolerance "as a better policy." Note, too, that Pius did not say that the "higher" norms operate to permit or require political toleration when intolerance would be impossible but precisely when restrictions on religious liberty are indeed physically possible.

But what are the "higher and more general norms" which are "ultimate" in this matter? Pius did not tell us specifically, but we may surmise from the context at least the one which Pius considered primary. Pius prefaced his discussion of the topic of tolerance by posing the problem in terms of plural belief systems existing within the same political community. It would be fair to assume, therefore, that the fact of pluralism constituted in the Pope's mind one of the "ultimate" norms to govern political action here. Moreover, since the fact of pluralism is intimately connected with the democratic political process—for which Pius had already indicated wide sympathy and understanding in his Christmas message of 1944—it would be a more developed but no less sound inference, we believe, to say that Pius numbered the unique political demands of democratic government among the "higher" norms.

For Pius, therefore, legal establishment simply was not an absolute and unconditional ideal of the state's relation to the Church. Pius emphatically subordinated legal establishment and legal restrictions on religious liberty to "higher and more general norms" which themselves constitute the "ultimate norm of action." Because Pius, unlike Leo, conceived the state as embracing more than the paternal principle of political organization, so Pius, unlike Leo, recognized the relevance of other than paternal norms as the ultimate basis of political decision in this matter. In other words, Pius did not recognize *either* establishment *or* nonestablishment as ideal for all situations. Rather, the ideal consisted in the prudent application by the Catholic jurist and statesman of the higher norms which govern political action. When circumstances permit or even require toleration "as a better policy," then nonestablishment becomes the ideal relationship between the Church and the state. Of course, Pius could not approve a complete separation of the two societies which would assume the hostility of the secular to the sacred. But he did approve of a cooperative interaction between the Church and the state which worked effectively without any proclamation of "common religious conviction" and with the peaceful coexistence in the community of the Church's faithful with men of other beliefs.

Pius did not develop the specific theme that the civic freedom of religious exercise is a condition of the religious freedom of the act of faith. Like Leo, of course, Pius did reject any semblance of direct public coercion of religious belief. But Pius did not go further and reject even the indirect pressures which the full rigor of legal establishment would work on the human conscience. The recent remarks of Cardinal Lercaro, however, may indicate that more will be heard from Rome on this theme in future years.[71]

To recapitulate briefly, Pius XII added a new dimension to the tradition of his papal predecessors of the nineteenth century on the issue of Church and state. The state about which Pius thought and spoke was not restricted to the paternal structure. He explicitly recognized the existence and desirability of, even the natural and rational exigency for, the democratic organization of modern political society. Moreover, he indicated a recognition of the necessary political characteristics of such a democratic organization. Consequently, Pius did not envision legal establishment to represent the ideal relationship between the Church and the state. The decision whether or not to establish the Catholic religion through public law is political in character and governed by higher and more general norms which are ultimate. "Certain circumstances"—including the fact of pluralism and the specific qualities of democratic government—permit or even require "as the better policy" the equality of all religions before the law. Pius' analysis and blueprint of the relationship between the Church and the state is applicable, and was specifically designed to apply, to modern democracies.

CONCLUSION

We must reject any suggestion, however, that Pius' exposition of the principles which govern the relations between the Church and the state in any way contradicted or opposed the teaching of Leo XIII and the popes of the nineteenth century. Rather, Pius explored an area of the problem which Leo never opened. Pius' comments, therefore, serve to complement and supplement the teaching of Leo. Pius did not deny the applicability of Leo's blueprint to paternal societies; but he did recognize the existence, the desirability, and the political implications of the democratic organization of society. Pius subsumed Leo's analysis in a much larger one which could apply to democratic and pluralistic as well as paternal and monistic societies. Where Leo spoke to the nineteenth century in terms of paternal society, then precariously dominant in Europe, Pius spoke to the twentieth century in terms of democratic society, now fully emerged. Historical events, of course, made this enlargement of principles necessary, and Pius responded to the necessity with clarity and initiative. Far from contradiction between the teaching of Leo and that of Pius on the Church-state question, there is only a genuine historical development and ideological complementarity.

What, then, is the theological status of the so-called "new

thesis"? Is the legal equality of all religions before the law under appropriate circumstances a relationship between the Church and the state which is fully compatible with Catholic principles and not some second-best solution? No authoritative statement from the teaching Church has yet settled the question. But enough evidence is at hand to indicate that the so-called "new thesis" is at least an acceptable theory within the framework of Catholic orthodoxy which may serve as the basis for continuing theological speculation and political practice. As one non-Catholic observer noted:

Roman Catholic literature representing this modern tendency [to defend religious liberty as first-best under appropriate circumstances] has lately been so voluminous and of such quality that it would be an understatement to say that, for one book or article in favour of the traditional doctrine, ten have been published defending . . . religious freedom. . . .[72]

While the *nihil obstat* which accompanied these books and articles does not represent a positive official endorsement of the content of the printed material, it does indicate that nothing in such material has been found to run counter to the teaching of the Church. Secondly and more authoritatively, Pius XII to all appearances enlarged and developed the principles on the relationship between the Church and the state at least far enough to permit an acceptable place within the framework of a Catholic orthodoxy for the defense of political tolerance as a first-best relationship under appropriate conditions.

If no theologian can close the question in favor of the so-called "new thesis" by an appeal to Pius, neither can any theologian close the question against the new thesis by an appeal to Leo. The theologian who genuinely seeks to illumine the problem must accept *all* the theological data from papal pronouncements of both the nineteenth and twentieth centuries. He must, moreover, accept all the relevant data from allied historical and political sources if he is to interpret the theological data accurately. The theological thesis of political tolerance for all religions as a first-best relationship of the Church to pluralistic and democratic societies, in our opinion, meets this test.

NOTES

1. "*Humani Generis,*" *Acta Apostolicae Sedis,* Vol. XVII (1950), p. 568. The translation is by Msgr. Ronald A. Knox, *The Tablet,* September 2, 1950, p. 188.

2. Fr. Murray, S.J., whose study of Leo XIII's thought on Church and state is the most exhaustive and penetrating study to date, has found "some ninety-seven documents" to be relevant to the problem and twenty of these to be "of major importance." "Leo XIII on Church and State: The General Structure of the Controversy," *Theological Studies,* Vol. XIV (1953), p. 1. Fr. Murray's analysis of Leo XIII's thought is elaborated in the latter and three suceeding articles: "Leo XIII: Separation of Church and State," *Theological Studies,* Vol. XIV (1953), pp. 145–214; "Leo XIII: Two Concepts of Government," *Theological Studies,* Vol. XIV (1953), pp. 551–567; and "Leo XIII: Government and the Order of Culture," *Theological Studies,* Vol. XV (1954), pp. 1–33. The three documents of the greatest significance are the encyclicals *Diuturnum* (1881), *Immortale Dei* (1885), and *Libertas Praestantissimum* (1888). In addition, the encyclical letters *Au milieu des solicitudes* (1892) and *Longinqua Oceani* (1895) are relevant to Leo's thought on the particular relationships between the Church and the state in France and the United States, respectively.

3. "*Libertas Praestantissimum,*" *Acta Sanctae Sedis,* Vol. XX (1888–1889), p. 599; the translation is from *The Church Speaks to the Modern World: The Social Teachings of Leo XIII,* ed. Etienne Gilson (Garden City, N.Y.: Image Books, 1954), p. 64.

4. *Ibid.*

5. "*Immortale Dei,*" *Acta Sanctae Sedis,* Vol. XVIII (1885), p. 162; the translation is from *The Church Speaks to the Modern World,* p. 162.

6. *Ibid.*

7. *Ibid.,* p. 164; *trans. cit.,* p. 165.

8. *Ibid.,* pp. 164–165; *trans. cit.,* p. 165.

9. *Ibid.,* p. 166; *trans. cit.,* pp. 168, 167.

10. *Ibid.,* p. 163; *trans. cit.,* p. 164.

11. *Ibid.,* p. 174; *trans. cit.,* p. 177.

12. *Ibid.,* p. 163; *trans. cit.,* p. 164.

13. *Ibid.,* p. 164; *trans. cit.,* p. 164.

14. *Ibid.,* p. 174; *trans. cit.,* p. 178.

15. *Ibid.,* pp. 174–175; *trans. cit.,* p. 178.

16. "*Libertas,*" *op. cit.,* p. 610; *trans. cit.,* p. 77.

17. *Ibid.*

18. *Ibid.,* p. 605; *trans. cit.,* p. 71.

19. "*Diuturnum,*" *Acta Sanctae Sedis,* Vol. XIV (1881), p. 13; the translation is from *The Church Speaks to the Modern World,* p. 153.

20. *"Immortale Dei," op. cit.,* p. 162; *trans. cit.,* p. 162.

21. *Ibid.,* pp. 162–163; *trans. cit.,* p. 163.

22. *Ibid.,* p. 162; *trans. cit.,* p. 163.

23. *"Libertas," op. cit.,* p. 605; *trans. cit.,* p. 71.

24. *Ibid.; trans. cit.,* pp. 71–72.

25. *"Immortale Dei", op. cit.,* p. 163; *trans. cit.,* p. 163.

26. *Ibid.,* pp. 172, 170; *trans. cit.,* pp. 174, 172.

27. *"Libertas," op. cit.,* p. 601; *trans. cit.,* p. 67.

28. *"Immortale Dei," op. cit.,* p. 162; *trans. cit.,* p. 163.

29. *"Libertas," op. cit.,* p. 613; the translation is my own from the Latin text which reads: "Atque etiam malle reipublicae statum populari temperatum genere, non est per se contra officium. . . ." The standard English translation (the Paulist Press) renders the Latin this way: "Again, it is not of itself wrong to prefer a democratic form of government. . . ." *Trans. cit.,* p. 81. The latter translation, however, is both misleading and inaccurate. It is misleading because Leo reserved the term "democratic" for the popular rule associated with the excesses of the Revolution. The term "democratic" for Leo, therefore, was a pejorative one. The standard translation is also inaccurate because Leo was in the context endorsing the ancient and medieval notion of mixed "polity" rather than the modern concept of democracy. The people constituted a *class* (*genus*) distinct from the aristocracy which would regulate or

temper (*temperatum*) the form of government. Thus the people shared rather than constituted the decision-making process. For a further confirmation of my analysis of this text examine the citation from *Immortale Dei* which immediately follows.

30. *"Immortale Dei," op. cit.,* p. 174; *trans. cit.,* p. 177.

31. This judgment is shared by two eminent ecclesiologists, Fr. Murray and Fr. Gustave Weigel, S.J., and by a prominent historian of Leo, Dr. Raymond Schmandt. According to Fr. Murray, Leo's theories "repose to some extent on a concept of government as paternal . . . a concept which is hypothetically and historically conditioned." "Leo XIII: Two Concepts of Government," *Theological Studies,* Vol. XIV (1953), p. 567. Fr. Weigel observed succinctly: "Leo by training conceived government as a paternalistic function." "Leo XIII and Contemporary Theology," *Leo XIII and the Modern World,* ed. Edward T. Gargan (New York: Sheed & Ward, 1961), p. 225. Dr. Schmandt commented: "Leo thought of government in paternalistic terms. For this reason he permitted broad powers in the regulation of the lives of the citizens. Here too his own experience was determinative, and his thoughts on liberty must be studied against this background." "The Life and Work of Leo XIII," *Leo XIII and the Modern World,* p. 43.

32. Anticlerical legislation dates in France from the fall of Mac-Mahon and in Switzerland from the days of the *Sunderbund.*

33. "Au milieu des solicitudes," Acta Sanctae Sedis, Vol. XXIV (1891–1892), pp. 519–529.

34. Ibid., p. 523; the translation is from The Great Encyclical Letters of Pope Leo XIII, ed. John J. Wynne, S.J. (New York: Benziger Bros., 1903), p. 255.

35. Ibid., p. 525; trans. cit., p. 258.

36. Ibid., p. 528; trans. cit., pp. 261–262.

37. Ibid., p. 528; trans. cit., p. 262.

38. "Longinqua Oceani," Acta Sanctae Sedis, Vol. XXVII (1895); p. 390; the translation is from The Great Encyclical Letters of Pope Leo XIII, p. 323.

39. Ibid.; trans. cit., pp. 323–324.

40. "Immortale Dei," op. cit., p. 174; trans. cit., p. 178.

41. "Libertas," op. cit., p. 603 et seq.; trans. cit., p. 70 et seq.

42. Another vital political movement at work in the nineteenth century whose significance escaped Leo was nationalism. "Leo totally missed the significance and underestimated the strength of nationalism. In all of his writings there is no passage that examines this elusive, potent factor in modern political life." Raymond H. Schmandt, "The Life and Work of Leo XIII," op. cit., p. 23.

43. "Summi Pontificatus," Acta Apostolicae Sedis, Vol. XXXI (1939), p. 431; the translation is from Selected Letters and Addresses of Pius XII, ed. Canon G. D. Smith (London: Catholic Truth Society, 1949), p. 22.

44. Ibid., p. 445; trans. cit., p. 37.

45. Ibid., p. 433; trans. cit., pp. 23–24.

46. "Già per la sesta volta," Acta Apostolicae Sedis, Vol. XXXVII (1944–1945), p. 13; the translation is from Selected Letters, p. 305.

47. Ibid., pp. 14, 13; trans. cit., pp. 306, 305.

48. Ibid., p. 18; trans. cit., p. 311.

49. Ibid., p. 17; trans. cit., p. 310.

50. Ibid.

51. Ibid., p. 22; trans. cit., p. 315.

52. Ibid.; trans. cit., p. 316.

53. Ibid.

54. "Allocution to the Roman Rota," Acta Apostolicae Sedis, Vol. XXXVIII (1946), p. 393; the translation is from the Clergy Review, Vol. XXVII (1947), p. 277.

55. "Allocution to the Roman Rota," Acta Apostolicae Sedis, Vol. XXXIX (1947), p. 494; the translation is from the Clergy Review, Vol. XXIX (1948), p. 197.

56. "Allocution to the Italian Jurists," Acta Apostolicae Sedis, Vol. XLV (1953), pp. 794–802.

57. Cardinal Ottaviani, art. cit.

58. "Allocution to the Italian Jurists," op. cit., p. 798; the translation is from The Catholic Mind, Vol. LII (1954), p. 247.

59. Ibid.

60. Ibid.

61. Ibid., pp. 798–799; trans. cit., p. 248.

62. Ibid., p. 799; trans. cit., p. 248.

63. Ibid. The italics are supplied from the original and are

not found in the translation.
  64. *Ibid.*, p. 801; *trans. cit.*,
p. 249.
  65. *Ibid.; trans. cit.*, p. 250.
  66. *Ibid.*
  67. *Ibid.*
  68. *Ibid.*, p. 802; *trans. cit.*,

p. 250.
  69. *Ibid.*
  70. *Ibid.*
  71. Cardinal Lercaro, *art. cit.*
  72. Carrillo de Albornoz, *op.
cit.*, p. 8.

4

American Democracy
and
Religious Freedom

The dogmatic intolerance of a Catholic belief, as we have seen, is compatible with the political tolerance of democratic government. But are the concrete dynamics of the American accommodation compatible with the beliefs and rights of Catholic citizens? Does the American formula of "separation of church and state" constitute a politically based "article of peace," or does it incorporate an "article of faith" theologically based on a Protestant or secularist creed? To answer this question it will be necessary to investigate here the basic principles of the American constitutional settlement and in succeeding chapters their application to particular problem areas.

First of all, we must recall that it is absolutely incumbent on
political society and its chief instrument, the state, to provide
conditions wherein men may freely fulfill God's salvific plans.
This involves the freedom of the Church to teach, sanctify, and
rule the faithful together with the correlative freedom of the
faithful to be taught, to be sanctified, and to be ruled. Secondly,
the polity must live in peace and harmony with the Church. And,
lastly, the polity must cooperate positively with the Church in
problems of mutual interest but always in accordance with the
proper finality and constitution of each.

These necessary goals of Church-state accommodation, as we
observed in the last several chapters, can be attained through
the guarantees of religious liberty and the equality of all religions
before the law, both of which a pluralistic, democratic form of
government requires. But we must not lose sight of the means-to-
end relationship involved. The peace, freedom, and well-being
of society are the ends of any political organization; the democratic process and all corollaries of the process are means to
these ends. Hence religious liberty and the equality of all religions before the law are political means to a political end.

Unfortunately the precise political character of religious freedom in American democracy is not always appreciated, and a
theological interpretation proper only to non-Catholic belief is
not infrequently substituted.[1] Protestants, for instance, may be
tempted to conceive the guarantee of religious liberty to be a
singular consequence of the authority of the individual conscience
to interpret divine revelation. This would make of the guarantee
of religious liberty an article of Protestant faith. Secularists, too,
may be tempted to conceive the guarantee of religious liberty to
be a singular consequence of the impossibility, or at least in-
actuality, of any special divine intervention in the affairs of man.
This would make of the guarantee of religious liberty an article
of secularist faith. Quite obviously, neither of these articles of
faith is consistent with Catholic belief in the Church's claim to a
unique authority from Jesus Christ to teach what God has revealed to man. The classical liberal's interpretation of the guarantee of religious liberty likewise denied its political character. The
classical liberal conceived the guarantee of religious liberty to
be a singular consequence of the autonomous sovereignty of the

individual, and, as we have commented before, this view is not so much in opposition to the claims of the Catholic Church to unique religious authority as to the claims of an objective social order in which the individual reaches fulfillment.

Protestant, secular, and liberal ideologies may rightfully claim credit for the historical influence which they have exerted in favor of the American guarantees of religious liberty. Yet the luster of these claims does not obscure or deny Catholic contributions to the historical origins of the same guarantees.[2] The Calverts in Catholic Maryland no less than Roger Williams in Baptist Rhode Island were precursors of the framers of the First Amendment. Moreover, it would be tragic if the American guarantees of religious liberty were regarded not as "articles of peace" but as "articles of faith." Protestant, secular, and liberal ideologies are indeed compatible with the principle of religious liberty, but that does not imply the truth of the converse, namely, that the principle of religious liberty is a unique consequence of Protestant, secular, or liberal ideology. Logic teaches us the fallacy of converting implications. The Catholic no less than his fellow citizens sees that religious liberty is an exigency of a pluralistic, democratic society.

INTERPRETING THE CONSTITUTION

What, then, do the American guarantees of religious liberty mean? To answer this question it is necessary to turn to the provisions of the United States Constitution, particularly the First Amendment, as authoritatively interpreted by the Supreme Court. In the provisions of fundamental law are contained the legal principles which define and govern church-state relations in the United States. The Constitution is indeed the "supreme law of the land," and an unbroken line of decisions by the Supreme Court has established the Court as its authoritative interpreter. Perhaps, as critics of the Court maintain, this power of judicial review is not clearly revealed in or demonstrable from the Constitution itself. But tradition, if not logic, has defined the Court's present position. By 1926 Charles Evans Hughes could say, without exaggerating the dominance of judicial review, that the Constitution is "what the Supreme Court says it is."[3]

The pages of American history are filled with the undulations of a seeming antithesis between "government under law" and "government under men." On the one hand, the Constitution is the "supreme law." "Judicial power," Chief Justice Marshall pronounced, "as contradistinguished from the power of the laws, has no existence. Courts are mere instruments of the law and can will nothing."[4] On the other hand, the Constitution must be interpreted authoritatively by men, and in the context of judicial review this human oracle is the Supreme Court. "While unconstitutional exercise of power by the executive and legislative branches of government is subject to judicial restraint," Justice Stone exclaimed in 1936, "the only check upon our own exercise is our own sense of self-restraint."[5]

In the controversy over the Court in the thirties, the reformers on one side complained of the intransigence of the Court and heralded the doctrine of an "evolving" Constitution. On the other side, at the inauguration of the "constitutional revolution" of 1937, Justice Sutherland protested that "the Constitution does not change with the ebb and flow of economic events."[6] And in the controversy over the Court in the fifties, on the one side Chief Justice Warren, speaking for the Court in the Segregation Cases asserted:

. . . We cannot turn the clock back to 1868 when the Amendment was adopted or even to 1896 when *Plessy* v. *Ferguson* was written. We must consider public education in the light of its full development and its present place in American life throughout the nation. . . .[7]

On the other side, his critics charged the Chief Justice not only with making but also with remaking history.

The advocates of an "unchanging" Constitution may be the victims of the popular misconception that constitutional determination is a mathematically precise and crystal-clear process of "squaring" the written word with the particular fact situation at hand.[8] There is no question of the importance of the wording of a constitutional provision; it is the heart of the American instrument of limited government. But, as Chief Justice Marshall said in *McCulloch* v. *Maryland,* "we must never forget that it is a *constitution* we are interpreting."[9] Since provisions of a constitution state general propositions which cannot envision all the particular areas of application, the meaning of key provisions of the Constitution requires interpretation.

Of course, the first guidepost for determining the meaning of a constitutional provision is not, as Justice Frankfurter reminded us in the Adamson case, the intention of the framers; it is what they wrote.[10] But when interpretation is required, as it normally is, the Court may have recourse to the debates and proceedings of the constitutive body which adopted or ratified the provision and to other facets of the historical background which place the debates and wording of the provision in the proper context. This, too, normally proves inconclusive or, if historically conclusive, not solely determinative. Since the Court is required to *interpret* the provision, it does so, at least in part, by examining the consequences of accepting alternative interpretations and by way of analogy to previous interpretations. When the Court does endorse a particular interpretation, this decision may establish a legal precedent. In a sense, therefore, any such decision will judicially amend the Constitution.

Time, however, may alter the conditions which make an interpretation and precedent realistic. Faced with this central problem of social change, the Supreme Court has followed the developmental tradition of the early common law. Excepting the protection extended to property interests from 1890 to 1937, the Court has generally approved a large degree of flexibility for constitutional interpretation to accord with social reality. The "constitutional revolution" of 1937 really signaled a return to Marshallian principles with an added recognition of the weight of social policy in the determination of constitutional questions. In the words of Justice Frankfurter, the judicial process is an "evolution of social policy by way of judicial application of Delphic provisions of the Constitution."[11] Or, as Simon Soboloff put it:

In our system the Supreme Court is not merely the adjudicator of controversies, but in the process of adjudication it is in many instances the final formulator of national policy.[12]

For the purposes of the question at hand there is no need to stir more deeply these live waters, to evaluate the relative importance of social policy in determining constitutional questions. It is sufficient to note that no discussion of a constitutional question as significant as the principle of religious liberty is complete without an examination of social policy.

The task of understanding the First Amendment in the light of decisions by the Supreme Court is circumscribed by several factors. One is that in the American system the Court decides no more than the individual case submitted to it. This means that the Court will not declare authoritatively more than is required for disposition of the individual case. We shall look in vain, therefore, for a treatise on church-state relations in the case law on the First Amendment. Another factor which makes an investigation more difficult is the number and diversity of Court personnel. In the course of decades of decisions many different personalities with many different philosophies have written, separately concurred in, or dissented from the Court's decisions. The past or present legal significance of the First Amendment in such circumstances is by no means fully transparent.

The guarantee of religious liberty by the First Amendment is twofold: (1) Congress shall make no law prohibiting the free exercise of religion, and (2) Congress shall make no law respecting an establishment of religion. We shall sketch first the most important cases relevant to the guarantee of religious freedom.

THE "FREE EXERCISE OF RELIGION"

For one hundred years following the Amendment's adoption the guarantee of free religious exercise against federal encroachment remained untested. The nature and scope of this prohibition of Congressional action was for the first time delineated by the Supreme Court in a case which involved the Mormon practice of polygamy, where the Court sustained a federal statute forbidding bigamy in the territory of Utah.[13] In answer to the defendant's appeal to the First Amendment's guarantee of the free exercise of his religious beliefs as a Mormon, the Court distinguished between legislation over religious belief and legislation over action violative of social duties or good order. Only the former was held beyond the pale of Congressional action. Nor, by virtue of the same distinction, did the Court in 1934 agree that the right to religious belief exempted a conscientious objector from military service although Congress might grant such immunity.[14]

Following the application of other First Amendment guarantees to state actions via the Fourteenth Amendment, the Supreme Court in 1940 affirmed the protection by the Fourteenth Amendment of the free exercise of religion against encroachment by the states.[15] Most of the cases which have arisen since 1940 on the free exercise clause have, like the Cantwell case, concerned state action and the small but dynamic sect known as the Jehovah's Witnesses.

In *Cantwell* v. *Connecticut* three Witnesses were convicted of violating a Connecticut statute requiring solicitors for religious causes to be certified by a local officer. Justice Roberts, speaking for a unanimous Court, held (1) that the due process clause of the Fourteenth Amendment protected the free exercise of religion against state restriction; (2) that free exercise of religion embraced two concepts, the freedom to believe, which is absolutely guaranteed by the Constitution, and the freedom to act according to conscience, which cannot be so guaranteed; and (3) that the Connecticut statute laid a forbidden burden upon the exercise of religious liberty. Justice Roberts reminded Connecticut that if any solicitation for religious causes was fraudulent, the state was free to punish such conduct subsequently. For a public official to determine whether a cause was religious antecedent to solicitation was a prior and prohibited restraint upon the exercise of religious liberty.

Several weeks after the Cantwell decision the Court decided the first of two controversial flag-saluting cases. In the Gobitis case, Justice Frankfurter, speaking for an 8-1 majority, declared that freedom of religious exercise was not violated by a Pennsylvania law requiring pupils of the public schools to salute the flag of the United States even when such a salute would be contrary to the dictates of conscience.[16] The Jehovah's Witnesses objected to the flag salute as worship of a "graven image," but Justice

Frankfurter deferred to the quest of the Pennsylvania legislature to promote the "cohesive sentiment" which is the foundation of national unity. Justice Stone alone argued that the First Amendment rights were constitutionally preferred and that the cause of national unity was insufficient to coerce students to act against their consciences.

Three years later and after heated criticism of the Gobitis decision, a similar case arose under a West Virginia statute. But in the Barnette case, Justice Jackson, speaking for a 6-3 majority, declared that the statute transcended constitutional limitations and "invaded the sphere of intellect and spirit which it is the purpose of the First Amendment to our Constitution to reserve from all official control."[17] The state may not compel utterance for the sake of "cohesive sentiment." Freedom of speech can be restricted, according to the majority here, only to prevent grave and immediate danger to interests which the state may lawfully protect. And the West Virginia statute aimed at no such danger to a community interest.

In several other cases during the 1940s characteristically involving both freedom of speech and freedom of religious exercise, the Supreme Court similarly wavered but finally consolidated the application of the guarantees of the Fourteenth Amendment to state action.[18] Moreover, despite sporadic statements that religious belief was entitled to greater constitutional protection than beliefs unrelated to religion, it may generally be assumed today that the guarantee of freedom of speech by the Fourteenth Amendment is no less extensive than the guarantee of freedom of religious exercise.

As the West Virginia flag-salute case shows, the Court is sensitive to the claims of the individual to freedom of religious exercise. Certain language by the Justices may appear to absolutize the exercise of religious liberty, but this freedom on balance has not been so treated. Only a substantial threat to the rights of others or of the community, however, has been held sufficient to justify its limitation. In short, there has been a consistent recognition of the relative, political, and yet paramount character of the guarantee of religious liberty in a democracy. Many current problems are arising under this clause, such as the debate over Sunday-closing laws, but we shall defer treatment of these to a later chapter. Let us first consider the general significance of the second part of the First Amendment's guarantee of religious liberty, namely, the prohibition against laws respecting an establishment of religion.

THREE VIEWS OF THE "ESTABLISHMENT OF RELIGION"

Only a decade and a half ago the Supreme Court squarely passed for the first time on the application of the religious establishment clause to the use of public funds to aid pupils attending denominational schools.[19] The Court's elaborate attempt to define and interpret the religious establishment clause in this and in the two succeeding cases which involved religious education and the public schools stirred wide controversy on and off the bench. One school of thought, not represented on the Court, would understand the religious establishment clause to express a "no preference" doctrine.[20] According to this view, "religious establishment" would mean to prefer by law one religion over another, and this Congress would be forbidden to do. But Congress would not be prevented from aiding all religions equally or supporting any religious activities provided only that it be done without discrimination.

Justice Black in the Everson case expressed a far more extensive view of the religious establishment clause:

Neither a state nor the Federal government can set up a church. Neither can pass laws which aid one religion, aid all religions, or prefer one religion over another. . . . No tax in any amount, large or small, can be levied to support any religious activities or institutions, whatever they may be called, or whatever form they may adopt to teach or practice religion. . . .[21]

Justice Rutledge, though disagreeing with Black's application in the Everson case, accepted the same principle of complete separation of church and state:

It [the Amendment's purpose] was to create a complete and permanent separation of the spheres of religious activity and civil authority by comprehensively forbidding every form of public aid or support for religion. . . .[22]

Somewhere between the "no preference" and the "complete separation" interpretations is the view that the First Amendment envisions a general but not total separation of the spheres of civil authority and religious activity. Justice Douglas summed up this view in the Zorach decision when he said:

The First Amendment, however, does not say that in every and all respects there shall be a separation of Church and State. Rather, it studiously defines the manner, the specific way, in which there shall be no concert or union or dependency one on the other. . . .[28]

Varying shades of opinion group under the flexible standard of "limited accommodation." But what did the framers of the First Amendment mean by the religious establishment clause?

THE VIRGINIA STRUGGLE AGAINST RELIGIOUS ESTABLISHMENT

Before taking up the framing and adoption of the First Amendment, we shall be wise to consider a celebrated and antecedent church-state controversy in Virginia closely associated with James Madison.[24] Madison was majority leader of the House of Representatives at the time of the adoption of the First Amendment, introduced the original set of amendments constituting the Bill of Rights, and was chairman of the House conferees that worked over the differences between the Senate and House versions of the Bill. This controversy in Virginia, Justice Rutledge claimed, showed both Madison's views on the First Amendment and the historical background of the Amendment in the states as a whole.[25]

Virginia, in company with eight of her sister states, had an establishd church before the Revolution. But in the course of the Scotch-Irish immigration and the Great Awakening, opposition developed to the aristocratic Episcopal church of the tidewater. When the Revolution made necessary a new state constitution,

Virginia, under the leadership of George Mason and the young Madison in the Convention of 1776, adopted a Declaration of Rights. One of these declarations established as part of the fundamental law of Virginia the natural right of men to practice religion according to the dictates of their conscience. Although this represented an advance over the principle of toleration insofar as it made freedom of religious exercise a matter of right, it left unchanged the discriminatory privileges of the Episcopal church. Madison hoped and worked for disestablishment but realistically, if not with finality, abandoned the fight.

When, in the fall of 1776, petitions of dissenters to end tithes to the Episcopal church began to devolve on the new Virginia Assembly, that body removed the civil disabilities of dissenters and suspended the general levies for the support of the Episcopal church. This suspension was made permanent in 1779.

In the fall of 1784 the battle was renewed. When the Episcopalians and Presbyterians united to seek the financial support of the state, Patrick Henry offered a resolution that the people "pay a moderate tax . . . for the support of the Christian religion or of some Christian church, denomination, or communion of Christians, or of some form of Christian worship."[26] This bill was intended to benefit the Christian churches and only later was labeled: "A bill establishing a provision for teachers of the Christian religion."[27] Since elementary education was largely in the hands of the parishes, the bill was somewhat disguised as an educational measure. Leading the opposition, Madison ultimately defeated the proposal and counterattacked by reviving and achieving the enactment of Jefferson's Statute of Religious Liberty. The statute states that "no man shall be compelled to frequent or support any religious worship, place or ministry whatsoever. . . ."[28] Although the established churches in Connecticut and Massachusetts continued well into the nineteenth century, controversies similar to that of Virginia occurred in other states prior to the adoption of the First Amendment.

Madison's victory was due to Fabian tactics, to the strategical elevation of Henry, the most influential proponent, to the weakest gubernatorial chair in the Confederation, and to the effective argumentation of Madison's *Memorial and Remonstrance Against Religious Assessments*. The point of Madison's objection was not simply the restriction of the bill to aiding the Christian religion; he objected to the fundamental character of general tax support of organized religion.[29]

But did he wish to extend his arguments to any proposal to aid eleemosynary institutions of religious character or wish to prohibit all interaction between civil authority and the activity of organized religion? Although it is difficult to conjecture Madison's unexpressed opinion, his later pronouncements indicate an affirmative reply. The long and short of it is, as Corwin has said, that Madison carried the principle of separation of church and state "to pedantic lengths."[30] In his *Essay on Monopolies,* Madison put himself on record against the incorporation of ecclesiastical bodies with the faculty of acquiring property, against the exemption of houses of worship from taxation, against the right of the houses of Congress to choose chaplains, against Army and Navy chaplains, and stated his misgivings about Thanksgiving Day proclamations.[31]

Madison, religious but not churchly, educated in the mildly anticlerical atmosphere of Princeton and repelled by the low estate and high privilege of the established clergy in Virginia, fought for the separation of religious activity and civil authority. Yet Madison failed to grasp the limitation on this separation and, as we shall see, the many areas where the two necessarily overlap.

We may reach two conclusions on the relation of the Virginia controversy to the First Amendment. First, although Virginia's experience throws much light on Madison's personal philosophy, it leaves open the all-important question of Madison's position as legislator in the framing of the First Amendment. Secondly, the Virginia controversy five years before the drafting of the First Amendment was a sharp battle against traditional discriminatory privilege and a narrow union of civil authority and religious activity. This contrasts pointedly with the record of the drafting and adoption of the First Amendment and the situation faced by the federal government in 1789. Therefore, since James Madison's personal opinions and Virginia's experience do not offer the full criteria for understanding the historical meaning of the religious establishment clause of the First Amendment, we shall now consult the legislative history of that clause.

THE DRAFTING OF THE FIRST AMENDMENT

In the wake of the successful fight for ratification of the Constitution, Madison introduced into the first House a set of amendments designed to satisfy several states on the matter of a bill of rights.[32] Relating to freedom of conscience, Madison asked the House to submit the following guarantee: "The civil rights of none shall be abridged on account of religious belief or worship, nor shall any national religion be established, nor shall the full and equal rights of conscience be in any manner, or on any pretext, abridged."[33] The committee shortened this to read: "No religion shall be established by law, nor shall the equal rights of conscience be infringed."[34]

In the course of the debate in the House on August 15, 1789, Madison replied to Congressman Sylvester's suspicion that this might have a "tendency to abolish religion altogether." "Mr. Madison said, he apprehended the meaning of the words to be, that Congress should not establish a religion, and enforce the legal observance of it by law, nor compel men to worship God in any manner contrary to their conscience."[35] To Congressman Huntington's fear that a broad interpretation of the clause would close the federal courts to suits to collect contributions pledged to the churches, "Mr. Madison thought, if the word national was inserted before religion, it would satisfy the minds of the honorable gentlemen. He believed that the people feared one sect might obtain such pre-eminence, or two combine together, and establish a religion to which they would compel others to conform."[36]

As the word "national" was unacceptable to the Anti-federalists, Madison was forced to withdraw his motion, and the House substituted a motion by Samuel Livermore of New Hanpshire: "Congress shall make no laws touching religion, or infringing the rights of conscience."[37] Later the House without debate substituted for this broad and vague motion still another version: "Congress shall make no law establishing religion, or to prevent the free exercise thereof, or to infringe the rights of conscience."[38] It must be pointed out that this last version of the House before conference with the Senate was introduced by Fisher Ames, a

conservative member from Massachusetts, a state with an established church, and was adopted without debate, that is, unanimously.

After specifically rejecting: "Congress shall make no law establishing any particular denomination of religion in preference
to another," the Senate motion read: "Congress shall make no
law establishing articles of faith or a mode of worship."[39] Following the Senate-House conference, of which Madison was a
member, the final version was adopted by Congress and ratified
by the states: "Congress shall make no law respecting an establishment of religion."

JUSTICE RUTLEDGE'S THESIS

Dissenting in the Everson case, Justice Rutledge contended that
the framers of the First Amendment envisioned a complete separation of church and state. To support this contention Justice
Rutledge appealed to the wording of the religious establishment
clause.[40] In the first place, Justice Rutledge pointed out, the
clause did not say simply that there shall be no establishment in
a technical sense but rather that there shall be no laws "*respecting* an establishment of religion." But this inference Professor
Corwin effectively rebutted:

This ["respecting"] is a two-edged sword: It forbids Congress to pass
any law *disfavoring* as well as any law favoring an establishment of
religion. . . . The word "respecting" was adopted as much to protect
the establishments which then existed in five States . . . as to prevent
Congress from setting up a national establishment.[41]

Justice Rutledge also argued from the use of the article "an"
rather than "the" before "establishment" and especially from the
reference to "religion" rather than to "church" that the nature of
the establishment prohibited should be read broadly and not tech-
nically. Yet, concentration on the meaning of verbal construction, on inferences based on different versions, obscures the
remarkable unity of thought and uniformity of expression of the
first Congress on the subject of the religious establishment clause.

The record of the framing of the Amendment, recounted here at length, bears the imprint of essential unity and reveals the absence of any such sharp ideological conflict as transpired in Virginia a few years before. All of Madison's statements as legislative leader are minimal and designed to appease; the New England and Virginia conservatives find no difficulty in acquiescing. Justice Rutledge agrees that "by contrast with the Virginia history, the congressional debates on consideration of the Amendment reveal only sparse discussion. . . ."[42] Thus Justice Story gives a rationale of the Amendment which most easily accords with the situation facing the federal government in 1789:

The situation . . . of the different states equally proclaimed the policy as well as the necessity of such an exclusion. In some of the States, episcopalians constituted the predominant sect; in others, congregationalists; in others, quakers; and in others again, there was a close numerical rivalry among contending sects. It was impossible that there should not arise perpetual strife and perpetual jealousy on the subject of ecclesiastical ascendency, if the national government were left free to create a religious establishment. The only security was in extirpating the power. . . .[43]

The framers, certainly the New Englanders, may have conceived the effect of the Amendment in this light. This lends historical credence to the "no preference" interpretation of the religious establishment clause. But while Congress may have intended the phrase "an establishment of religion" only to prohibit the legal preference of one religion over another, still, as Justice Reed observed, passing years "have brought about the acceptance of a broader meaning. . . ."[44] The prohibition of "laws respecting an establishment of religion" has grown in content to express more than merely a prohibition of preferential aid to one or more religions. Vast changes in the religious and political consciousness of our society have brought a new content to the general term "religious establishment." Justice Douglas limited the constitutionally permissible accommodation of governmental authority, of course nonpreferential, to religious activities related to specific civic interests. His view may express better the desirable force of the religious establishment clause today. This but illustrates the organic character of constitutional provisions.

Altogether unacceptable as a historical thesis is the Rutledge doctrine of "complete separation" of church and state. Neither the record of the framing of the religious establishment clause nor its subsequent history supports the contention that the framers intended "complete separation." Previous to the adoption of the Amendment, church property was exempted from taxation; the same Congress that framed the Amendment provided for military and legislative chaplaincies; subsequent to the adoption, almost throughout the course of the nineteenth century, the federal government in the administration of the territories, the District of Columbia, and Indian affairs bestowed grants on sectarian education.[45]

The Rutledge doctrine of complete separation of church and state, while avoiding the excess of the Jacobin tradition where a mistitled separation involved outright suppression of the Church's freedom, does rest on assumptions less malevolent yet still foreign to sound principles. First, the Rutledge doctrine assumes that religious and civic activities should not intersect because religious activity is simply individual and private, not social and public. This point Justice Rutledge made quite explicit:

To say that [New Jersey's appropriations for the bus transportation of parochial school children] . . . are not for public purposes but . . . for private ends, is to say that they are for the support of religion and religious teaching. Conversely, to say that they are for public purposes is to say that they are not for religious ones.[46]

Secondly, the Rutledge doctrine supposes that the state's attitude toward religion must be one of indifference or tolerant hostility because religious activity is at best a civic frill and at worst a civic threat. "To hold that it [the state] may not [cooperate with religious authorities]," Justice Douglas observed, "would be to find in the Constitution a requirement that the government show a callous indifference to religious groups."[47]

The assumptions of Justice Rutledge are not shared, of course, by the Catholic. The Catholic holds that because religious activities, like man himself, are social as well as individual, religious and civic activities must intersect, and that because religious activities are both paramount and complementary to the goals of civic activity, the state's attitude toward religion must be one of cooperation and friendship. The prohibition of a religious establishment is a political principle no less than the guarantee of religious liberty which it serves. We must never forget that the prohibition of a religious establishment is an exigency of democratic government, a means of ensuring equality of citizens. Those who speak of a "wall of separation" make an end of what is a means, an absolute of what is relative.

Further, to interpret the religious establishment clause in an absolute manner is unrealistic in view of the many actually existing intersections of religious and civic activities in American life. Mindful of this, Justice Reed, dissenting in the McCollum case, protested the interpretation of the religious establishment clause as prohibiting "those incidental advantages that religious bodies, with other groups similarly situated, obtain as a byproduct of organized society."[48] Among other instances, Justice Reed pointed out that all churches are free from taxation; that the National School Lunch Act includes aid to parochial school children; that the armed forces have commissioned chaplains; and that, under the Servicemen's Readjustment Act of 1944, eligible veterans may receive instruction at government expense at denominational schools. In any culture where religion plays a prominent role the same men make up both civil and religious societies whose interaction is inevitable.

The real question, therefore, is to what degree and in what manner, consonant with the political principle of religious freedom, civil authority in a particular case may or should cooperate with a religious institution or activity related to a specific civic interest. We shall take up this question more explicitly with the Everson, McCollum, Zorach, and McGowan cases. But first a brief examination of the historical background of these cases.

BACKGROUND TO EVERSON

The areas of federal interaction with religious activities were and are relatively few. In the case of Indians (who were wards of the United States), of the territories, and of the military services the federal government undertook both direct and indirect aid to religious activities. In addition, there were many incidental tangents, such as the opening of legislative sessions with prayers and the coinage imprint: "In God we trust." So well accepted were these activities in the nineteenth century that no cases directly involving the religious establishment clause came before the Supreme Court until the advent of the present century. Then the Court upheld the payment of District of Columbia funds to a hospital corporation operated by a religious sisterhood in exchange for services to the indigent, and approved the use of federal funds, which under a treaty were due to a group of Indians, for the support of Catholic schools.[49]

As long as the federal relationships with religious activities were restricted to so few areas and the attitude of Americans was so uniformly favorable to these relationships, there was little likelihood of resort to the federal courts. However, the Fourteenth Amendment in time applied the prohibitions of the First Amendment to the more numerous interactions between local government and religious activity, and American religious thinking developed to widen the margin of dissent. The result has been the case law of the last decade and a half: Everson, McCollum, Zorach, and McGowan.

Prior to the Fourteenth Amendment, of course, the "no establishment" clause of the First Amendment applied only to the federal government; it was Congress that was prohibited from making a law "respecting an establishment of religion." By the adoption of the Fourteenth Amendment in 1868, no state was permitted by the federal Constitution to deprive any person of "life, liberty, or property without due process of law." But what is the meaning of deprivation of life or liberty or property "without due process of law"? Justice Frankfurter called the due process clause a "slippery slope" for the judicial function of government, and our brief excursion into legal history will justify extending the label to the meaning of the clause as well.[50]

After 1890 the Court attributed to the due process clause a substantive limitation upon the power of a state to abridge property rights. This meant that the Court would determine in each instance the reasonableness of action taken by a state to circumscribe the use of property.

The Court, however, did not restrict to economic legislation its application of substantive limitation of state action; state action affecting personal liberty as well came within its scope. In the field of religion and education, the Court struck down an Oregon statute requiring attendance of all children of school age at the public school because the statute denied the primacy of parental right in the education of children.[51] The dramatic opening, however, for the greatly expanded federal judicial review of personal liberties affected by state action was provided by the Gitlow case:

. . . We may and do assume that freedom of speech and of press— which are protected by the First Amendment from abridgement by Congress—are among the fundamental personal rights and liberties protected by the due process clause of the Fourteenth Amendment from impairment by the states.[52]

This offered the prospect that other sections of the First Amendment—including the religious establishment clause—might come within the compass of the due process clause of the Fourteenth Amendment.

Although the Roosevelt Court was more sympathetic in its review of state economic legislation, the application of the Fourteenth Amendment prohibitions to state action infringing civil liberties received fresh impetus. By 1940 freedom of religious exercise was included under the guarantees of the Fourteenth Amendment, and in 1947 the Everson case rounded out the process of piecemeal inclusion of the First Amendment guarantees by prohibiting to the states laws "respecting an establishment of religion."[53]

As a result of these decisions the Fourteenth Amendment protected the individual against religious establishment and encroachment of religious freedom by state action. Those devoted to the concept of an inflexible Constitution of course were not pleased with the expansion of the protection afforded by the Fourteenth Amendment. But the possibility, indeed the necessity, of organic growth is nowhere more evident than in a constitutional provision which so generically prohibits a state from depriving any person of "life, liberty or property without due process of law." The Fourteenth Amendment, no less than other general provisions of the Constitution, is subject to the evolutionary process of human institutions.

The United States Constitution envisions a federal system of government: both federal and state governments are sovereign in their proper spheres. And the First Amendment, as we have seen, was designed as much to define federal-state relations as to protect the rights of the individual against federal encroachment. Latitude of experiment forbidden to the federal government was permitted to the states. But if we follow the Twining and Palko view that the due process clause of the Fourteenth Amendment protects the "fundamental liberties" of the individual against encroachment by the states, we should find little difficulty in concluding with the Court that the prohibition of religious establishment and the guarantee of religious freedom are fundamental liberties.[54] They are fundamental because they are exigencies of a democratic form of government. The conclusion that the Fourteenth Amendment revolutionized federal-state relations is unavoidable.

The Court has not said that there is absolutely no distinction between the degree of protection afforded the individual against federal establishment or federal encroachment of religious liberty and the degree of protection afforded the individual against similar action by state governments. But the Court has assumed, and in our opinion wisely, that at least approximately the same degree of protection is afforded the individual against both federal and state establishments of religion and infringements of religious liberty.

Paralleling this legal evolution of the First Amendment's religious establishment clause into a prohibition on local government were the developments in education that brought local governments into new relationships with religious activity. Two developments especially underlie the local governmental actions out of which the recent cases arose: the growth of the predominantly secular public school and the rise of the Catholic parochial school system.

Although education in early colonial America, even where supported by public funds as in Massachusetts, was largely dominated by religious inspiration and clerical authority, a transition developed in the years following the Revolution. Under the stimulus of the new ideas of eighteenth-century liberalism and the authority of such prominent American thinkers as Franklin and Jefferson, the goal of a common school which would be open to all eligible students, supported by state funds, and free of sectarian instruction received increasing acceptance in American communities. Other more practical forces were also at work: the multiplication of Protestant sects, the presence in American society of religious but unchurched groups, and the rise of non-Protestant religious minorities. Since this diversity of religious belief accompanied the rise of the public school, the measure of public education's contribution to religious formation became the least common denominator of the various creeds. By the middle of the twentieth century the disorganization of Protestantism in the cities, the development of secularist influences, and the devotion of an intellectual élite to the ideal of completely nontheistic public education had radically reduced the contribution of the public schools to religious formation.[55]

The nineteenth century saw not only the birth of the public school system but the concomitant introduction of the Catholic parochial school. As Professor Cushman observed, the Catholic Church, mushrooming with successive waves of immigration, could not give up to the public schools her role as educator. The latter, in her eyes, bestowed religious training inadequately and usually with a Protestant coloration.[56] Nor were Catholics content with a compartmentalized program of religious education such as released-time. Other parochial systems, though not of comparable size, also developed among Protestant and Jewish groups.

Individuals and groups believing in the fundamentally religious character of education viewed with alarm the secular trend of public education in the twentieth century. For their part, supporters of parochial school systems were not complacent about the burden of supporting two school systems. Therefore, it is not surprising that, as Justice Rutledge said:

. . . two great drives . . . are in motion. . . . One is to introduce religious education and observance into the public schools. The other, to obtain public funds for the aid and support of various private religious schools.[57]

Since the actions of local governments did not go unchallenged by those of secular persuasion, the case law has burgeoned more in one period of a decade and a half than in all previous American history.

EVERSON, McCOLLUM AND ZORACH

Everson v. *Board of Education* was the first in this series of cases involving the religious establishment clause to be reviewed by the Court. A local board had acted in accordance with a New Jersey statute and reimbursed parents for money spent in sending their children to school on local buses, including parents whose children attended Catholic parochial schools. When taxpayer Everson challenged the school board's decision in the state courts and, by appeal, in the United States Supreme Court, a bare majority of the latter sustained the action of the local authorities.

Both majority and minority agreed that the First Amendment comprehensively forbade every form of support or aid by government to religious activity, but disagreed on whether public transportation of parochial school children constituted governmental support of religious activity. The majority maintained that the state's contribution of free transportation constituted no more than an aid to the individual child, not support of the denominational school. But Justice Rutledge argued in dissent:

The funds used here were raised by taxation. . . . This not only helps the children to get to school and the parents to send them. It aids them in a substantial way to get the very thing they are sent to the particular school to secure, namely religious training and teaching.[58]

Justice Jackson remarked that the majority, like Byron's Julia, "Whispering 'I will ne'er consent':—consented."[59]

We submit, however, that both majority and minority were asking the wrong question. The Court, by accepting the thesis of complete separation of church and state, could debate only the consistency of its application. This thesis, we believe, is historically, politically, and theologically unacceptable. The real question, as we have observed, is to what degree and in what manner, consistent with the democratic exigency of religious liberty, civil authority may or should cooperate with a religious activity related to a specific civic interest.

The federal government was never permitted to prefer one religion over another; for over one hundred years state churches have been disestablished; indeed, the day has long passed since either federal or state governments felt constrained to aid religious activity simply because religious. Hence the question faced today is whether particular circumstances permit or warrant the use of governmental power to aid incidentally a religious institution or activity related to a specific civic interest.

A few examples may serve to illustrate this proposition. Since the Revolution the federal government has supported military chaplains. Why? Not necessarily to prefer religion over non-religion but rather to provide for the spiritual needs of personnel isolated by the demands of military service from the religious opportunities of their civilian communities. Similarly, a hospital operated by a religious corporation in the District of Columbia might receive federal aid because, as a hospital, it was vitally linked to the community welfare. In each instance there was an appropriate civic reason to warrant the particular federal action. The Court might have reached the Everson result more realistically, therefore, by distinguishing the rational basis of the principle of church-state separation and by accepting as legal precedents the decisions which upheld both public aid to hospitals operated by religious corporations and state grants of free textbooks to parochial school children.[60]

Although the immediate decision in the Everson case favored reimbursement under state authority for the expenditure in bus transportation of parochial school children, the principles there enunciated bore fruit in the McCollum decision one year later. The case arose from an action by the Champaign (Illinois) school board in 1940 permitting religious instruction in the local schools during school hours for children whose parents signed request cards. Mrs. McCollum, the mother of a son attending one of the local schools but not the religious instruction classes, objected to the classes as an infringement of freedom of conscience and a religious establishment within the meaning of the First Amendment. After defeat in the state courts she carried her appeal to the United States Supreme Court, where the case was decided on the religious establishment clause. "This," said Justice Black, "is not separation of church and state."[61] Once again the Court chose to make the test of constitutionality any use of civil power to aid religious activity.

We have already criticized the principle of "complete" separation of church and state by which the Court reached the McCollum decision, and in Chapter VI we shall consider the problem of how to reconcile community efforts to achieve moral and religious instruction in the public schools with the requirements of religious freedom. But here it suffices to note the reversal by the Zorach case of the principle on which the McCollum decision rested. The Court, without specifically overruling the McCollum decision, upheld the action of the New York City Board of Education in providing a "released time" program for religious instruction during public school hours off the school premises. Cutting through the premise of the previous two cases, Justice Douglas said:

When the state encourages religious instruction or cooperates with religious authorities by adjusting the schedule of public events to sectarian needs, it follows the best of our traditions. For then it respects the religious nature of our people and accommodates the public service to their spiritual needs. . . .[62]

Those words echo the thought of Justice Reed in the single dissent of the McCollum case:

A state is entitled to have great leeway in its legislation when dealing with the important social problems of its population. A definite violation of legislative limits must be established. . . . Devotion to the great principle of religious liberty should not lead us into a rigid interpretation of the Constitutional guarantee that conflicts with accepted habits of our people. . . .[63]

The alternative is, like Frost's mender of walls, to set up a constitutional absolute whose rational and empirical bases we do not understand and refuse to investigate.

McGOWAN v. *MARYLAND*

The recent series of cases involving Sunday laws provided the Court with a fresh opportunity to probe the general structure of the religious establishment clause.[64] Complainants in three states —Maryland, Massachusetts, and Pennsylvania—objected to the Sunday laws of their respective states as, *inter alia,* religious establishments of the orthodox Christian religions. The states countered with a defense of the laws as day-of-rest statutes based on the police power over community health and welfare. In the course of the decisions in favor of the constitutionality of the laws, both Chief Justice Warren, speaking for the court, and Justice Frankfurter, speaking for himself and Justice Harlan, made some observations on the religious establishment clause which must be noted.[65] Only Justice Douglas dissented on the religious establishment issue, and his disagreement was based solely on what he judged to be the religious character of the Sunday laws in question, not on the general meaning of the establishment clause.

Chief Justice Warren's remarks on the religious establishment clause contributed nothing new. In fact, he repeated without analysis the Everson formula. The Chief Justice accepted the thesis elaborately developed by Justice Rutledge in the Everson case that the struggle in Virginia for religious freedom was "particularly relevant in the search for the First Amendment's meaning."[66] The Chief Justice, however, did not claim that the events in Virginia alone would be dispositive without a "brief review of the First Amendment's background."[67] The review of the legislative record completed, the Chief Justice concluded that "the First Amendment, in its final form, did not simply bar a congressional enactment *establishing a church*; it forbade all laws *respecting an establishment of religion.*"[68] The Chief Justice then cited with apparent approval "the most extensive discussion of the 'Establishment' Clause's latitude" found in the Everson decision.[69] He further cited in a footnote the still more comprehensive definition of religious establishment by Justice Rutledge in his dissenting opinion in the same case.[70] No mention at all was made of the Zorach decision or opinion.

Now, in the context of the Sunday laws controversy, the Chief Justice may have had a good tactical reason for accepting the relevance of the Virginia struggle and the Everson view on the meaning of the religious establishment clause. In 1785, the same year in which the Virginia legislators passed the "Bill for Establishing Religious Freedom," Madison presented a "Bill for Punishing . . . Sabbath Breakers," which was enacted the next year.[71] And the Everson majority upheld public support for the bus transportation of parochial school pupils as a public welfare measure. Thus, neither the Virginia view of religious liberty in 1785 nor the Everson view of the religious establishment clause in 1947 was incompatible with the validity of Sunday laws as public welfare legislation.

Unfortunately, however, Chief Justice Warren did more than make a tactical move with respect to the struggle in Virginia and the Everson opinion. On the one hand, he accepted from the hands of Justice Rutledge, a dissenter in Everson, the questionable hypothesis that events in Virginia in 1785 revealed the import of the First Amendment's establishment clause to its framers in 1789. On the other hand, he followed the sweeping dicta of the Everson opinion in interpreting the religious establishment clause without any consideration of the modifying effects of the Zorach decision. The circumstances of the Sunday law cases, of course, did not demand the refinements here suggested in order to resolve the issues at stake.

More original and somewhat more penetrating were the remarks of Justice Frankfurter on the general structure of the religious establishment clause. Justice Frankfurter was keenly aware in these cases, as he may not have been in Everson, that " 'separation' is not a self-defining concept."[72] The spheres of religious and civic activity are sure to intersect: "As the state's interest in the individual becomes more comprehensive, its concerns and the concerns of religion perforce overlap."[73] Justice Frankfurter, too, found the "battle in Virginia . . . a vital and compelling memory in 1789," and he made an attempt to express the essence of the separation principle.[74] "The purpose of the Establishment Clause was to assure that the national legislature would not exert its power in the service of any purely religious end; that it would not . . . make of religion, as religion, an object of legislation."[75] Justice Frankfurter developed from this expression of the principle two corollaries:

If the primary end achieved by a form of regulation is the affirmation or promotion of religious doctrine— primary, in the sense that all secular ends which it purportedly serves are derivative from, not wholly independent of, the advancement of religion—the regulation is beyond the power of the state. . . . Or if a statute furthers both secular and religious ends by means unnecessary to the effectuation of the secular ends alone—where the same secular ends could equally be attained by means which do not have consequences for the promotion of religion—the statute cannot stand.[76]

But "not every regulation some of whose practical effects may facilitate the observance of religion . . . affronts the requirement of church-state separation."[77]

Justice Frankfurter rightly emphasized that the religious establishment clause, at least as now understood, prohibits civic accommodation to religious ends simply because they are religious. The day has long since passed, and passed quite necessarily in virtue of the rise of secular humanism, when the government might be expected to aim at fostering religion even without preference among different creeds. And Justice Frankfurter rightly saw that incidental effects favorable to one or all religions do not by that fact alone invalidate a civil enactment.

However, Justice Frankfurter's corollaries were not without ambiguity, even imprecision. Justice Frankfurter would not allow a statute to stand unless it served a secular end which was "wholly independent of the advancement of religion" or which could not "equally be attained by means" which would "not have consequences for the promotion of religion." But should all such statutes necessarily be considered to violate the separation of church and state? It would be difficult to say that provision for military chaplains or tax exemption for church property served secular ends "wholly independent" of religious ends. Yet these actions can in no way be construed as a *preferment* of religion over nonreligion. The government provides military chaplains not to prefer religion over nonreligion but to duplicate for servicemen as far as morally possible the religious conditions which were available to them in the civilian communities from which they are removed in the service of the nation. The government exempts church property from taxation not to prefer religion above nonreligion but because the government favors all charitable institutions, whether religious or not, with exemption. To hold that the government may not provide military chaplains or exempt church property from taxation would oblige the government to penalize servicemen who wished the opportunity for religious worship and to penalize charitable institutions which were religious. That would be to establish secularism as the religion of the state. We believe that the government may enact legislation even for an end not "wholly independent of the advancement of religion" where justified by equitable considerations which exclude the intention to prefer religion over nonreligion. Surely a state is not forbidden to exempt Jews and other Sabbatarians from the observance of Sunday laws although the end of the exemption would not be "wholly independent" of the religious end. Such a conclusion would be an unreasonable and impolitic construction of the religious establishment clause.

We might attempt to express these criticisms in a revision of Justice Frankfurter's formula. The purpose of the religious establishment clause is to ensure that neither a state nor the federal government may exert its power in the service of any purely religious end *simply because religious* or make of religion, as religion, an *object of preference*. The two corollaries that follow from this revised principle are these: (1) If the primary end achieved by a form of legislation is the preferment of a religious activity—primary in the sense that the aim of the legislation is to aid a religious activity simply because religious—the legislation is beyond the power of the state; and (2) if a statute seeks to further a secular end *through* the preferment of religion, the statute cannot stand. This revision, we submit, gives a more reasonable and more precise interpretation to the religious establishment clause.

Less than a month after the decisions upholding the constitutionality of Sunday laws, the Court again commented on the general nature of the religious establishment clause in the

Torcaso case.[78] There the Court unanimously struck down as unconstitutional a Maryland statute which required all office-holders to declare their belief in the existence of God. Justice Black, speaking for the Court, specifically reaffirmed and expanded the Everson definition of the religious establishment clause to serve as the basis for the decision.[79] Neither a state nor the federal government "can constitutionally pass laws nor impose requirements which aid all religions as against non-believers."[80] This conclusion, in our view, is an entirely reasonable and even necessary interpretation of the religious establishment clause for a present-day American society which includes secular humanists. It need not, however, suppose or imply any acceptance of the doctrine of the "absolute" separation of church and state, although Justice Black's reaffirmation of the broad language of the Everson decision did suppose or imply such an acceptance.

CONCLUSION

Thus far, of course, we have been concerned only in a general way with the standard by which particular problems involving church and state may be evaluated. We conclude that the religious establishment clause is best interpreted to mean that neither a state nor the federal government may prefer one religion over another or all religion over nonreligion. Note that we do not say that the government under no circumstances may *accommodate* or *aid* a religious or a religiously oriented activity but rather that the government under no circumstances may *prefer* one religion over another or all religions over nonreligion. In our view, a state or the federal government may aid religiously oriented institutions performing secular functions or accommodate religious activities in specific circumstances where this implies no preference of one religion over another or of all religion over nonreligion. To determine further what relations of civic authority to specific activities or institutions are permissible or desirable, we must examine the particular problem areas themselves.

NOTES

1. This substitution and transformation is usually implicit. But note the following incredibly explicit identification of the First Amendment with religious beliefs incompatible with the authoritative claims of the Catholic Church: "It is usually said that the common faith of America is the democratic faith. One article of this democratic faith, embodied in the separation principle, is that freedom of belief had priority over any ecclesiastical institution and its claim to authority. American democracy therefore presupposes a particular doctrine of the institutional church as not supremely authoritative and as not coextensive with religion. This is a *theological* doctrine (historically derived from Protestantism) to which all Americans tacitly subscribe, as part of their common democratic faith." Philip H. Phenix, "Religion in American Public Education" in *Public Education in America,* eds. George Z. F. Bereday and Luigi Volpicelli (New York: Harper & Brothers, 1958), pp. 93–94. Quite obviously, no Catholic can conscientiously subscribe to the First Amendment as a theological doctrine denying that the Church is "supremely authoritative" in matters of faith and morals.

2. For an account of the contribution of Catholics in Maryland see Thomas O'B. Hanley, S.J., *Their Rights and Liberties: The Beginnings of Religious and Political Freedom in Maryland* (Westminster, Md.: The Newman Press, 1959).

3. Cited by Alfred H. Kelly and Winifred A. Harbison, *The American Constitution: Its Origins and Development,* rev. ed. (New York: W. W. Norton & Company, Inc., 1955), p. 4.

4. *Osborn* v. *Bank of the United States,* 9 Wheaton 737, 865 (1824).

5. *United States* v. *Butler,* 297 U.S. 1, 78–79 (1936).

6. *West Coast Hotel Co.* v. *Parrish,* 300 U.S. 379, 402 (1937).

7. *Brown* v. *Board of Education,* Topeka, Kans., 347 U.S. 483, 489 (1954).

8. Cf. *United States* v. *Butler,* p. 62.

9. *McCulloch* v. *Maryland,* 4 Wheaton 316, 407 (1819).

10. *Adamson* v. *California,* 332 U.S. 46, 64 (1947).

11. Felix Frankfurter, "John Marshall and the Judicial Function," *Harvard Law Review,* Vol. LXIX (1955), p. 231.

12. Quoted by Arthur Krock, *The New York Times,* May 24, 1956, p. 30.

13. *Reynolds* v. *U.S.,* 98 U.S. 145 (1878).

14. *Hamilton* v. *Regents of the University of California,* 293 U.S. 245 (1934).

15. *Cantwell* v. *Conn.,* 310 U.S. 296 (1940).

16. *Minersville School District* v. *Gobitis,* 310 U.S. 586 (1940).

17. *West Virginia State Board of Education* v. *Barnette,* 319 U.S. 624, 642 (1943).

18. *Jones* v. *Opelika,* 316 U.S. 584 (1942), reversed by *Murdock* v. *Pennsylvania,* 319 U.S. 105 (1943); *Follett* v. *Town of McCormick,* 321 U.S. 573 (1944) extended the application of the Murdock principle [invalidity of license fees for door-to-door peddling of religious tracts]. *Martin* v. *Struthers,* 319 U.S. 141 (1943) [invalidity of ordinances against summoning occupants to the door for the distribution of pamphlets]. *Tucker* v. *Texas,* 326 U.S. 517 (1946) and *Marsh* v. *Alabama,* 326 U.S. 501 (1946) [right to distribute literature on the premises of a federal housing project and a company town].

19. *Everson* v. *Board of Education,* 330 U.S. 1 (1947).

20. Edward S. Corwin, "The Supreme Court as National School Board," *Thought,* Vol. XXIII (1948), pp. 665–683.

21. *Everson* v. *Board of Education,* pp. 15–16.

22. *Ibid.,* p. 32.

23. *Zorach* v. *Clauson,* 343 U.S. 306, 312 (1952).

24. Irving Brant, *James Madison* (Indianapolis-New York: The Bobbs-Merrill Company, Inc., 1941, 1948), I, 241–250; II 343–350.

25. *Everson* v. *Board of Education,* p. 33 ff.

26. Brant, *op. cit.,* p. 343.

27. *Ibid.,* p. 346.

28. Henry Steele Commager, ed., *Documents of American History,* 5th ed. (New York: Apple-ton-Century-Crofts, Inc., 1949), I, 126.

29. Brant, *op. cit.,* p. 350.

30. Corwin, *art. cit.,* p. 671.

31. *Harper's Magazine,* March 1914, pp. 489–495.

32. Gales and Seaton, eds., *The Debates and Proceedings in the Congress of the United States* (Washington, 1834), I, 434.

33. *Ibid.*

34-37. *Ibid.,* pp. 729–731.

38. *Ibid.,* p. 766.

39. Anson Phelps Stokes, *Church and State in the United States* (New York: Harper & Brothers, 1950), I, 546–548.

40. *Everson* v. *Board of Education,* p. 33 ff.

41. Corwin, *art. cit.,* p. 671.

42. *Everson* v. *Board of Education,* p. 42.

43. Joseph Story, *Commentaries on the Constitution,* ed. M. Bigelow (Boston: Little, Brown & Co., 1891), II, 634.

44. *Ill.* ex rel. *McCollum* v. *Board of Education,* 333 U.S. 203, 244 (1948).

45. Richard J. Gabel, *Public Funds for Church and Private Schools* (Washington: Catholic University of America, 1937), Chs. VI, XI, and XVII.

46. *Everson* v. *Board of Education,* p. 51.

47. *Zorach* v. *Clauson,* p. 314.

48. *McCollum* v. *Board of Education,* p. 249.

49. *Bradford* v. *Roberts,* 175 U.S. 291 (1899); *Quick Bear* v. *Leupp,* 210 U.S. 50 (1908).

50. Frankfurter, *art. cit.,* p. 227.

51. *Pierce* v. *Society of Sisters,* 268 U.S. 510 (1925).

52. *Gitlow* v. *New York*, 268 U.S. 652, 666 (1925).

53. *Cantwell* v. *Conn.* and *Everson* v. *Board of Education*, respectively.

54. *Twining* v. *New Jersey*, 211 U.S. 78 (1908); *Palko* v. *Conn.*, 302 U.S. 319 (1937). Prof. Mark A. DeWolfe Howe, however, would distinguish significantly between the degrees of protection afforded the individual against federal and state establishments of religion. "Religion and Race in Public Relations," *Buffalo Law Review*, Vol. VIII (1959), pp. 245–247.

55. Edwin H. Rian, *Christianity and American Education* (San Antonio: Naylor Co., 1949), pp. 23–65.

56. Robert E. Cushman, *Leading Constitutional Decisions*, 9th ed. (New York: Appleton-Century-Crofts, Inc., 1950), pp. 144–145.

57. *Everson* v. *Board of Education*, p. 63.

58. *Ibid.*, p. 45.

59. *Ibid.*, p. 19.

60. *Bradford* v. *Roberts; Cochran* v. *Louisiana*, 281 U.S. 370 (1930).

61. *McCollum* v. *Board of Education*, p. 212.

62. *Zorach* v. *Clauson*, pp. 313–314.

63. *McCollum* v. *Board of Education*, p. 256.

64. *McGowan* v. *Maryland*, 366 U.S. 420 (1961); *Two Guys From Harrison* v. *McGinley*, 366 U.S. 522 (1961); *Braunfeld* v. *Brown*, 366 U.S. 599 (1961); *Gallagher* v. *Crown Kosher Supermarket*, 366 U.S. 617 (1961).

65. *McGowan* v. *Maryland*, pp. 437–445, 460–467.

66. *Ibid.*, p. 437.

67. *Ibid.*, p. 440.

68. *Ibid.*, pp. 441–442.

69. *Ibid.*, p. 442.

70. *Ibid.*, p. 444.

71. *Ibid.*, p. 438.

72. *Ibid.*, p. 461.

73. *Ibid.*

74. *Ibid.*, pp. 464–465.

75. *Ibid.*, p. 465.

76. *Ibid.*, pp. 466–467.

77. *Ibid.*, p. 467.

78. *Torcaso* v. *Watkins*, 367 U.S. 488 (1961).

79. *Ibid.*, pp. 492–493, 495.

80. *Ibid.*, p. 495.

5

Public Support
and the
Parochial Schools

No issue is more sure to bring Americans of different religious creeds and philosophical convictions to a fever pitch of emotional response than what is euphemistically styled "the school question." This question of course concerns government aid to private, including church-related, primary and secondary schools. It is an issue on which American Catholics are separated quite distinctly from the viewpoint of most of their fellow citizens.[1] In fact, many non-Catholics consider the school question the crucial test by which they can judge how sincerely American Catholics accept the principle of separation of church and state.[2] For this reason the issue of government aid to church-related schools must be explored here if we are to presume to speak at all meaningfully or comprehensively of the concordance of the Catholic Church and American democracy.

To most non-Catholics, government aid to church-related schools is "undebatable" because "clearly unconstitutional"—as President Kennedy, himself a Roman Catholic, expressed it.[3] To most Catholics, on the other hand, government aid to church-related schools is right, necessary, and wise public policy, and therefore either is or should become constitutional. Marvelous to say, neither the non-Catholic nor the Catholic admits to any doubts about the correctness of his views. Few matters of constitutional law or public policy allow a comparable clarity to diametrically opposed interpretations. This alone should be sufficient to warn us that the most significant clarity in the matter may consist in the open nerve endings which so many Americans expose in the heat of controversy. We cannot escape the conclusion that the issue of government aid to church-related schools elicits from Americans of different religious beliefs and philosophical convictions a basic identification with the most deep-seated interests and ideals of their human personalities. We cherish the hope that our consideration of this troublesome issue will reflect some light of reason rather than generate more heat of emotion.

STATISTICAL DIMENSIONS

President Kennedy, the first Roman Catholic to occupy the White House, was caught in the throes of the school question very early in his administration. The President was quite surprised, embarrassed, even annoyed, to find that the forces in favor of government loans to parochial schools were so vocal and so strong. The President complained that only in his administration was there any large-scale effort to obtain government aid to parochial schools.[4] Actually the President had a point. Cardinal Spellman had gone so far, in fact, in August, 1949, as to deny that Catholic parochial schools sought from the government other than "child-benefit" aid in such fringe areas as bus transportation and school lunches.[5] And Cardinal Cushing's lack of enthusiasm for government aid has been well publicized.[6]

Yet the President should not really have been too surprised.

His own successful accession to the office of chief executive of the United States in part attested to the growth of influence of Catholics on American political, economic, and social life. Today American Catholics are in a far better position to articulate their views on current problems than in the past, and even a casual perusal of statistics and trends in education will reveal why Catholics are expressing themselves so specifically, effectively, and insistently on the school question.

In the fall of the 1960–61 school year Catholic elementary and secondary schools in the United States enrolled over 5.3 million full-time day students.[7] National public school enrollment at the same time numbered 36.3 million students.[8] This means that the Catholic schools in 1960 enrolled better than one student for every seven in the public schools. Also significant is the growth of the Catholic school population since 1900, both in terms of absolute numbers and in relation to the growth of the public school population. In the first sixty years of this century the Catholic school enrollment increased more than sixfold, while the public school enrollment doubled once.

CATHOLIC AND PUBLIC (ELEMENTARY-SECONDARY)
SCHOOL ENROLLMENTS IN THE UNITED STATES, 1900–1960

Year	Catholic School Enrollment[9] (millions)	Catholic School Percentage of Public School Enrollment	Public School Enrollment[10] (millions)
1899–1900	0.8	5.2	15.5
1919–1920	1.8	8.3	21.6
1939–1940	2.6	10.2	25.4
1959–1960	5.1	14.5	35.2

But these statistics and trends are cold reflections of the concrete reality. Each year Catholic parents, teachers, and administrators enact a human drama as parochial schools attempt to stretch their facilities, faculties, and resources to cope with the phenomenal problem which the statistics indicate. Each year Catholic parents experience anxiety over the admission of their children to parochial schools. The Catholic population of school age is increasing even more rapidly than the capacity of the

Catholic schools, with the result that more and more Catholic children are turned away from the parochial schools each year. Today almost one out of every two Catholic children of school age attends a parochial school, but it is quite doubtful in the opinion of many experts whether the present proportion can be long maintained.[11]

Each year, too, the parochial school faculties struggle with more disadvantageous student-teacher ratios. The National Education Association regards a student-teacher ratio of 25 to 1 as ideal, and the National Catholic Education Association a ratio of 35 to 1, but many Catholic schools actually have 60 or even 90 to 1 ratios.[12] In fact, the enrollment in Catholic elementary schools alone is growing 3.7 times as fast as the number of teaching sisters.[13] Today lay men and women comprise over one-fourth of the parochial school faculties.[14]

This brings us to the more demanding task of finance which parochial school administrators confront each year. Construction funds for augmenting classroom facilities is only one aspect of the financial problem; teachers' salaries are a far more critical aspect. This expense is growing heavier because of inflation, because more teachers are needed for more pupils, and because the parochial schools today require more lay teachers who, of course, receive higher salaries than teaching sisters. Catholics in general fall among the lowest economic ranking of religious groups, and as a result the burden of educational development rests heavily on members of American society least able to support it.[15]

The import of this situation on the harmonious activity and cohesive aspiration of the community should be transparent. The Catholic parent contrasts the relatively green pasture which the public school enjoys through tax support—his own taxes included—with the plight of the parochial school which he supports through voluntary contributions. The Catholic grows restive under the "double burden," complains of the injustice to him and his children, and claims that the present system of school tax distribution cripples his "freedom of choice" in educating his children unless he is rich enough to afford it.

On the other hand, the non-Catholic reacts to the same situation in exactly the opposite way. The non-Catholic bristles at the charge of injustice and points out that the doors of the public school are open to all. He looks apprehensively at the growth of an educational system which he fears may some day threaten the security of the public school. He is suspicious that public school budgets will encounter difficulty in winning acceptance in many communities where Catholic schools are numerous.[16] Most of all, he fears that government aid to parochial schools will benefit the Catholic Church almost exclusively, violate the separation of church and state, and encourage an unhealthy divisiveness among Americans.

WHY PUBLIC SUPPORT?

At the outset let us clearly note, however, that the issue should not be narrowed to one of aid to Catholic school pupils. There are, in addition to the 5.3 million students in Catholic elementary and secondary schools, over a half-million students enrolled in non-Catholic private schools.[17] The issue of public support concerns not only those who attend Catholic schools but *all* who attend nonprofit private schools—whether Catholic or not, whether church-related or nonsectarian.

One good reason in favor of government aid to private, including church-related, schools is simply the community's interest and investment in private education. When over 13 per cent of the nation's children attend nonpublic schools, the nation can ill afford to ignore the facilities and faculties of these schools. The community should find in private, including church-related, schools too great and too vital an educational stake to maintain a disinterested aloofness to their welfare. The educational needs of the space age and the Soviet challenge serve no less to reinforce this basic contention. Hence, advocates of public support conclude, government aid to all private nonprofit educational institutions is necessary and wise policy.

But such aid is not only wise and useful social policy; it is also the fair and necessary implementation of the basic right and responsibility of parents to choose the education of their children. Since the right of parents is primary, then the state's role in education is secondary, substitutional in character, and subordinate to the choice of parents. The state therefore should not supplant but rather support, as far as the common good permits, the choice of parents for the education of their children. This, of course, is only a restatement of the fundamental principle of subsidiarity which governs all action by the state: the state must do for citizens only what citizens through subordinate, responsible organizations cannot conveniently do for themselves. To abridge the principle of subsidiarity is to violate the right of individuals; to deny it is to endorse the totalitarian Leviathan.

The primacy of parental rights in education is sound political theory, but it has also received the authoritative endorsement of the United States Supreme Court as a part of the fundamental law of the land. In *Pierce* v. *Society of Sisters* the Supreme Court struck down an Oregon statute which would have obliged all children to attend public schools.[18] Justice James McReynolds, speaking for a unanimous court, explained why the Oregon statute was unconstitutional:

The child is not the mere creature of the state; those who nurture him and direct his destiny have the right, coupled with the high duty, to recognize and prepare him for additional obligations.[19]

The Pierce decision, to be sure, established only the general right of parents to send their children to the schools of their choice. Few would be inclined today to question the correctness of this decision. But many would challenge whether private school apologetes can successfully argue from the Pierce principle to the obligation of government support for private schools as a matter of right. They do not see that the denial of government support to private schools is in fact a denial of parents' freedom of choice in education. But what are the chief results of such a denial of governmental support on freedom of parental choice in education? If parents wish to send their children to private, nonprofit educational institutions, they must pay the tuition or its equivalent to the private school over and above the taxes which they must pay to support the public school. Now, wealthy parents who wish can afford to do this, but less affluent parents can ill afford this additional financial burden. Moreover, less affluent parents who desire a religiously oriented education for their children may find themselves forced to exercise a hard choice between the superior facilities and faculties which public support may provide for public schools and the more restricted educational opportunities which the voluntary resources of private schools may be able to offer. Thus the freedom of choice which parents may wish to exercise in favor of a religiously oriented education for their children may be seriously and effectively limited by the harshness of financial burden and the inequality of educational opportunity. In other words, the system of distributing tax funds only for the support of public schools tends effectively to make children the "mere creatures of the state" against which the Pierce decision was directed. The effect of the state's action is to supplant and not to support the choice of parents in education; the state is acting in a way calculated to assume the primary and not the secondary role in education.

Further analysis will show more exactly why the present system is inequitable. If parents have the right to choose a private, especially a religiously oriented, education for their children, they have the right to expect that tax burdens and tax benefits in support of education will be levied and distributed equitably. This does not mean that tax burdens and tax benefits must be *equal*, for this would be to accept the antisocial philosophy of radical individualism and to deny the very structure of a common good to which all citizens contribute and in which all citizens participate. But it does mean that the levy of tax burdens and the distributions of tax benefits should be equitable, that is, proportionate to the capacities, needs, and merits of the citizens. This means, in the matter of education, that tax burdens and tax benefits should be shared equitably or proportionately by all students. Hence the parents of the 13 per cent of the nation's children who attend private schools have every right to expect that the tax benefits of public support will not exclude the nonprofit schools to which they choose to send them. Students at private, including religiously oriented, schools should not be excluded as a class from the distribution of tax benefits. This is especially true when, as at present, their need may be greater than that of students at public educational institutions.

In the nineteenth century, public expenditures, whether specifically for education or generally, may have had little impact on the survival and vitality of private institutions. Today, however, the situation is far altered. The vastness of public expenditures in recent times gives to the government a much more effective control over private institutions through the power of the public purse. If individual freedom of choice is to survive in an age of big government, then a responsible government must ensure that it does not distribute benefits in a way calculated to make it difficult or virtually impossible for the individual who so desires to use the facilities of any welfare institution—whether public or private, whether church-related or not. Yet the systematic and total exclusion of the private, including church-related, schools from the distribution of public funds for education inevitably works to produce this unhappy result.

THE CHURCH-STATE ISSUE

But is government support of church-related schools consistent with public policy or even constitutional principle? The First and Fourteenth Amendments as interpreted in the Everson case would appear to condemn the use of tax monies for the support of all religious activities or institutions.[20] Critics of public aid to religiously oriented schools contend that, since church-related schools are *ex professo* religious institutions, government support of such schools would be inconsistent with the American principle of separation of church and state. Surely, the government is not obliged to distribute tax benefits to religious education when there is a public policy, even a constitutional principle, against such a distribution.

No one who professes the conviction that private, including religiously oriented, schools should share proportionately in the benefits of public support can ignore the pertinence of the objection. If in fact sound public policy or sound constitutional principle weighs against government aid to church-related schools, then no claim in equity or convenience can be forcefully urged. It would be difficult, for example, to convince right-thinking citizens of the necessity or the wisdom of aiding private schools instituted to block racial integration or to teach subversive doctrine. But does government aid to church-related schools really run counter to any sound public policy or constitutional principle? Is religiously oriented education to be classed with segregation and subversion as a social vice?

In the preceding chapter we contended that the First Amendment should not be interpreted to mean a complete and absolute separation of civil authority and religious activity. To do so would establish secularism as our national religion and would misconceive the historical basis, political wisdom, and legal realism of the American principle of separation of church and state. The First Amendment ordains a general rather than a total separation of the civil and religious spheres of activity. Where, therefore, circumstances related to a specific civic interest urge cooperation between public authority and religious activity, the First Amendment should not be interpreted as a barrier to such cooperation. Military chaplains provide but one historical example of the permissible cooperation which Americans quite universally accept. We do, indeed, assume that the American principle of separation of church and state excludes general support by the government of religious activity, any preference of one religion over another or any preference of all religion over nonreligion. We do not assume, however, that the principle excludes government support of *any* activity, however concretely related to a specific civic interest, simply because the activity is religious or religiously oriented. The First Amendment should not be interpreted to prohibit the public authority from contributing an incidental benefit to religious activity or religious institutions for a specific cause or motive which excludes the preference of one religion over another or of all religion over nonreligion.

To refer to church-related schools as "religious schools" can be particularly misleading, for the term "religious school" may connote that the school instructs pupils solely in religious doctrine. A church-related school does possess a religious character that penetrates the marrow of its academic life. That presumably is the reason for its existence. But it is not *merely* a religious institution; it serves the community in an educational capacity and conveys a secular benefit. All states in fact accept attendance at church-related schools as fulfilling compulsory school attendance laws. Over a quarter of a century ago Archbishop Alter pointed out the essence of the request for public support of church-related schools:

We merely ask that the State help us to teach the secular branches which the state compels all children to study in order to prepare adequately for the duties of citizenship.[21]

A school should not be less acceptable as an educational institution because it is religiously oriented. Those who argue otherwise gratuitously assume, perhaps unwittingly, the secularist principle that religious activity is essentially superfluous or even dangerous to the cause of civic virtue, that religious activity is at best a civic frill or at worst a civic threat. To read such a principle into the First Amendment is to establish secularism as the national religion.

In several ways, indeed, the attitude of opponents of government aid to church-related schools is remarkably inconsistent. On the one hand, the government cannot assist church-related schools because they are *religious* institutions; on the other hand, attendance at a church-related school will fulfill the *educational* requirements of the school attendance laws. Nor may a parent who pays tuition to a church-related school deduct the whole of this expense from his taxable income as a religious contribution, because he has received an educational benefit in exchange for the money expended. Now, the resulting situation is quite paradoxical for parents who choose to send their children to church-related schools. If they seek tax support, they are told that the church-related school is essentially a religious enterprise; if they seek to deduct tuition from taxable income, they are told that the church-related school is essentially an educational institution. As a religious enterprise, the church-related school is ineligible for tax support; as an educational institution, the church-related school cannot provide a tax deduction for the parent who pays tuition.

Public aid to denominational schools would provide, to be sure, an incidental benefit to some religious groups and institutions. Roman Catholics would profit more than others since loyalty to the public school, principles of doctrine, and difficulties of organization would prevent many religious groups from participating in tax benefits through a parochial school program. Yet, incidental benefit implies no formal preference by the state. If the public authorities made grants to one or more denominational medical schools because of well-developed programs for cancer research, the aid given on the basis of community interest and without discriminatory design would seem unexceptionable. The question of public aid, therefore, really hinges on the nondiscriminatory design of the aid and on the nature of the community interest in the project aided. It is difficult to see why—without the establishment of a secular covenant—an incidental benefit to religious groups or institutions should negate the primary rights of parents to educate their children. In the matter of government aid to pupils attending church-related schools Americans must examine their conscience and determine just how sincerely they accept the primacy of parental rights in education.[22]

THE COURT AND THE CHURCH-STATE ISSUE

The constitutional issue of public support of church related institutions has been raised before the United States Supreme Court in a number of cases beginning with *Bradford* v. *Roberts*.[23] There the Court unanimously upheld the validity of a contract between the District of Columbia and Providence Hospital, a religious corporation controlled and operated by the Sisters of Charity. The District agreed to pay money to the hospital to help finance the construction of an isolation ward for the treatment of contagious diseases, and the hospital promised to reserve two-thirds of the ward for poor patients sent and supported by the District. On the basis of the religious establishment clause of the First Amendment, Bradford sued to prohibit payment to the hospital. Justice Peckham, speaking for the Court, rejected the petitioner's contention:

If we were to assume, for the purpose of this question only, that under this appropriation an agreement with a religious corporation of the tenor of this agreement would be invalid, as resulting indirectly in the passage of an act respecting an establishment of religion, we are unable to see that . . . the corporation is of the kind described. . . .[24]

Thus, the Bradford decision rested essentially on the Court's contention that the hospital was not really sectarian. Now, this contention is somewhat disingenuous and unrealistic, but perhaps the Court was simply groping to give expression to the crucial fact that the contract was concretely related to a significant civic interest and the benefit to the religious corporation was in consequence only incidental. At any rate, the Court did not see in the religious establishment clause any "absolute" separation of church and state.

The Bradford case concerned the appropriation of federal funds for a sectarian hospital. But in 1930 the Supreme Court for the first time faced the issue of whether state funds may be used to benefit pupils attending sectarian educational institutions.[25] The case of *Cochran* v. *Louisiana* did not come to the Court on the basis of any immediate appeal to the First Amendment's prohibition of a religious establishment. Rather, Cochran contended that in providing free textbooks in secular subjects for parochial school pupils the state was expending funds for a private and not a public use. Nonetheless, the church-state issue was implicitly involved. Chief Justice Hughes, speaking for a unanimous Court, rejected Cochran's claim and cited with approval the conclusion of the Louisiana Supreme Court:

The appropriations were made for the specific purpose of purchasing school books for the use of the school children of the state, free of cost to them. It was for their benefit and for the resulting benefit to the state that the appropriations were made. . . . The schools, however, are not the beneficiaries of these appropriations. They obtain nothing from them, nor are they relieved of a single obligation because of them. The school children and the state alone are the beneficiaries.[26]

The Cochran decision appears to rest on the Court's contention that the school pupils and not the sectarian institutions were the beneficiaries of the state's purchase of textbooks. Now, this proposition, like the one in the Bradford case, is a considerable oversimplification, but perhaps, again as in the Bradford case, the Court was attempting to articulate the crucial fact that the public support was genuinely related to an important civic

interest and the benefit to the religious institution was in consequence only incidental. In the Cochran opinion we have the
seeds of the distinction decisively expressed in *Everson* v. *Board
of Education* between direct and indirect aid to religious institutions and activities by civil authority.

Unquestionably the Everson decision is the current and controlling expression of American constitutional law on the issue
of public support for church-related schools. A local school board
acting under a New Jersey statute reimbursed parents for the
cost of transporting their children to school by bus and included
in the reimbursement the parents of parochial school children.
Taxpayer Everson challenged the school board's action and
carried his appeal to the United States Supreme Court. There a
bare majority sustained the action of the school board. For the
first time the Court squarely considered the intent and extent
of the First Amendment's prohibition of a religious establishment
and explicitly applied the prohibition to the state governments.
We have already had occasion to note and criticize the "absolute"
interpretation which the Everson court—majority and minority—
gave to the religious establishment clause. Here we wish only to
indicate Justice Black's application of the doctrine of "absolute"
separation of church and state to the problem of public support
of church-related schools:

No tax in any amount, large or small, can be levied to support any
religious activities or institutions, whatever they may be called or
whatever form they may adopt to teach or practice religion.[27]

And again:

New Jersey cannot consistently with the "establishment of religion"
clause of the First Amendment contribute tax-raised funds to the support of an institution which teaches the tenets and faith of any
church.[28]

Nonetheless, Justice Black upheld the New Jersey statute as a
public welfare measure:

[The New Jersey statute] does no more than provide a general program to help parents get their children, regardless of their religion,
safely and expeditiously to and from accredited schools.[29]

Justice Black appears in the Everson case to have carried forward the "child benefit" theory of the Cochran decision but in the context of a doctrine of "absolute" separation of church and state never expressed by the Cochran court. The Everson majority attempted to distinguish as a matter of constitutional principle between direct and indirect aid to religious activities and institutions. The former would be unconstitutional, whereas the latter would conform acceptably to the mandate of the First Amendment. Thus, the majority concluded, public support for the transportation of parochial school pupils—the issue at stake in the Everson case—was constitutional because directly a "child benefit" and only indirectly an aid to religion.

As a constitutional principle the distinction between direct and indirect aid has many difficulties, but the principal one is the intrinsic ambiguity of the terms "direct" and "indirect." This difficulty is quite analogous to the attempt of the Court in the 1930s to measure the "direct" and "indirect" effects on interstate commerce. If aid to religion is "indirect" when the aid is designed to benefit the child, then not only bus rides or textbooks but also support of the whole enterprise of a church-related school could be called a benefit to the child and incidentally an aid to religion. But this logic extends further than Justice Black would wish to follow. Thus "indirect" aid in the minds of the Everson majority may refer as much to the fringe character or remote connection of bus transportation to sectarian education as to its benefit to the child.

Actually, of course, Justice Black arrived at the rigid distinction between direct and indirect aid only after he first accepted as a premise the linguistic strait jacket of an "absolute" separation of church and state. Had Justice Black not believed aid to religiously oriented activities and institutions, as such, howsoever related to a civic interest, unconstitutional, he would not have been forced to make so ironclad a distinction between direct and indirect aid in order to uphold public support for the transportation of parochial school pupils. To reach the right answer one must ask the right question, and Justice Black, unfortunately, did not ask the right question.

The McCollum and Zorach decisions are relevant here only because of their general treatment of the First Amendment's religious establishment clause.[30] Their immediate concern was with religious instruction and the public schools. McCollum etched the high-water mark of the "absolute separation" theory, while Zorach substituted a more realistic "limited accommodation" approach to church-state relations. After Zorach we must wait almost a decade for any national legal precedent on the issue of public aid to church-related schools.

The most recent and somewhat ambiguous case, *Swart* v. *South Burlington School District,* arose in Vermont.[31] A 1915 statute permitted towns with no high schools of their own to pay for the tuition of pupils of the district to other public or private schools. Acting under the statute, the South Burlington school district undertook to pay the tuition for a number of children who attended three Roman Catholic high schools. A taxpayer, C. Raymond Swart, objected to the practice and brought suit to enjoin the district from continuing the tuition payment for parochial school pupils. The Vermont Supreme Court sustained petitioner Swart at least in part on the basis of the federal prohibition of an establishment of religion.

The Supreme Court of Vermont relied heavily on the Everson, McCollum and, ironically enough, the Zorach decisions.[32] The Vermont court apparently was impressed by the following section of the Zorach decision:

Government may not finance religious groups nor undertake religious instruction nor blend secular and sectarian education nor use secular institutions to force one or some religion on any person.[33]

Yet in the context Justice Douglas was speaking not of government support of church-related schools but of what was permissible in schools owned and operated by the public authority and open to citizens of any or no religious belief. And the Vermont court neglected to cite the very next sentence of the majority opinion which rather more conclusively indicated the significance of the Zorach case:

But we find no constitutional requirement which makes it necessary for government to be hostile to religion and to throw its weight against efforts to widen the effective scope of religious influence.[34]

What the Supreme Court of Vermont chose to think of the First Amendment would have remained, in the usual course of events, of interest only to the citizens of Vermont. But on May 15, 1961, the United States Supreme Court declined without comment to grant the review of the South Burlington case which some of the affected parents had sought.[35] It is inevitable that the high Court's action will color future discussions and prospects of the "school question."

Did the United States Supreme Court, in effect, endorse the Vermont court's sweeping application of the First Amendment to prohibit any tuition payment by public authorities for children attending parochial schools? The case might appear to have confronted the high Court with a clear-cut issue to which the Court replied unequivocally. Yet a more profound consciousness of the historical practice of the Supreme Court will suggest that the meaning of the case is not quite so clear and not quite so decisive.

The fact that the Court said nothing—and said it unanimously —should arouse more than a shadow of suspicion against any attempt to attribute too decisive an intent to the action of the Court. Had the Court wished to endorse the reasoning of the Vermont court, it could easily have made clear that there was no need of further review of the constitutional issue. But had the Court so expressed itself, there would have been the likely prospect of dissent or at least elaborate articulation of views in concurring opinions. The record of the Everson, McCollum, and Zorach cases well indicates how expressive the Court is on the meaning of the First Amendment's religious establishment clause. The Court, however, said nothing except to deny review.

The shadow of doubt further lengthens when we recall the significance which the Court attaches to cases which involve First Amendment freedoms. It is difficult to believe that the Supreme Court would acquiesce in an interpretation by a state court of so important a clause as that prohibiting a religious establishment without hearing a single argument and without uttering a single comment. We must look elsewhere if we wish adequately to understand the meaning of the Court's action.

The Justices may have differed among themselves on the reasons for declining to review the case, but the technicality of the South Burlington school district's failure to join the parents' petition to the Supreme Court for review may have proved decisive. The effect of the school district's inaction was that the principal party to the original action and the party directly affected by the Vermont decision did not seek review. Some of the justices, at least, may have felt that there was no compelling reason for the Supreme Court to hear the case when the local authorities responsible for the stricken program did not wish a review. It was the South Burlington school district which was enjoined from reimbursing the parents of parochial school children and the South Burlington school district acquiesced in the Vermont decision. There was in the high Court's action, therefore, no new, unequivocal, and authoritative statement on the constitutionality of tuition payments by public authorities for children attending parochial schools.

In the light of the precedents, then, what conclusions may we reach concerning the constitutionality of public aid for church-related schools or their pupils? There is, as we have indicated, some ambiguity in the precedents themselves, and the precedents, of course, do not foreclose the possibility of modification or reversal by future decisions of the Court. Yet we shall hazard the following generalizations without any elaborate attempt to justify their accuracy. On the one hand, "child benefit" aid in such areas as bus transportation, textbooks, school lunches, and health services are undoubtedly constitutional.[36] Tax deductions authorized by Congress for tuition paid to church-related schools would also appear to be consistent with the religious establishment clause at least by analogy with the long-accepted practice of tax exemption for church property and tax deduction of contributions made for charitable or religious purposes. Whether the analogy extends far enough to embrace the less publicized tax credit and certificate plans, both of which would directly reimburse individual parents rather than religious institutions, is less certain in view of dicta in the Everson case.[37] On the other hand, the Court's interpretation of the First Amendment's religious establishment clause, especially in Everson, would appear to proscribe any direct government grants or loans to church-related schools for purposes of general construction or faculty salaries. But direct government grants or loans to church-related schools for the specific purpose of constructing dormitories, gymnasia, cafeterias, science laboratories, or language facilities may fall within the legitimate sphere of implementing national defense and welfare objectives.[38]

THE PUBLIC PROCESS AND THE CONSTITUTION

At this point it may be well to make an important observation on the nature of the judicial decision-making process by which the Court resolves constitutional issues. Americans by and large tend too strongly to absolutize interpretations by the Court without reflecting sufficiently on how closely these fragile and human judgments are related to the political order. Let us suppose, for example, that the United States Supreme Court in clear and unequivocal language decided that no aid of any kind to church-related schools or their pupils would be constitutional. Would citizens be obliged to accept the decision as irreversible? We know that the Court reversed itself on the constitutionality of New Deal legislation in 1938 and of racial segregation in 1954. The Constitution itself, therefore, recognizes the principle of judicial as well as other forms of change. A minority which believes a goal right, wise, and constitutional may and should attempt to convince the majority of the merits of its contentions.

To judge by past history, the public view of the propriety, wisdom, and necessity of a legislative course of action has proved decisive in the resolution of a constitutional question. A public convinced of the correctness of a course of action will resolve the constitutional issue in one of three ways: (1) by formal amendment of the Constitution (e.g., the income tax amendment adopted in 1913); (2) by judicial reinterpretation (e.g., the Segregation Cases of 1954); or (3) by tailoring the legislative form to fit specific constitutional objections (e.g., the Agricultural Adjustment Act of 1938). The practical genius of the American people has made them unwilling to believe that a right, wise, and necessary course of action could fail to be constitutional in some form or other. In a classic remark John Marshall noted the organic and vital character of the American Constitution: ". . . we must never forget that it is a *constitution* we are expounding."[39]

Ultimately, therefore, the constitutional issue of aid to church-related schools will hinge on whether or not this nation is convinced of its wisdom. Aid to church-related schools, like any other proposal for government action, is debatable in the first place precisely on the level of necessity and wisdom. Opinions may, of course, differ on the question, but the opinions should be voiced for the public to hear. If such aid is wise, the American people will accept it as constitutional in some form or other.[40] Where there is a will there is a way.

This is not to suggest that all forms of government aid to church-related schools or their pupils are equally desirable. The legislature should adopt a form of public support which not only promotes educational values and promises successful administration but also mutually safeguards the integrity of church and state from possible encroachment. Whether or not differences in the form of government aid should add up to a distinction based on constitutional principle, sound public policy at least should recognize the merits and demerits of various forms of public support, including their effect on the institutional relationship of church and state. We shall make only a few cursory comments on this topic here.

Direct government grants or loans have the advantage of efficiency: the government may designate and ensure the educational purposes for which the appropriation will be used. But such a method of government support would also set up a rather direct relationship between the public authority and religious institutions. Tax credit plans for their part, while avoiding the difficulty of direct government grants or loans, would assist only those parents who pay an income tax larger than the potential tax credit. As a result the poorer citizens, who most need the assistance, would not benefit substantially. A family with four children, for example, with an income of less than four thousand dollars a year already pays so small an income tax that a credit against the tax would be of negligible help. Tax deductions, of course, would even more decisively favor parents in higher income brackets. Among all methods of reimbursing parents, the certificate plan is perhaps the most equitable to

citizens of lesser means. We should insist, by way of conclusion
to this whole matter of choosing among different forms of public
support for church-related schools or their pupils, that the legislature, as Justice Reed observed, "is entitled to great leeway . . .
when dealing with important social problems of its population."[41]

ARE PRIVATE SCHOOLS DEMOCRATIC?

Another and less explicitly articulated argument of public
policy against the wisdom of government aid to nonprofit educational institutions centers not on the church-state issue but rather
on an assertedly divisive, even undemocratic, character of private
schools in American life. The public school, it is often suggested,
serves as the unique vehicle to unite the many diverse religious,
cultural, economic, and social elements in our pluralistic society,
and fulfills the unique educational function of transmitting to
successive generations the democratic values of human liberty,
equality, and solidarity without respect to race, wealth, or religion.
If this be the unique mission of the public school, then the private
school, of course, must be regarded as a splinter force that may
be tolerated but should not be encouraged by public support.
Nor may parents who seek a private education for their children
make a just claim to the distribution of tax benefits beyond the
support of the public schools; they themselves have chosen not
to make use of the public schools which are open to, and designed for, all American children.

If we are to determine, in the light of the above criticism, how
beneficial or harmful private schools are in American life, we
must first consider the role and function of the public school.
The consensus of American opinion today believes elementary
and secondary education (a consensus on some measure of college education may also be emerging) essential to the development and formation of every citizen. The advantages and necessity
of education for citizens are well recognized in our day. Education offers citizens the opportunity to develop the resources of
their personality, to harness their vital potential, and thus to
lead the "good life" to which men aspire. Moreover, education

helps provide the community with the intelligent and informed electorate which democratic government requires as well as with the broader base for intelligent and vigorous leadership in all fields by which democratic society can meet the challenges of the present and the future. Now, the public school exists to ensure the fulfillment of these goals. The public school exists to supplement—not supplant—the limited capacity and limited interest of private education in "the many." These are the solid reasons why all Americans wholeheartedly support a system of public education. Thus public and private education are partners in the common task of developing the citizens to whom America will entrust the future.

Unfortunately, many philosophers of education claim that more than this is essential to the role and function of the public school. They see the public school as absolutely essential and solely qualified to transmit democratic values in a pluralistic society and to achieve the political and social unity of the American community. Such a claim, needless to say, makes private education not an honored partner but a scarcely tolerated pariah in American society. Amid differences, especially of religious belief, the public school becomes the symbol of national unity and the ark of a secular covenant. In the name of democracy and freedom these philosophers would establish the public schools as the temple in which all Americans should worship.[42]

Political unity and community harmony are indeed values to be cherished but they should not be purchased at the price of parents' freedom of choice in pursuit of educational excellence or in devotion to religious belief. Were the cause of educational diversity a doctrine of racial supremacy or a desire for class distinctions, the undemocratic character of such educational pluralism would hardly be consistent with public support. But nothing in the democratic tradition opposes an educational pluralism which is religiously inspired or motivated by a desire for educational excellence; indeed, our heritage has been one of diversity, and our zeal has been directed toward the protection of the rights of those holding views with which we disagree. Where educational institutions are fulfilling their civic responsibilities, whatever their religious inspiration and our opinion of it, we ought to recognize the effective right of parents to choose this educational diversity.

Any real attempt, then, to achieve political harmony and cohesive unity in a pluralistic society like America must respect the right of parents to choose a suitable education, especially a religiously oriented education, for their children. This rule, of course, is subject to the standards and criteria which the public authority may be required to specify or determine for the common good. To recognize the equality of schools which parents in a pluralistic society may choose for worthy purposes is not merely sound democratic theory; it also makes for wise and even necessary political practice. Private, including church-related, institutions today enroll over 13 per cent of the nation's elementary and secondary school population. The student enrollment in private schools, as we have observed before, has increased rapidly in this century in terms both of absolute numbers and of relative proportion to public school enrollment. Simply to read this sizable segment of the American educational structure out of the democratic pale by the tag "divisive," therefore, is not at all helpful in achieving the very goal of a united community which critics of the private schools desire. From a merely practical point of view, those genuinely dedicated to the goal of shaping political unity in a pluralistic community must take full account of the diversity in education at least as a matter of empirical realism. This is a pluralistic structure which citizens in a democratic polity must accept and work with.

However fatuous (and, ironically enough, even undemocratic) the argument that the public school is the sole educational workshop in the transmission of democratic values, whereas the private school is a "divisive" force, it does reveal a real and serious problem of how to associate citizens of different beliefs, classes, and means in a democratic and cohesive political unity of aspiration and action. The public school, of course, performs an indisputably distinguished service in its efforts to deal effectively with this problem. The private school has no less devotion to American ideals and should have no less sensitivity to the issue of a harmonious and integrated community life. Yet it cannot be denied that a private, especially a church-related, school may lead to a certain amount of religious and cultural isolation. The private school, therefore, should be solicitous to give a more sympathetic understanding to the values and aspirations of all citizens, and the private school should particularly seek to promote a fuller cooperation with the educational efforts of the public schools. There is no easy panacea for this problem, but we can hope that dedication, experiment, and application will help lay a sure groundwork for the future. Such a groundwork, however, can be secure only if it begins with a recognition of the fact of, and the right to, diversity, including educational diversity.

PRIVATE SCHOOLS AND PUBLIC PURPOSES

But why should the public support private education—however equal and legitimate its place in American life? Why should private institutions have any claim to public support? This question may stem, of course, from a statist preconception at odds with the principle of subsidiarity, which, as we have observed, requires the state to function in education where necessary to support, not to supplant, parental choice. Yet, the exclusive reservation of public support for public institutions may also arise from an ambiguous use of the polar terms "public" and "private." Private, nonprofit schools in a real sense are quite as truly public as public schools. They seek no private gain but rather dedicate themselves unselfishly to the cause of American education—a cause which benefits not only the minority of students they educate but also, through them, the entire public. The privacy of private schools consists only in their operation and control; in other respects they are quite genuinely public.

Even in the sphere of operation and control the private school is not fully autonomous. The public authorities may exercise both nonscholastic and scholastic controls over private education. With respect to nonscholastic controls, the state supervises the health and safety of pupils attending the private schools; with respect to scholastic controls, the state may demand of private schools the certification of teachers, minimum attendance, submission of records to the state, prescribed courses in secular subjects, and/or the examination of pupils in the same. It is in the realm of scholastic or curricular regulation, of course, that the risk of governmental abuse is highest. Yet the possibility of abuse does not destroy the proper role of governmental regulation. Private schools are not divorced from the common good, and the state may rightfully insist on their fulfilling adequate standards of educational excellence.

Public support in itself neither increases nor decreases the potential risks of substantive public control of private institutions. Even without the lever of public support, public authorities may and do insist on adequate standards for private schools. They may, of course, abuse their power. But we should not too easily assume either that the American people can be persuaded to abandon their tradition of limited government and individual freedom or that the United States Supreme Court would acquiesce in such an abandonment. The record written by the federal government in support of local welfare projects and by local governments in support of private welfare activities indicates that public support can avoid the danger of usurping the functions and responsibilities of local and private institutions. If Americans come to accept some measure of public support for private schools, they will do so because they recognize the primacy of parental choice in education. And if Americans come to recognize the implications of the basic right of parents to determine the education which their children should receive, then there will be little likelihood that they will tolerate the transformation of public support into public encroachment on private schools.

Justice Jackson, in particular, seemed to labor under the too common misapprehension that aid to church-related schools constituted a unique title to regulation and that absence of aid ensured the private schools against regulation. In the Everson case he commented: "If the state may aid . . . religious schools, it may therefore regulate them."[43] Yet the state may legitimately regulate private schools within defined bounds with or without public support, for its claim derives not from its support but from its concern for the common good. Justice Jackson misidentified the power to regulate with the power of the purse and confused the right to regulate with the right to abuse. To adapt Justice Holmes' well-known aphorism, the power to distribute tax benefits to private schools is not the power to destroy those schools as long as Americans love liberty and the Supreme Court exercises vigilance.

RATIONAL COOPERATION AND THE DEMOCRATIC PROCESS

The history of recent legislative efforts to secure federal aid to education reveals how much the rivalry between public and private institutions can undermine the over-all educational goals of both.[44] Worse still, the unnecessary and irrational friction between public and private education poisons the community atmosphere and thus multiplies tensions beyond the single area of education. Each fights the other to be the first at the public trough instead of supporting generously any justified and demonstrated claim of the other to government assistance. Both public and private schools serve the cause of American education, and both should cooperate to see this cause forwarded. America is not so poor that she does not have the resources to support the education of her entire school population.

The private school is not a competitor but a cooperator with the public schools in the task of educating the nation's children. Many commentators worry that private schools, if aided by public support, would undermine the community's commitment to the public school. First of all, it should be observed in response that public aid to private schools does not indicate any lessening of the commitment to the public schools. The public schools must be maintained and supported in all localities to ensure the educational opportunity of citizens for whom private schools are unable or unwilling to provide. This commitment is absolute. Secondly, public aid to private schools is not at all likely to encourage widespread splinter movements in education. Public aid would support parental choice only where private schools were already educationally viable and fully operational. It takes a strong force of human aspiration and activity to create educational institutions, which none but those strongly motivated can achieve on any large scale. There are no signs outside of existing systems that such a sustained force would be extensively forthcoming.

What should be the attitude of those who favor public support for private, including church-related, schools if legislators continue to exclude the private schools totally from participation in public support? Hotheads are tempted to play a desperate game of power politics in an effort to scuttle support of public education unless and until private schools or their pupils are invited to share in public support. Even in this age of man's inhumanity to man, a suggestion to play Russian roulette with so many of the nation's children would be an affront to conscience and a violent disruption of community harmony. If any claim of public education is urgent and demonstrated, then all citizens should give the claim their wholehearted backing.

Where, on the other hand, the claim of public education to public support is not urgent, though desirable, advocates of government aid to private schools might feel justified in making their support contingent on an end to the discrimination against private schools. They could feel justified in so bargaining, however, only if they had a proximate hope of success that both public and private education would receive their reasonable claims to support, and only if the pressure applied would not create more harmful effects within the community than the benefit desired, namely, an end to governmental discrimination against private schools. The whole tactic of pressure is one fraught with danger, and those who undertake to use it may not be able to stop at the narrow line which reason imposes as the limit.

At any rate, advocates of public support for private, including church-related, schools or their pupils may and should continue to press their cause. Perhaps the objective is a long way from realization, but advocates will continue to urge their reasons in all calmness on the public and the public's legislative representatives. Under no circumstances will they permit rational discussion to be foreclosed by the question-begging description of public support as "undebatable" because "unconstitutional" or "divisive." And they will continue to participate in all legitimate political processes which may influence suitable legislative fulfillment of their aims. This is no less than the very essence of the democratic process.

NOTES

1. Many non-Catholics, however, endorse government aid to private, including church-related, schools even as a matter of justice. Rabbi Morris Sherer, executive director of Agudath Israel of America, and Glen Andreas of the Christian Reformed Church, vice-president of Citizens for Educational Freedom, both testified in favor of government support of private religious schools. *The New York Times*, March 30, 1961, p. 16; *America*, April 1, 1961, pp. 4–5.

2. See the questioning of candidate Kennedy by the Houston ministers. *The New York Times*, September 13, 1960, p. 22.

3. The President made this remark at his weekly news conference, March 1, 1961. *The New York Times*, March 2, 1961, p. 18.

4. The President's news conference of March 8, 1961. *The New York Times*, March 9, 1961, p. 16.

5. *The New York Times*, August 6, 1949, p. 1.

6. See *The Brooklyn Tablet*, March 24, 1956.

7. *Official Catholic Directory* (New York: P. J. Kenedy & Sons, 1961).

8. Samuel Schloss and Carol J. Hobson, *Fall 1960 Statistics on Enrollment, Teachers and School-housing* (Washington: U.S. Department of Health, Education and Welfare, 1961), p. 3.

9. See the *Official Catholic Directory* for 1900, 1920, 1940, and 1960.

10. The figures for the 1899–1900, 1919–1920 and 1939–1940 public school enrollments represent cumulative counts of the total number of different pupils registered at any time during the school year in each state. Hence pupils enrolled in two or more states during the school year are counted more than once and the net total is some 3 per cent less according to the estimates of the U.S. Office of Education. See the *Biennial Survey of Education in the United States, 1956–1958* (Washington: U.S. Department of Health, Education and Welfare, 1961), Ch. II, p. 6, for an explanation of the enrollment statistics and p. 18 for the statistics themselves. The 1959–1960 figure, on the other hand, represents fall enrollment. See Schloss and Hobson, *op. cit.*, p. 3.

11. Neil McCluskey, S.J., "How to Find and Pay Teachers," *America*, April 27, 1957, pp. 121, 124.

12. *Ibid.*, p. 122.

13. *Ibid.*, p. 121.

14. Kenedy, *op. cit.*

15. E. G. Homrighausen, "Social Status of Religious Con-

stituencies," *Theology Today,* January, 1946, p. 543.

16. This complaint gained sufficient credence to lead the New York State Department of Education to study some thirty districts which rejected school budgets in the spring of 1959. The study sought to determine whether there was any link between voter rejection and the size of the district's parochial school population. *The New York Times,* September 20, 1959, p. 64. The Department found no such link. *The New York Times,* May 23, 1960, p. 26.

17. The Office of Education estimates the non-Catholic private elementary and secondary school enrollment at about 10 per cent of the total nonpublic registration. See the *Biennial Survey of Education, 1956–1958, loc. cit.,* p. 15.

18. *Pierce* v. *Society of Sisters,* 268 U.S. 510 (1925).

19. *Ibid.,* p. 535.

20. *Everson* v. *Board of Education,* 330 U.S. 1 (1947).

21. Most Rev. Karl J. Alter, "Does State Aid to Education Mean Union of Church and State?" *Catholic Education Review,* Vol. XXXIII (1935), p. 69.

22. Americans should consider in this respect the now universal practice of democratic Europe. There, countries including traditionally separatist France, grant some measure of public support for students who attend denominational schools. The practice has constituted no "establishment of religion" and involved no political control of church-related schools. See *The New York Times* survey by Fred M. Hechinger, March 27, 1961, pp. 1, 23.

23. *Bradford* v. *Roberts,* 175 U.S. 291 (1899).

24. *Ibid.,* p. 297.

25. *Cochran* v. *Louisiana,* 281 U.S. 370 (1930).

26. *Ibid.,* pp. 374–375; 168 La. 1030 (1929).

27. *Everson,* p. 16.

28. *Ibid.*

29. *Ibid.,* p. 18.

30. *Ill.* ex rel. *McCollum* v. *Board of Education; Zorach* v. *Clauson.*

31. *Swart* v. *South Burlington School District,* 122 Vt. 177 (1961).

32. Interestingly enough, the Vermont Supreme Court accepted without discussion Justice Rutledge's historical exposition of the meaning of the First Amendment although that exposition was expressed in a minority opinion in the Everson case and has been severely criticized subsequently by many scholars.

33. *Zorach* v. *Clauson,* p. 314.

34. *Ibid.*

35. *Anderson* v. *Swart,* 366 U.S. 925 (1961).

36. *Everson* v. *Board of Education.*

37. Tax-credit plans would provide a credit against individual income taxes for all or part of student tuition and fees paid to tax-exempt public and private educational institutions. It differs from a tax deduction in that the credit is against the actual tax and not against taxable income.

The certificate plan, on the other hand, would provide to

parents government vouchers redeemable for a specified annual maximum sum per child if spent for approved educational purposes. Parents could then spend this sum and any additional amount for educational purposes at the institution of their choice. The G.I. bills of 1944 and 1952 as well as many state scholarship programs incorporate the principle of the cerificate plan. But the veteran and scholarship programs aid only a special rather than the general student population.

38. At least this was the opinion of the Health, Education and Welfare Department legal staff expressed in the memo of March 28, 1961. *The New York Times,* March 29, 1961, p. 22.

39. *McCulloch* v. *Maryland,* 4 Wheat. 316, 407 (1819).

40. In addition to the federal constitutional provisions affecting government action, forty state constitutions bar public funds for sectarian or nonstate controlled schools. Fringe benefits, such as school lunches or bus transportation, however, are often construed not to constitute support for church-related schools.

41. *Ill.* ex rel. *McCollum* v. *Board of Education,* p. 256. While in the context Justice Reed spoke of the state legislature, the remainder of his opinion made clear that the logic of his arguments extends to federal legislation as well.

42. President Kennedy, himself the product of private schools, seemed to acquiesce in this view. At his weekly news conference of March 8, 1961, the President sought to clarify his administration's distinction between construction loans to church-related elementary and secondary schools (which the President opposed) and construction loans to church-related colleges (which the President favored). The difference, he indicated, lay in the fact that "secondary education is compulsory. It is provided for every student, every citizen. Every citizen must attend school." *The New York Times,* March 9, 1961, p. 16. The Health, Education and Welfare memo echoed this point. *The New York Times,* March 29, 1961, p. 22.

43. *Everson* v. *Board of Education,* p. 27.

44. The necessity of a general program of federal assistance to education, of course, has been disputed. Ninety per cent of public school administrators, for example, indicated opposition to further federal aid in the spring of 1961. See *The New York Times,* May 6, 1961, p. 31.

6

Religion
and
the Public Schools

INTRODUCTION

The institutional relationship between religion and education is a two-edged sword. In the previous chapter we examined one edge, namely, public support for church-related schools; here we shall take up the other edge, namely, the role of religious activity in public education. Now, though the second edge isolates the Catholic less from his fellow citizens than the first, it is nonetheless a divisive issue which deeply agitates the American community. The secularist at least has identified the Catholic as the disciplined and articulate spearhead of the religionist position. The issue is not simply a "Catholic" issue, to be sure, but Catholic principles and power are so prominently

involved or believed to be involved that no adequate consideration of the Church's relation today to American democracy
can prudently afford to ignore it.

In less than a century the attitude of Catholics toward the
public school has undergone a radical change of direction. The
Church in the nineteenth century, for the most part, fought
to *remove* religious instruction and observances from the public
schools on the grounds that they were Protestant-oriented; today
Catholics seem to be far more intent on *inserting* religious instruction and observances into the framework of public education.
The major cause of this change of attitude is twofold: first, the
present-day public schools are much freer than in the past of
any specifically Protestant orientation; and, secondly, a secular
humanism hostile or at least indifferent to revealed religion has
progressively gained an ascendancy in public education.

Many Protestants, especially those of more traditional conviction, and many Catholics have become disturbed at the asserted "religious illiteracy" of the recent graduates of public
schools. Protestants, quite understandably in view of the historical record, had come to regard the public school as somehow
their own, and consequently were slow to grasp the disparity
between the idealized picture of the public school as Protestant
and the increasingly secularized reality which came to prevail
in many areas of the country, especially the urban centers. But
by the early decades of this century the Protestant could no
longer avoid the conclusion that secular humanism had replaced
Protestantism as the dominant force in the public school. As
a result many Protestants and Catholics today share an apprehension concerning the secularist trend both in American society
in general and in the public school in particular. This has led
to the many recent efforts to preserve or restore a religious orientation in public elementary and secondary education.

Jews, on the other hand, have generally opposed efforts to
retain or increase religious, particularly sectarian, influences in
the public schools. Even Orthodox Jews, who strongly regret
secularization, are reluctant to support such efforts. The record
of religious persecution of Jewish minorities has long led the
Jew to identify himself with liberal causes. This reaction has

often had the effect of aligning Jews with militant secularists, particularly on the issue of religion and the public schools.

Lastly, there exists alongside the Protestant, Catholic, and Jewish "conspiracies"—to use Fr. Murray's felicitous term—the fourth "conspiracy" of secular humanism itself.[1] The modern tradition of secular humanism began with the deistic influences of the Age of Enlightenment, and, if not explicitly professed by large numbers of citizens, nonetheless finds expression in a very articulate and educated minority. More important than numbers is the influence which the leaven of nontheistic secular humanism has had on the mass of American society. In every respect secular humanism must be reckoned a vital, fourth "faith" in the modern American social structure.

Thus, where Jews, liberal Protestants, and, of course, secular humanists tend to oppose, conservatively minded Protestants and Catholics tend to support religious instruction and practices in public education. The issue is complex and cuts deeply into the social and political life of the community. The citizen and statesman can fail to investigate the complexities of the issue only at their own peril.

Advocates of religious instruction and observances in public education contend that morality and ultimately religion constitute indispensable prerequisites for good citizenship, that moral and ultimately religious formation of character are necessary to educate young and impressionable citizens for their future responsibilities, that the religious establishment clause of the First Amendment prohibits the public authorities from preferring one religious belief over another but not from preferring religious belief over nonbelief, that religious freedom is properly a freedom for religious belief, that public education must ineluctably choose between a religious and a secular orientation, that the majority as well as the minority of parents have rights in public education, and, lastly, that the affirmation of a national religious heritage extends from Washington to Kennedy and finds judicial endorsement in the Zorach profession that "we are a religious people."[2]

Opponents of religious instruction and observances in public education, of course, disagree with one or more of the above contentions from a number of different, sometimes even contradictory, points of view. Militant secularists not only deny that religion constitutes the backbone of good citizenship but may even affirm positively that religion is inimical to any true commitment to human values and that the young should not be prejudiced or in any social way induced into religious conformity. Others, of less secularistic inclination and more Protestant inspiration, emphasize that religious influences belong exclusively to the home and to the church. Still others lay stress on the political and legal complexities involved in attempts to bring or keep religious influences in public schools. Separation of church and state guarantees the right of all citizens—whether they believe in God or not—to send their children to the common school under public auspices without fear that the educational experience there received will in any way offend their susceptibilities.

This, then, is the dilemma of public education. Is the public school to be religiously oriented or not? If it is, to what extent and by what means could the orientation be accomplished in a way compatible with democratic traditions? It appears on first blush either that we must establish religious belief over secular nonbelief or else that we must establish secular nonbelief over religious belief. But perhaps the dilemma is not so overpowering as appearances may at first suggest.

The general question of how to relate religious education and the public authority is reflected in the quite interesting and often paradoxical positions which each of the four major "conspiracies" adopts in an attempt to resolve the dilemma. Protestants in general want a public school not only accessible to all citizens but specifically designed for all citizens to attend. At the same time they want a "nonsectarian" religious orientation for the public school, including Bible reading from the King James Version! The Protestant will oppose public support of church-related schools as a violation of the separation of church and state and will simultaneously defend sectarian instruction of public school pupils on a released or dismissed time basis. Catholics, for their part, insist on a parochial school system on the grounds that the public school is essentially unfitted to provide adequate religious education for Catholics. Religious instruction and exercises either would be Protestant and thus unacceptable, or else "nonsectarian" and thus so watered down as to be ineffective, sentimental, and indifferent to the unique mysteries of Catholic belief. Notwithstanding this critique, Catholics today will generally contend for the inclusion of more "nonsectarian" religious instruction in the public schools. Catholics insist on the primacy of parental rights in education when they argue for public support of Catholic children at parochial schools; yet Catholics generally remain almost insensitive to, or unconcerned with, the interests of nontheistic parents whose children attend the public schools.

Nontheistic secular humanists together with most Jews cannot be accused of any like inconsistency. They want all citizens to attend the public schools and want absolutely no religious orientation or accommodation within these schools. This stand, though highly consistent, passionately commits the public authority beyond dispute to an exclusively secular humanism. Such a militant stand cannot be described as neutral in any meaningful sense and in reality would establish the secular creed as the faith of the nation.

Before we proceed to define and analyze more precisely the principal issues involved, several peripheral clarifications are of consequence. First, there is need of perspective on the potential value of religious instruction and exercises in public education. The theist quite often exaggerates what religious orientation will contribute to the practice of civic virtues. In fact, untoward emphasis on the utilitarian results of religious conviction can undermine the unique significance of religious faith. But the nontheist, too, errs by an excessively superficial attempt to measure the contribution of religion to public life. His a priori, exclusive commitment to secular values may blind him to the genuine, if imperceptible, influences which religious belief can exercise in men of faith.

In this connection it is opportune here to sustain a clear perspective on the present status and role of public education in the American social framework. It is all too easy to paint a dark picture of the public schools as breeding places for juvenile delinquency, immorality, and crime. Yet any evaluation of the public schools must take care to include all relevant data on the harmful influences of social forces other than the public schools. The public schools may much more reflect than create unhealthy social patterns. The mere introduction or strengthening of religious influences in the public schools, therefore, will be no cure-all if the defects complained of flow more fundamentally from other vital forces at work in American society. On the other hand, experience clearly teaches the wisdom of coordinating as many forces as possible to achieve a necessary and desirable goal.

Nor are the family and the church today able to shoulder alone the burden of religious education. The complexity of modern life will allow only the most naive optimist to think that the family and the church are adequate in the present social framework for the transmission of religious values. How many parents today are prepared to give solid and thorough religious instruction? How many families have the structure and stability to sustain such instruction? The institution of the school is the most efficient instrument for religious education; it can accomplish what neither the home nor the church can effect by themselves. This is why parents of religious conviction seek a place for religious instruction in the formal education to which they submit their children.

The liberal mind has always sought to draw a sharp distinction between belief and action. Traditionalists, on the other hand, have insisted with equal vigor on the intimate relation between conviction and social action. Now, as a matter of psychological insight, the traditionalist may have the better of the liberals, but, as a matter of political wisdom, the liberals show more perspective. Consequently the secularist invites just criticism if he is naive enough to think that the sanctuary of conviction can be totally divorced from the world of action. But the theist invites no less just criticism if he is simplistic enough to think that belief and action are equally subject to the prescription of the public authority.

Again, the liberal mind tends to deny a place to sound morals within the common scheme which public action should create and support. This divorce of moral climate from public concern the traditionalist has vigorously opposed but often without any healthy regard for political realities and legal complexities. The result in the field of public education is for the liberal secularist to deny any legitimate locus of the religious or moral within the aspirational ambit of public education, while the traditional theist tends to confuse philosophical or theological principle with political wisdom or even possibility. We shall speak at much greater length on this topic, but it will suffice here to observe that any true solution of the issue of religion and public education must come to grips in the first place with the reality of political pluralism and not merely be content with impolitic programs because they reflect acceptable philosophical and theological values.

The role of religion in public education poses a twofold question: (1) To what extent, if any, may or should the public authority in control of the operation of a common school *permit* sectarian religious instruction or exercises designed for those who desire them? and (2) to what extent, if any, may or should the public authority in control of the operation of a common school *sponsor* "nonsectarian" religious instruction or exercises designed for all students? Each question must be considered separately because the issues involved, though related, are nonetheless distinct. A few general principles, however, may be profitably set forth now to govern both sectarian and "nonsectarian" practices in the public schools.

The first general principle is that religious belief is not, and cannot be, a criterion or test of citizenship in a pluralistic democracy. This is the only acceptable meaning of the First Amendment which is politically consistent with the present pluralistic value structure of American society. This is not a philosophical principle which reflects secularist presuppositions but a political principle—elevated, of course, to legal and constitutional status by the First Amendment—which reflects the exigencies of a pluralistic democracy. If citizens are to have an equal voice in the decision-making process as the theory of democratic process requires, they cannot be distinguished on the grounds of the basic value commitment which will serve as the principal motor force in concrete exercises of the decision-making function. And if theoretical political analyses leave any theist unconvinced, still the practical impossibility of acting in any other way in twentieth-century America will prove persuasive enough. The plain fact is that with American society a fragile composite of four often conflicting "conspiracies" on fundamental and ultimate value commitments, "articles of peace" among the "conspiracies" are an essential and necessary prerequisite to the fulfillment of any civic aspirations.

The second general principle is that parents enjoy the primary right, duty, and responsibility in the education of children. The public authority in the operation and control of public schools acts as the surrogate of parental authority. The public school offers educational instruction to citizens of all beliefs, and the public schools should respect the wishes of all parents in the matter of religious instruction as far as this is consistent with the common good. Just how the public authority can satisfy the desires of all parents in the matter of religious instruction is, to be sure, the heart of the public school dilemma. The distinction between instruction sponsored for all students and instruction permitted for those whose parents request it may offer the key to resolving the dilemma.

SECTARIAN RELIGIOUS INSTRUCTION AND THE PUBLIC SCHOOLS

To what extent and under what conditions, if any, should the public school cooperate with sectarian religious instruction designed for those who desire it? This was the question which many communities and states faced when from the early decades of the twentieth century they sought to join sectarian instruction to public education on a voluntary basis. Two programs involving released and dismissed time, in fact, were ultimately carried to the United States Supreme Court to determine whether they violated the religious establishment clause of the First Amendment.

The first consideration is to understand on exactly what basis the public authority is involved in a program of sectarian instruction made available to those who request it. Here we have recourse to the general principle echoed in the Pierce decision that the child is not the "mere creature of the state" and that parents have the primary right, duty, and responsibility to educate the child.[3] The public role in education, therefore, is secondary and subordinate to that of the parents. If the public school offers its pupils the opportunity of sectarian religious instruction at the request of the pupils' parents, then the public authority is simply executing its substitutional relationship to the parents insofar as this is consistent with the common good. The public authority is not imposing anything; rather, it is permitting pupils to obtain the education which their parents have chosen for them insofar as this is curricularly feasible within the general civic aims of public education.

The effort of public school authorities to allow programs of sectarian religious instruction to be available to pupils who wish to participate is, of course, incompatible with any doctrine of an absolute separation of church and state. But then any doctrine of an absolute separation of church and state—as we have had occasion to remark more than once—is itself an establishment of the secularist creed and is to make civil authority hostile to religious activity. In the case of public education we have concrete conditions related to a specific civic interest which urge the wisdom of an accommodation of civil authority to the incidental benefit of religious activity. The public authority operates and controls the educational framework as the surrogate of the parents, and parents of religious belief seek to specify religious instruction for their own children. Are we to say that the public authority cannot accommodate itself as far as feasible to this reasonable parental specification? If so, then it is difficult to see by what logic the federal government could provide military chaplains and permit religious services for servicemen.

To deny that public schools may allow parents to choose an "elective" of religious instruction is in fact to establish secularism as our national religion. The public authority would then act to prevent parents from selecting a feasible amount of religious instruction as part of the formal education of their children. In other words, the public schools would be required to exclude religious instruction from the education even of those who desire it. Now, the end product of such a policy would not be the neutrality of the government in public education either between religious groups or between religion and nonreligion;

the end product would, rather, be that the government would place the heavy weight of its authority in public education solely on the side of the secularist creed.

The parents who do not wish their children to participate in any program of sectarian religious instruction often complain that their children are coerced into conformity by the psychological and social pressures of the religious majority. They might have a legitimate complaint if the public school authorities allowed them no choice with respect to the inclusion or exclusion of sectarian religious instruction in the educational curriculum of their children. But the public school authorities do permit nontheist parents to choose secular instruction at the time when theist parents choose religious instruction for their children. The nontheist parent does in fact exercise choice in favor of secular instruction for his own child. What the nontheist really objects to is the opportunity for theist parents to choose a period of religious instruction for their children.

Such psychological and social pressures as come to bear on the children of nonbelievers derive from the religious nature of the American people rather than from any coercion on the part of the public authority. The public authority merely cooperates with the wishes of believers with reference to the education of *their* children. Whether there exists any coercion on the part of the public authority can be tested quite simply by considering upon whom the burden of psychological and social pressures would fall if the majority of parents opted against sectarian religious instruction. Obviously the psychological and social pressures would then operate against the children of believers. Yet no secularist would allow a believer to complain that the public authority under these circumstances was illegally coercing his children against religious instruction. The separation of the children of believers from the children of nonbelievers by released or dismissed time programs does not stamp the nonbelieving minority with any stigma unless the minority chooses to put that construction upon it.

Two typical programs of sectarian religious instruction for public school pupils were brought to the United States Supreme Court for constitutional adjudication. In the McCollum case of 1948 the Court was asked to review an Illinois program for religious instruction which was popularly known as "released time."[4] The Champaign (Illinois) Board of Education permitted a voluntary association of interested Protestants, Catholics, and Jews called the Champaign Council on Religious Education to offer classes in sectarian religious instruction to public school pupils in grades 4 to 9 inclusive. The classes were composed of pupils whose parents signed printed cards signifying their desire to have their children attend, and were held weekly in public school classrooms for from thirty to forty-five minutes. The school authorities did not pay the religious instructors, but the instructors were subject to the approval and supervision of the superintendent of schools. Students who did not wish to participate in the religious instruction were required to pursue secular studies at the time appointed for religious instruction classes. Likewise, students released at their parents' request were required to be present at the religious instruction classes.

Justice Black decided the McCollum case on the premise of an "absolute" separation of church and state. From that premise it was not hard to reach the conclusion that the Champaign system violated the constitutional prohibition of a religious establishment:

The . . . facts . . . show the use of tax-supported property for religious instruction and the close cooperation between the school authorities and the religious council in promoting religious education. The operation of the State's compulsory education system thus assists and is integrated with the program of religious instruction carried on by separate religious sects. Pupils compelled by law to go to school for secular education are released in part from their duty upon the condition that they attend the religious classes. This is beyond question a utilization of the tax-established and tax-supported public school system to aid religious groups to spread their faith.[5]

This narrow and doctrinaire analysis saw the released-time program only as an aid to religion and not as cooperation with parents whose children were being educated. Justice Reed, in the single dissent in the case, complained that constitutionally prohibited aid to religion should not include "those incidental advantages that religious bodies, with other groups similarly situated, obtain as a by-product of organized society."[6] After reviewing the many historical instances of cooperation between church and state, Justice Reed objected pointedly to the majority's premise:

The prohibition of enactments respecting an establishment of religion do [sic] not bar every friendly gesture between church and state. It is not an absolute prohibition against every conceivable situation where the two may work together, any more than the other provisions of the First Amendment—free speech, free press—are absolutes.[7]

One point in the Champaign released-time program deserves close scrutiny: the subjection of the religious instructors to the approval and supervision of the public school authorities. Here the Champaign Board of Education might have set up a potentially dangerous and inadmissible link between the public authority and the religious instruction made available. Of course, the Board of Education might have intended the approval and supervision on the part of the school authorities as a procedural regulation rather than as a substantive control on the religious instruction. The Board of Education might have designed the approval and supervision simply to ascertain that the religious instructors would cooperate in the observance of school regulations and in the maintenance of an orderly classroom. But the Champaign Board of Education should have been quite careful to spell that out and make quite clear what constituted approval and supervision by the public school authorities. Otherwise, arbitrary action by public authorities could easily transform a procedural regulation into a a substantial control of the religious instruction. This would surely violate the constitutional guarantee of separation of church and state. At any rate Justice Black and the majority never focused on this point, and it did not figure prominently in the decision.

As a result of the McCollum decision a flurry of suits in different parts of the country attacked programs of sectarian religious instruction for public school pupils. In 1952 the United States Supreme Court reviewed a second type of program in force in New York City which was popularly known as "dismissed time."[8] The New York City public schools permitted pupils to leave the school buildings and grounds during school hours to attend classes or devotions at religious centers. The pupils were re-leased on written request of their parents, and those not released stayed in the public school classrooms. The religious instructors made weekly reports of the children who were released from the public school but who did not attend the instruction.

Justice Douglas, speaking for the majority, found the New York City program constitutional. The vital facts, apparently, which distinguished this program from that of Champaign, Illinois, were that the New York City program did not involve religious instruction in public school classrooms or the expenditure of public funds for the dismissed-time application blanks. The religious instruction took place at religious centers, and all costs, including the cost of application blanks, were paid by the religious organization. The issue, as the Court saw it, was whether the state might "encourage religious instruction or cooperate with religious authorities by adjusting the schedule of public events to sectarian needs."[9] And the Court resolved the issue decisively:

To hold that it may not would be to find in the Constitution a require-ment that the government show a callous indifference to religious groups. That would be preferring those who believe in no religion over those who do believe.[10]

The Court also rejected as "obtuse reasoning" any claim that the nonbeliever was coerced into religious instruction by the New York City program.[11]

Quite obviously, Justice Douglas and the Zorach majority had rejected the rigid standard of an "absolute" separation of church and state. This rejection dissenting Justice Black discerned and criticized.[12] Moreover, Black pointed out that the majority was feebly attempting to distinguish the McCollum result, which they professed to accept, from the New York City program, which they found unexceptionable in Zorach. Justice Black succinctly observed: "I see no significant difference between the invalid Illinois system and that of New York here sustained."[13] Justices Frankfurter and Jackson, for their part, were more con-cerned with the coercive effects of the New York City program on students who did not attend the religious instruction classes.

The public school classroom under the New York City program, concluded Justice Jackson, "serves as a temporary jail for a pupil who will not go to Church."[14]

The minority was on particularly strong grounds when they attacked the Zorach majority for professing to accept the Mc-Collum decision while upholding the quite similar New York City pattern of sectarian religious instruction for public school pupils. Does the fact that the Illinois program of religious in-struction took place in public school classrooms distinguish it significantly from its New York City cousin? Presumably civil authorities may permit religious organizations along with all civic groups to make an orderly use of public parks and other public property without any suggestion except from the most extreme secularist that this would constitute an establishment of religion. Nor does the expenditure of public funds in the Illinois program for application blanks appear as anything other than an appro-priation which secures an orderly procedure in the administra-tion of the program. The essential issue is whether the public authorities may provide a place for voluntary sectarian religious instruction within the framework of public education. If they may do so, then it is difficult to see why the location of the classes or the cost of application blanks should affect the result.

Neither the majority nor, a fortiori, the minority developed the relationship of civil authority to parental choice in public education. Had they done so, there might have been less abstract discussion of the government program as an "aid to religion" and more emphasis on the government action as an implementation of parents' rights and responsibilities in education. The govern-ment as public educator is the surrogate of the parents, and the government action which serves as an aid to religion in released-time and dismissed-time programs is incidental to the fulfillment of parents' wishes in the education of their children.

NONSECTARIAN RELIGIOUS INSTRUCTION AND THE PUBLIC SCHOOLS

The role of religion in public education raises a second basic question: To what extent, if any, may or should the public authorities in control of the operation of a common school sponsor nonsectarian religious instruction? This question must be divided into three components: (1) Is there any genuinely nonsectarian religious instruction? (2) If there is, may or should the state sponsor it? and (3) If the state sponsors nonsectarian religious instruction, may or should the state compel participation or attendance? To comment summarily on the last point first, it is difficult to see how either compulsory participation or compulsory attendance at nonsectarian religious instruction would be consistent with the freedom of conscience implied in the democratic political structure and guaranteed by the First and Fourteenth Amendments. But the other two components of the nonsectarian religious instruction question are far more controversial.

For any asserted claim that religious instruction is nonsectarian, the inevitable problem of defining "nonsectarian" arises. "Nonsectarian" could serve to indicate religious teachings derived not from any special divine intervention or revelation but solely from the operation of human intelligence on the data of experience. This would be a difficult definition to apply empirically because "natural religion" has been colored irrevocably by the historical influence of the Judeo-Christian revelational religions on Western thought and civilization. More empirical and more commonly employed is the definition of "nonsectarian" by reference to teachings acceptable to the traditional American religions: Protestant, Catholic, and Jewish. But this definition leaves no room for other revelational religions, like the Moslem, or for possible theistic beliefs, like the Unitarian, which deny any special divine intervention or revelation. If nonsectarian religious instruction indicates teachings acceptable to Protestants, Catholics, and Jews, then we face the rather strange paradox that teachings by other sects could be inconsistent with the so-called "nonsectarian" teachings.

As if this effort at limiting "nonsectarian" were not difficult enough, some speak of the common teachings of *Christian* sects as "nonsectarian" religious instruction proper for public school sponsorship. The confusion palpably at work here is between the ideal of a Christian society and the concept of a Christian state. This confusion is embodied in the ambiguous phrase

"Christian nation," which many invoke as justification for an avowedly Christian—but "nonsectarian"!—religious instruction in the public schools. Christians should indeed work and pray fervently for the dynamic influence of Christian ideals in American life, but this hope is not synonymous with preference by the public authority for Christian teachings and practices. The political structure of American democracy based on the equality of all citizens makes such preference of one religion over another impossible. Nor can "nonsectarian" signify a Christianity free of dogma. "Nonsectarian" religious teaching of this type would really be nothing less than a Harnackian brand of liberal Protestantism, which Jews, Catholics, and orthodox Protestants alike would find offensive.

The problem of nonsectarian religious instruction in the public schools classically has focused on the practice of reading a few verses of the Bible at the beginning of each school day. Eleven states and the District of Columbia have statutes which require daily Bible reading without comment in the public schools.[15] Twenty-six states, either by constitutional provision (Mississippi) or by statute or by judicial decision or as an uncontested matter of practice, permit daily Bible reading in the public schools.[16] All together, then, thirty-seven states require or permit Bible reading in the public schools. Thirteen of these states do so despite statutory prohibition of sectarian instruction in the public schools.[17] On the other hand, eleven states with similar prohibitions on sectarian instruction have held Bible reading sectarian and therefore illegal.[18] It is clear that the problem of defining "nonsectarian" is one of the central points at issue concerning Bible reading in the public schools.

All the latent difficulties of interpreting the term "nonsectarian" are brought forcefully to light when the peculiar nature of Bible reading is considered. Mandatory and permissive statutes quite frequently refer to the Bible as the "Holy Bible," and the practice of many states is to include both the Old and the New Testament within the reading program. However, even if the Old Testament alone were read, the nature of the Bible is such that it would appear sectarian to one who, like the Unitarian, is neither a Jew nor a Christian. To the Jew, the Bible is the record of God's special covenant with Israel, and to the Christian, the Bible is salvation history fulfilled in Jesus Christ. To the Catholic, the Bible is the instrument of the Church's teaching, and to the Protestant, the Bible is the vehicle of God's communication to the individual. The Bible is for Protestants, Catholics, and Jews an *inspired* book, and thus even the Old Testament will be unacceptable to other theists who either do not believe in the special divine intervention recorded in the Old Testament or who do not believe in any special divine revelation through an inspired writing. It is difficult to see how Bible reading as religious instruction can be called truly nonsectarian.

Less crucial today is the selection of a text acceptable to Christians and Jews. At one time the contest between the Catholic Douai and the Protestant King James versions was particularly acute. But today, as a result of the newer editions which modern scriptural scholarship has made available, this difficulty does not appear as critical as of old. Protestant, ·Catholic, and Jewish scholars—and even nonbelievers in the field, for that matter—could reach a large measure of agreement on a common text. Or at any rate their disagreements would be based principally on scientific rather than on religious grounds.

But let us suppose—difficult as the supposition is—that a nonsectarian religious instruction can be achieved on which all sects agree and to which only nontheistic secular humanists are opposed. Let us assume that a common Bible reader can be composed which is acceptable to all men of religious conviction. If such a program of nonsectarian religious instruction is designed for the public schools, it will pose quite unequivocally the question whether the state may or should sponsor such instruction, whether the public authority may or should prefer religious belief over nonbelief.

Parenthetically we may note how ineffective and incomplete such an instruction would be for orthodox Christians and Jews. For the Christian and Jewish religions are historical religions in which prophetic personalities and miraculous events are central to belief, worship, and salvation. It is understandable that Protestants influenced by the liberal theology of the last century would be more easily attracted to a religion without dogma, a religion of the heart. But it is ironic that Catholics, who have so insisted on the ineffectiveness and incompleteness of a nonsectarian religious approach that they have instituted and supported an entire school system of their own, should play a leading role in the present fight for nonsectarian religious programs in the public schools. At any rate, presumably on the grounds that something is better than nothing, Protestants and Catholics have generally supported the efforts on behalf of these programs.

Advocates of nonsectarian religious programs contend that the public schools may transmit the spiritual heritage of our forefathers as the basis of American laws and morality. The nonbeliever or nontheist is free not to attend the instruction or, if in attendance, not to participate. But though no coercion should be imposed on the nonbeliever, the majority has the right to include religious training as part of the curriculum of public education because such training is necessary to invigorate the moral fiber of the citizen.

Unfortunately for the theist, the issue of nonsectarian religious instruction is more complex than its advocates often indicate. No religious person would be inclined to disagree with the view that religious training and the transmission of our spiritual heritage make for sound citizens. But public sponsorship of nonsectarian religious instruction in the public schools presents a primarily political issue. The public authorities do not merely permit children whose parents wish it to participate in such instruction but rather integrate the program into the common curriculum of the public school from which an individual pupil must be "excused." The nonbeliever either must come in late or, if he attends, must stand out as a nonparticipant in the common program. The nonbeliever is not legally compelled to attend or participate, but acceptation of the religious instruction constitutes a test of good, or at least better, student participation in public education.

Now, whatever the abstract merits of religious instruction under public sponsorship in other forms of government, such a program is incompatible with a democracy that genuinely accepts the equality of citizens. "Articles of peace" which incorporate the legal equality of plural value systems are necessary for cohesive political aspiration and activity. The public authorities may permit religious instruction for those who wish it, but they may not sponsor religious instruction as a program designed for all students. Even the freedom of the nontheist or nonbeliever from compulsion to attend will not cure the essential defect of legal preferment of religious belief over nonbelief. This is the establishment of a religious test of citizenship which leaves the nontheist or nonbeliever unable to participate fully in the common public school curriculum.

In the recent Torcaso case the United States Supreme Court gave a clear indication of its attitude toward legal preference for religious belief over nonbelief.[19] The Governor of Maryland appointed plaintiff Torcaso to the office of notary public, but Torcaso refused to declare his belief in the existence of God as Maryland required of all officeholders. The plaintiff then brought suit to obtain his commission and contended that the Maryland requirement violated the religious guarantees of the federal Constitution. The Supreme Court unanimously upheld the plaintiff's right to the commission without declaring his belief in the existence of God. Justice Black expanded on the Everson decision to reach the Court's holding:

We repeat and again reaffirm that neither a state nor the Federal Government can constitutionally force a person "to profess a belief or disbelief in any religion." Neither can constitutionally pass laws nor impose requirements which aid all religious as against non-believers, and neither can aid those religions based on a belief in the existence of God as against those religions founded on different beliefs.[20]

The Torcaso decision, of course, says nothing about publicly sponsored religious instruction in the public schools. In fact, the Maryland requirement on officeholders coerced and penalized Torcaso far beyond any coercive or punitive effect which common religious instruction in the public schools would have on the nonbeliever. Yet the general principle which Justice Black outlined in the Torcaso decision would seem to apply with equal logic to religious instruction in the public school under public sponsorship.

The nature of the legal neutrality of the public authority in relation to religious activity is bitterly contested. The religionist insists that the public authority should not prefer nonbelief over religious belief, while the secularist no less insists that the public authority should not prefer religious belief over nonbelief. The plain truth is that the neutrality of the public authority in relation to religious activity includes both ordinances. Thus the religionist wrongly demands preferment of religious instruction under public sponsorship, and the secularist opposing released time for those who wish it wrongly seeks to prefer religious unbelief over religious belief. And what is said here of religious instruction and public education applies, *mutatis mutandis,* to public support of parents' choice of a religiously oriented private education, to public support of military chaplains for servicemen uprooted from their civilian communities, and to tax exemption of church property as part of a scheme of exempting the property of all philanthropic organizations.

Nonsectarian religious instruction also does not really honor the primacy of parental rights in education. The majority of parents, of course, will be satisfied with the instruction as compatible with their religious convictions, but the nonbelieving parent cannot accept the public school curriculum for his child if it includes religious instruction. True, the children of nonbelievers are not forced to attend or to participate, but the curriculum includes as an integral feature the religious instruction which the parent does not accept. Admittedly the principle of minority parental rights in public education could raise problems even in the teaching of secular subjects. Public school instruction in health or biology, for instance, might run counter to the belief of Christian Scientists. But in such cases at least the public school could justifiably argue that the instruction was simply part of a secular science and was presented only as the opinion of reputable scientists. No such defense is possible when the public authority sponsors purely religious instruction.

Catholics have been strangely slow to translate to the field of public education the principle of parental primacy which they stress in behalf of parochial education. Catholic commentators too often are oblivious of the strictly political implications of nonsectarian religious instruction in the public schools for a pluralistic society which embraces secularists as well as theists. Few voices have risen above the commonplace. Without any attempt at thorough analysis, Catholics are accustomed to conclude that the public school must prefer religious belief to nonbelief in order to escape preferring nonbelief over religious belief. It is to be hoped that they will come to see that the public authority in a democracy can and should avoid any legal preference.

The inconsistency of many Catholics is matched, to be sure, by the inconsistency of many non-Catholic religionists who favor religious instruction in the public schools but who find public support of parochial schools a violation of the separation of church and state. It is matched by the inconsistency of the non-Catholic secularist who trumpets the rights of the minority nonbeliever in the public school but who remains quite callous to the rights of minority believers in parochial schools. Is it too much to hope that all four of America's "conspiracies"—Protestant, Catholic, Jewish, and secular humanist—will become more solicitous of the rights of their brethren?

Released or dismissed time is both more effective and more equitable to the rights of parents. It is more effective because the instructor has the freedom and the time to give full expression to his religious convictions; it is more equitable because each child participates in the religious "elective" only through the express choice of his parents. The short temporal duration of the nonsectarian religious instruction makes it unamenable to the released-time and, a fortiori, the dismissed-time techniques.

The problem of nonsectarian religious instruction in the public schools is related to but distinct from the communication of moral values. Certain restrictions on freedom, certain principles of action are implicit in the concept of an ordered, democratic society. Americans of whatever religious or ethical persuasion agree at least on maintaining societal intercourse and democratic process. The implications of such a commitment will be felt in the sphere of civic action. Good citizenship is distinguishable from bad citizenship at least by adherence to constitutional processes, by obedience to the laws of nation and state, by social concern, and by respect for individual rights and liberties. Insofar as any virtue can be taught, good citizenship can be taught. Men of religious conviction know well that a living religious faith has been throughout our history and is now the sure foundation of good citizenship. Yet, although the nature of a common school sponsored by the public authority in a pluralistic society may preclude common instruction in that foundation, this does not make pragmatic instruction in civic virtues meaningless or valueless. What believers—Protestants, Catholics, and Jews—accept on varying theological bases the nonbeliever accepts at least on a pragmatic basis. If the public schools communicate this consensus on civic virtue, they will make a contribution, albeit radically incomplete from the viewpoint of the believer.

We have suggested that the pluralistic nature of the American polity precludes public sponsorship of nonsectarian religious instruction in public education. But this is not to say that the public schools may not teach *about* religion. Instruction about religion is not religious instruction. No adequate study of history or literature, for instance, can really avoid dealing with the religious beliefs of an age or of an author. Religious beliefs are part and parcel of any civilization or literature. Those who would study history or literature without a consideration of religious or ethical perspective would radically emasculate the raw data of those disciplines.

Thus the public schools can indirectly transmit the spiritual heritage about which the religionist is concerned through an adequate exposition of the historical and literary record of Western, including American, civilization. Indeed, even so religious a work as the Bible can be studied both from the viewpoint of its intrinsic matter and form as well as from the viewpoint of its profound ideological and stylistic impact on life in the West and in America. Bible study confined to such purposes would cause no theoretical objection involving the separation of church and state, for the study would be secular and not religious in character. Alabama and Texas are unique among the states in offering high school credit for the study of the Bible as history and literature.[21]

BIBLE READING AND THE COURTS

Since public education in the United States is the traditional concern of local governments, most of the judicial actions on Bible reading have taken place in state courts. Of the twenty state high courts which have passed on the issue, thirteen have expressly upheld and seven have overturned the practice.[22] The courts which approved Bible reading in the public schools stressed the nonsectarian and noncoercive character of the practice while the courts disapproving held the practice sectarian even if noncoercive.

Of particular significance are two cases which have reached the United States Supreme Court, although that forum has yet to pass on the substantive issue.[23] In the first case, two taxpayers, Donald Doremus and Anna Klein, sought a declaratory judgment in the Superior Court against the practice of reading the Bible and reciting the Lord's Prayer in New Jersey's public schools. A New Jersey statute provided:

At least five verses taken from that portion of the Holy Bible known as the Old Testament shall be read or caused to be read, without comment, in each public school classroom, in the presence of the pupils therein assembled, by the teacher in charge, at the opening of school upon every school day. . . .[24]

And the succeeding section permitted "the reciting of the Lord's Prayer."[25] The Hawthorne Board of Education issued a directive that any student might be excused during the reading of the Bible upon request, but in fact no student, not even plaintiff Klein's seventeen-year-old daughter, so requested. The plaintiffs complained that the program of reading the Bible and reciting the Lord's Prayer violated the federal prohibition against an establishment of religion.

Justice Clarence Case, speaking for the unanimous New Jersey Supreme Court, rejected the plaintiffs' contentions.[26] Justice Case first noted that the cost of the Bible-reading program was negligible to the taxpayer-plaintiffs and that plaintiff Klein did not object to the program as offensive to her daughter. Nonetheless, Justice Case proceeded to consider the plaintiffs' claims on their substantive merits. The court reported: "We consider that the Old Testament, because of its antiquity, its content, and its wide acceptance, is not a sectarian book when read without comment."[27] And: *"We find nothing in the Lord's Prayer that is controversial, ritualistic or dogmatic"* [italics *sic*].[28] If the Bible or the Lord's Prayer was unacceptable to religions other than the Protestant, Catholic, and Jewish, the court observed, the impact of their beliefs on our national life and character was insignificant by comparison. The court then concluded that, since the New Jersey program was nonsectarian, it was permissible. Theism is "the warp and woof of the social and governmental fabric," and a public-sponsored theistic program is not, in consequence, prohibited by the religious guarantees of the federal Constitution.[29] The government may acknowledge God as God. Otherwise how would the persistent practice of legislative chaplaincies be explained?

The New Jersey Supreme Court decision hinged on two findings: (1) The New Jersey program was nonsectarian in character, and (2) the public authorities may sponsor theistic religious instruction and observance in the public schools. Enough has already been said about the difficulties inherent in the characterization of Bible reading as nonsectarian. But Christians should be quite surprised to hear that the Lord's Prayer, which contains doctrinal assertions about God as Father, heaven, the forgiveness of sins, the danger of temptation, and the power of evil, is undogmatic! And Jews must wince to hear that the Lord's Prayer, so intimately linked to the founder of Christianity, is "nonsectarian." The court's second finding was also open to criticism, and Justice Case's reference to legislative chaplaincies in particular was inapposite. Doremus and Klein complained that New Jersey sponsored religious instruction as an integral part of the common curriculum of public education. Legislative chaplains, on the other hand, are not sponsored by the legislators as religious instructors of the public. Rather, the chaplains give expression to the prayerful sentiments of the legislators in the same way as invocations at a presidential inauguration reflect the President's choice. Moreover, the legislature is the sole judge of its own procedure, and no one but a legislator may object to it, any more than a private citizen may bring judicial action against invocations at presidential inaugurations.

Defeated in the state courts, plaintiffs Doremus and Klein appealed to the United States Supreme Court. There Justice Jackson, speaking for a six-man majority, dismissed the appeal on jurisdictional grounds.[30] By the time the case reached the high Court, Mrs. Klein's daughter had been graduated from high school and the case was now moot with respect to her. As for the standing of Doremus and Klein as "citizens and taxpayers," Justice Jackson found that the plaintiffs had failed to demonstrate direct financial injury or the involvement of "measurable appropriations." Doremus, moreover, was a resident of Rutherford, not of Hawthorne, whose tax uses were attacked in court. Justice Douglas dissented with Justices Reed and Burton on the ground that taxpayers have a vital interest in the operation of public schools and that New Jersey had consented to hear the suit. Under the circumstances the Doremus decision cannot be regarded as the Supreme Court's final, or even first, word on the subject of Bible reading in the public schools.

Both more recent and more significant is the second case to reach the Supreme Court. Edward and Sidney Schempp, Unitarians, brought suit as parents and guardians of three children attending the public schools of Abington Township, Pennsylvania, to prohibit the program of reading the Bible and reciting the Lord's Prayer. They initiated the suit in the federal district court, and a three-judge panel heard the case. Pennsylvania required that "at least ten verses from the Holy Bible" be read without comment in the public schools at the beginning of the school day.[31] The Abington schools joined to the statutory Bible reading the practice of reciting the Lord's Prayer, both of which were usually followed by the pledge of allegiance. The plaintiffs complained that the Bible-reading program, whether alone or in conjunction with the Lord's Prayer, violated the federal prohibition against an establishment of religion.

Of the three Schempp children, only the eldest, Ellory, had clearly made known to the public school authorities his objections to the Bible-reading program. In November, 1956, Ellory read the Koran privately while the Bible was read publicly, and he refused to stand during the recitation of the Lord's Prayer. Subsequently, after discussing the matter with the school authorities, he waited out the period of morning exercises in the office of the school's guidance counselor for the remainder of his junior year. He returned the next year and again asked to be excused from the Bible-reading period. The assistant principal told Ellory to remain in the homeroom with the other students, and he obeyed the instruction for the remainder of the year. Since Ellory has been graduated from the Abington schools, the issue of Bible reading was now moot as to him.

On September 16, 1959, Chief Judge Biggs delivered the opinion of the court in favor of the plaintiffs.[32] With respect to the children other than Ellory the court judged that the parents had an immediate and direct interest in the Abington program. On the substantive merits of the plaintiffs' claims the court first noted that Pennsylvania did not indicate what version constituted the "Holy Bible" and that Protestant and Jewish authorities at the hearing respectively affirmed and denied the nonsectarian nature of the Bible. The court concluded that the Bible, whether nonsectarian or not, had "its essential character as a religious document."[33] The statutory requirement of Bible reading sponsored a daily reminder of man's relation to God and thus preferred religious belief over nonbelief:

If the study of the Bible as an artistic work, a treasure of moral truths, a historical text can be separated from the espousal of doctrinal matters and religiousness, we should find no objection. But the manner in which the Bible is employed as required by legislative fiat does not effect this division.[34]

Indeed, "inasmuch as the 'Holy Bible' is a Christian document, the practice aids and prefers that Christian religion" and, when joined with the Lord's Prayer, invested the morning exercises with a "devotional and religious aspect."[35] The court stated its conclusion on the religious establishment issue unequivocally:

. . . [Even if the Abington program is "non-sectarian,"] the religion which is established is either sectless or all-embracing, or . . . different religions are established equally. But none of these conditions, assuming them to exist, purges the use of the Bible as prescribed by the statutes of its constitutional infirmities.[36]

Judge Biggs also laid stress on the compulsory character of the religious program. The facts indicated that the school authorities had successfully induced Ellory Schempp to attend the morning exercises against his expressed wishes. Moreover, the statute required administrators, teachers, and students to cooperate in the Bible-reading program. The court concluded that "the arguments made by the defendants that there was no compulsion ignores reality in the face of social suasion."[37]

Lastly, the court called attention to the primary rights of parents in the education of their children. If the public authorities offered religious instruction to children inconsistent "with the faith of the parent and contrary to the wishes of the parent, interference with the familial right of the parent to inculcate in the child the religion the parent desires is clear beyond doubt."[38] But "the right of the parent to teach his own faith to his child, or to teach him no religion at all," the court observed, "is one of the foundations of our way of life and enjoys full constitutional protection."[39]

The Schempp decision held the Pennsylvania Bible-reading program unconstitutional both as an establishment of religion and as an infringement of the free exercise of religion. It is difficult to see how the court could have reached any other result on the substantive merits of the case. The court judged that the use of the Bible "as a religious document" determined the religious establishment issue. Even an essentially religious document, the court admitted, may be studied for its secular significance. But the Bible reading in the Abington schools was by design religious and not historical, literary, or moral instruction. The court well indicated that, when Bible reading is designed as religious instruction, the public authorities are the sponsors, whether the instruction be considered sectarian or not. It is this condition that constituted the Abington program an establishment of religion.

The court's decision also rested on the compulsory character of the Bible reading at Abington. In Ellory's case the facts may fairly be said to support the claims of coercion. But for Ellory the case was now completely moot. It is difficult to see by what right the court could use evidence cited as to Ellory to support the claim of coercion against the other children in whose interest the case was heard. Nor might the court buttress its argument by reference to the statutory mandate on school administrators and teachers to carry out the program. There was no evidence that any student presently in the Abington schools was coerced by such a mandate.

The most significant part of Judge Biggs' opinion, I believe, was his closing observation on the primary right of parents in the education of their children. This observation hews closely to the principle of the Pierce decision and offers the best hope of clarifying the application of the general prohibition against a religious establishment to the sphere of education. Analysis of parental rights in education suggests a more fruitful and realistic approach to the relation of religion and education than does the abstract dissection of the religious establishment clause on which the Everson, McCollum, and Zorach opinions so exclusively focused. Judge Biggs' introduction of this perspective marks a return to the Pierce principle and, if consistently applied, a salutary effort at realism.

Abington Township, vanquished in the federal district court, now appealed to the United States Supreme Court for review. The Commonwealth of Pennsylvania, meanwhile, sought to make its statute more palatable by expressly authorizing any pupil to be excused from the required Bible reading in the public schools upon the written request of his parent or guardian.[40] The intent of this amendment, which went into effect on December 17, 1959, was to remove any basis for the claim that the statute compelled pupils to participate in the Bible-reading program. The device proved successful enough to force a rehearing. On October 24, 1960, the Supreme Court vacated the district court judgment in a brief *per curiam* opinion and remanded the case for further proceedings in the light of the newly amended Pennsylvania statute.[41] While the Court's action may seem unduly cautious, the purpose was to make clear the primary basis of the lower-court ruling. The Supreme Court was unwilling to review the Schempps' complaint until the lower court indicated that religious establishment and not freedom of religious exercise was the determinative issue in its earlier ruling.

On February 1, 1962, the three-judge federal panel again decided, despite the amendment of the Pennsylvania statute, that the Bible-reading program in force at Abington constituted a violation of the federal prohibition against a religious establishment.[42] The Court agreed with the plaintiffs that nonparticipation in the Bible-reading program would penalize the Schempp children. Failure to participate in the program would label nonparticipants "odd balls," as the plaintiffs put it. The Court again insisted that the "reading of the verses, even without comment, possesses a devotional and religious character."[43] This was all the more apparent because the Bible reading was followed immediately by recitation of the Lord's Prayer. Some, even all, pupils "might be excused from attendance at the exercises," but this "does not mitigate the obligatory nature of the ceremony."[44] The amended statute "unequivocally requires the exercises to be held every school day . . . in the school buildings . . . by and under the authority of the local school authorities and during school sessions."[45] The Court likewise repeated its conclusion in the earlier ruling that the "Holy Bible" was "a Christian document" and the practice of Bible reading therefore "prefers the Christian religion."[46]

Judge Biggs noted that the Schempp case was "quite similar" to that of McCollum but declined to compare them further.[47] The failure to distinguish the two cases was unfortunate. The essence of the Schempp case, unlike that of the McCollum, was the public sponsorship of a program of religious instruction designed for all students and from which nonbelievers had to petition to be excused. Public sponsorship of Bible reading as religious instruction was sufficient to constitute the Abington program an establishment of religion because the public authority sought thereby to prefer religious belief over nonbelief. As a result of the Court's failure to distinguish the two cases, needless reference to the location of religious instruction within the public school was introduced and the Court allowed unreflective religionists the opportunity to apply justifiable criticism of the McCollum decision to the Schempp case. At any rate, though, the Court did reach the right over-all result here and basically for the right reason.

OTHER RELIGIOUS PRACTICES
IN THE PUBLIC SCHOOLS

There are many other assertedly religious practices in the public schools which are the subject of controversy. Almost all of them, in fact, have appeared in litigation and even collectively in a current Florida suit.[48] But the principles already delineated in

the consideration of nonsectarian religious instruction in the public schools will also prove decisive, for the most part, in resolving
the constitutional questions which these practices raise. We shall
abbreviate to a large extent, therefore, our notation and discussion of these practices.

Next to Bible reading, the recitation of nonsectarian prayers is
the most controversial of the religious activities in the public
schools. This practice figured in the Doremus and Schempp cases
and was the sole point of contest in the Engel case involving the
New York State Regents' prayer.[49] There is one important aspect
of prayer recitation in the public schools which distinguishes it
from the kindred practice of Bible reading: recital of a prayer
is a religious exercise and not a religious instruction. Whether or
not this fact is vital will be evaluated subsequently; it will be
necessary first to turn to the genesis of the case of the Regents'
prayer.

On November 30, 1951, the New York State Board of Regents
recommended that the following prayer be recited at the beginning of each school day after the pledge of allegiance to the flag:
"Almighty God, we acknowledge our dependence upon Thee,
and we beg Thy blessings upon us, our parents, our teachers, and
our country." On July 8, 1958, the North Hempstead (Long Island) Board of Education adopted the Regents' prayer. Engel
and four other taxpayers and parents sought the prohibition of
the recitation of the prayer as an establishment of religion contrary to the federal Constitution. New York Supreme Court Justice Bernard Meyer heard the suit and on August 24, 1959, ruled
against the plaintiffs' petition.[50]

Justice Meyer's opinion, a serious and studious effort running
some 35,000 words and 187 footnotes, rested its argument on the
weight of tradition. The Justice pointed out that the Regents'
prayer was not a religious instruction but a religious exercise,
nonsectarian and noncompulsory in character. Such an exercise,
he felt, was a traditional and therefore acceptable accommodation to the spiritual needs of the people. The custom of public
prayer was deeply rooted in historical American practice, and, in
fact, "prayers in our legislative halls" were cited with approval
in the Zorach decision. But the public authorities may in no way
compel any student to attend or to recite the prayer. "The par-

ents of each child" should be advised "of the adoption of the resolution [to recite the prayer in the school district] . . . , of the wording of the prayer and of the procedure to be followed when it is said and requested to indicate whether the child shall or shall not participate in the exercise."[51]

On July 7, 1961, the New York Court of Appeals upheld Justice Meyer's decision by a margin of five to two.[52] Chief Judge Charles Desmond concluded that the nonsectarian and noncompulsory prayer was "not 'religious education' nor is it the practice of or the establishment of religion in any responsible meaning of those phrases."[53] But Associate Judge Marvin Dye, dissenting, characterized the Regents' prayer as "a form of state-sponsored religious education."[54] The plaintiffs then carried their case to the United States Supreme Court.[55]

On June 25, 1962, by a margin of six to one, the Supreme Court held the recitation of the Regents' prayer in the New York public schools to violate the Constitution.[56] Justice Black, speaking for himself, the Chief Justice, Justice Clark, Justice Harlan, and Justice Brennan, argued that "the state laws requiring or permitting use of the Regents' prayer must be struck down as a violation of the Establishment Clause because that prayer was composed by governmental officials as part of a governmental program to further religious beliefs."[57] Neither the states nor the federal government, he concluded, has the power to prescribe by law "an official prayer in carrying on any program of governmentally sponsored religious activity."[58] In the view of the majority there was no doubt that the New York program did officially establish the religious beliefs expressed in the Regents' prayer. "Neither the fact that the prayer may be denominationally neutral, nor the fact that its observance on the part of the students is voluntary can serve to free it from the limitations of the Establishment Clause."[59] Moreover, laws officially prescribing a particular form of religious worship involve indirect coercion on individuals not participating:

When the power, prestige and financial support of government is placed behind a particular religious belief, the indirect coercive pressure upon religious minorities to conform to the prevailing officially approved religion is plain.[60]

Justice Black rejected any characterization of the decision as "antireligious":

> It is neither sacrilegious nor antireligious to say that each separate government in this country should stay out of the business of writing or sanctioning official prayers and leave that purely religious function to the people themselves and to those the people choose to look to for religious guidance.[61]

A significant footnote at this point dissociated the "unquestioned religious exercise" of the New York program from those "patriotic or ceremonial occasions" in which "school children and others are officially encouraged" to recite "historical documents such as the Declaration of Independence which contain references to the Deity" or to sing "officially espoused anthems which include the composer's professions of faith in a Supreme Being," or in which there are "manifestations in our public life of belief in God."[62]

The sixth member of the majority, Justice Douglas, concurred in a separate opinion. For him the issue was "whether the Government can constitutionally finance a religious exercise."[63] Justice Douglas saw more at stake than the New York Regents' prayer: "What New York does on the opening of its public schools is what we do when we open court" and "what each House of Congress does at the opening of each day's business."[64] In each instance "the person praying is a public official on the public payroll, performing a religious exercise in a governmental institution."[65] Justice Douglas found "in retrospect" that even the Everson decision, which he had supported at the time, was "out of line with the First Amendment."[66]

The sole dissent was that of Justice Stewart. In his view of the facts a local school board had simply provided an opportunity for "those pupils who wish to do so" to "join in a brief prayer at the beginning of each school day."[67] There was therefore no establishment of an "official religion" involved in the New York Regents' prayer. "On the contrary," he observed, "to deny the wish of these children to join in reciting this prayer is to deny them the opportunity of sharing in the spiritual heritage of our Nation."[68]

Understandably this decision aroused a storm of controversy.

In fact, several constitutional amendments to overrule the decision were introduced in Congress.[69] Yet it is difficult to see how the Court could have reached any other decision in the case. Sponsors claimed that the Regents' prayer was nonsectarian, but the prayer implicitly professed belief at least in the existence of God, His providence over the affairs of men, and the meaningfulness of prayer to Him. Just how nonsectarian that complexus of religious affirmations is may be questioned. Indeed, Justice Meyer conceded that the prayer might be offensive to some sects but affirmed nonetheless that the prayer was nonsectarian![70]

However nonsectarian the Regents' prayer, it was beyond doubt a religious exercise which the public authorities were sponsoring as an integral part of the common public school curriculum and from which the nonbeliever had to petition to be "excused." Justice Meyer and others correctly pointed out that the Regents' prayer was not religious instruction. It was, however, a religious exercise, and for the public authorities to sponsor even a nonsectarian religious exercise as a program designed for all students is to set up a religious qualification on full participation in the public school curriculum. The nonbeliever must either come in late or noticeably remain silent while the other students pray. In short, the Regents' prayer was an "official prayer" for the public schools of New York.

Justice Douglas' concurring opinion, however, casts a real shadow over the decision. In many respects it marks a regression to the simplistic interpretation of the religious establishment clause which Justice Douglas himself had done so much to correct in the Zorach case. Financial support of a religious activity or institution for whatsoever reason is unrealistically offered as the inflexible standard of unconstitutionality.

Nor does the opinion of Justice Douglas leave an opening for any distinction between prayer in the public school and prayer in Congress or the Court. Yet there is a vital difference: prayer in the public school is sponsored by the government for public hearing or recitation, while prayers in the legislature and the Court are designed by the legislators and justices for their own hearing. Surely Congress and the Court may hear a prayer if they wish to do so.

The issue of legislative chaplains is further complicated by the fact that they receive salaries from the government. This may well constitute a prohibited public preference of religious belief. But public support of legislative chaplains must be carefully distinguished from that of military chaplains. (Significantly, perhaps, the majority and concurring opinions did not even mention support of the latter.) The government pays for the support of military chaplains, not to prefer religion over nonreligion, but rather to provide for the spiritual needs of personnel whom, because of the demands of military service, the government itself has isolated from the religious opportunities of their civilian communities.

Whatever can be said of the constitutional infirmities of the Regents' prayer a fortiori can be predicated of familiar prayers like the Lord's Prayer. But one possibility that is free from constitutional objection may remain open to the public schools: to offer pupils the opportunity for a moment of silent prayer. If the public authorities were to provide an opportunity at the beginning of the school day for the student to lift up his mind and heart to God or not as he chose, it is difficult to see how they could be accused of sponsoring or endorsing a religious exercise. The public school authorities would offer prayer or nonprayer on a basis of complete equality. There would be neither sponsorship nor endorsement of any use to which an individual student wished to make of that time. Unlike the recitation of the Regents' prayer, a moment of silence does not single out the one who abstains from prayer as not fully participating in the public school curriculum. The student may pray on his own or not without the slightest inconvenience. This is the suggestion of Canon Stokes and the practice of the United Nations.

Another assertedly religious practice which has been the subject of litigation concerns the pledge of allegiance to the flag of the United States. Prior to June 14, 1954, the pledge of allegiance read as follows: "I pledge allegiance to the flag of the United States of America and to the Republic for which it stands, one nation indivisible, with liberty and justice for all." But in 1954 Congress amended the pledge of allegiance to insert the phrase "under God" after the word "nation."[71] The New York State Commissioner of Education recommended the new version for the public schools of the state, and a prominent freethinker well known to the courts of New York brought suit with others to compel the Commissioner to revoke or revise his recommendation.[72]

The plaintiffs had no other interest except as taxpayers and citizens. Moreover, they sought to compel the Commissioner to revoke or revise what was merely a recommendation; they did not object to any actualized practice. On the basis of these points alone, the court was entitled to deny the plaintiffs' petition. But Justice Bookstein went beyond procedural elements to comment on the substantive issue presented. He felt that the federal guarantee against a religious establishment did not mean that belief in God could not be preferred to nonbelief. The First Amendment, the Justice contended, does not prohibit a religious state but a state religion.

More relevant to the particular case of the pledge, however, were the observations which the Justice made in the latter part of his opinion. He called attention to what the amended pledge actually effected. The amendment simply permitted those who believe in God the opportunity to express that belief, while those who do not believe may omit the words "under God" without any pressure or embarrassment:

Petitioners' right to disbelieve is guaranteed by the First Amendment, and neither they nor their children can be compelled to recite the words "under God" in the pledge of allegiance. But the First Amendment affords them no preference over those who do believe in God and who, in pledging their allegiance, choose to express that belief.[73]

The words "under God" do not constitute a publicly sponsored religious instruction or exercise; they simply constitute an expression of belief. Congress and the Commissioner of Education did not sponsor the amended pledge as a religious exercise; rather, Congress and the Commissioner authorized that an opportunity be available to a believer in God to express that belief when he pledges allegiance to the flag of the United States. At any rate there is little need here to be too fastidious: *de minimis non curat praetor.*

Public school baccalaureate exercises in many areas are also said to violate the federal prohibition against a religious estab-

lishment and the guarantee of free religious exercise. In some
localities, apparently, nonsectarian hymns are sung and the grad-
uation itself is held in a church. It is unnecessary, in the light of
previous comments, to conclude here that such practices under
public sponsorship would constitute a prohibited religious exercise. One factor, however, which distinguishes these practices
from others is worthy of notice. Baccalaureate exercises are not
so much a part of the public educational curriculum as a social
event consequent upon the completion of some phase of the curriculum. The religious aspect of baccalaureate exercises, therefore, cannot fairly be characterized as a religious instruction or
even a religious exercise within a strictly curricular framework.
Nonetheless, the public authorities do sponsor the baccalaureate
exercises and must comply there, as elsewhere, with the basic
implications of the plural value structure of American democracy.

The last practice to consider is that of religious displays and
symbols in the public schools, especially those connected with
Christmas. Again, consistent with principles previously suggested, the public school authorities may not sponsor such displays or symbols as part of a religious program designed for all
students. This does not prevent display of materials which students have submitted voluntarily in connection with school work.
Classrooms may display drawings or compositions on religious
subjects which the students themselves choose to produce within
the discretionary limits of an artistic or literary assignment. But
the public school authorities may not sponsor displays or symbols
as part of a religious program designed for all students.

CONCLUSION

No writer on the topic of religion and education can hope to
satisfy all critics. About the best guarantee that he has of success
will be his failure to satisfy all of them completely. Consistency
is not a kindly master, and consistency in so controversial a matter as religion and education is unlikely to appeal to many. Each
of the four great "conspiracies" seeks freedom for its own creed,

and each shows a disinclination to be concerned with the freedom of the others. If Americans cannot resolve the relation of plural value structures to education, they cannot resolve the overall problem of pluralism and democracy.

Religionists often proclaim that the public school cannot be truly neutral between belief and nonbelief. Silence on matters of religion, they say, is to prefer nonbelief to belief. Therefore the public school should rightfully prefer religious belief over nonbelief. Secularists, on the other hand, often define "neutrality" in such a way that the public school must prefer nonbelief to religious belief. Even to permit religious instruction for those who wish it becomes a preference of religious belief. In effect, therefore, both religionists and secularists deny genuine neutrality to the public school. Yet the genuine neutrality of the public authority is an absolutely necessary political implication of pluralistic, democratic process, and no effort must be spared to clarify the application of this necessary implication to the operations of the public school.

An accurate understanding of the place of religion in the public schools depends on two principles: the absolute equality of all citizens in the matter of belief or nonbelief and the primacy of parental rights in the education of children. The former is fundamental to the democratic process, and the latter is a basic human right as well as an expression of pluralism. If the government sponsors a program of religious instruction or exercise for all, then it will violate the principle of equality and establish religious belief over nonbelief; if the government cannot permit parents to choose religious instruction on an elective basis, then the government will deny the primacy of parental rights in education and establish nonbelief over religious belief. It is our conclusion that the public school authorities should have the constitutional power to permit but not to sponsor religious instruction.

One last observation will close this discussion of religion and the public schools. The limits in the role which religion can play in public education derive from the nature of a common school in a pluralistic society. Of necessity neither religionist nor secularist can be completely satisfied with the deference which each must make to the other in public education. This is precisely why Catholics and other religious groups have made sacrifices to support parochial school systems in which religious instruction and religious orientation can be freely imparted. If considerations of the democratic process, by and large, favor the secularist's contentions against public sponsorship of religious instruction or exercises in common schools, no like factor argues against public support of private, religiously oriented but secularly competent education when parents choose such for their own children. The secularist cannot have his cake and eat it too; he cannot exclude government sponsored religious instruction in the common schools and simultaneously deny the propriety of government support of religiously oriented education for those who wish it. At least the secularist cannot do so without thoroughly and completely establishing a confessional state based on the secularist creed. This would not be neutrality toward religion; it would be a declaration of war.

NOTES

1. J.C. Murray, S.J., *We Hold These Truths* (New York: Sheed & Ward, 1960), p. 22.

2. The literature on this subject is voluminous. But for one typical and forceful presentation of the religionist position, see Joseph F. Costanzo, S.J., "Religion in Public School Education," *Thought*, Vol. XXXI (1956), pp. 1–29. For the Zorach profession that "we are a religious people," see *Zorach* v. *Clauson*, p. 313.

3. *Pierce* v. *Society of Sisters*, 268 U.S. 510, 535 (1925).

4. *Ill.* ex rel. *McCollum* v. *Board of Education*, 333 U.S. 203 (1948). The first released-time program in the United States was adopted in Gary, Indiana, in 1914.

5. *Ibid.*, pp. 209, 210.

6. *Ibid.*, p. 249.

7. *Ibid.*, pp. 255, 256.

8. *Zorach* v. *Clauson*.

9. *Ibid.*, p. 314.

10. *Ibid.*

11. *Ibid.*, p. 311.

12. *Ibid.*, pp. 315, 316.

13. *Ibid.*, p. 316.

14. *Ibid.*, p. 324.

15. Donald E. Boles, *The Bible, Religion and the Public Schools* (Ames: Iowa State University Press, 1961), pp. 48, 53.

16. *Ibid.*

17. *Ibid.*, p. 48.

18. *Ibid.*, p. 53.

19. *Torcaso* v. *Watkins*, 367 U.S. 488 (1961).

20. *Ibid.*, p. 495.

21. Boles, *op. cit.*, p. 57.

22. *Ibid.*, pp. 58 and 100.

23. *Doremus* v. *Board of Education*, 342 U.S. 429 (1952) and

School District of Abington v. *Schempp,* 364 U.S. 298 (1960).

24. N.J.R.S. 18: 14–77.

25. N.J.R.S. 18: 14–78.

26. *Doremus* v. *Board of Education,* 5 N.J. 435 (1950).

27. *Ibid.,* p. 448.

28. *Ibid.,* p. 451.

29. *Ibid.,* p. 449.

30. *Doremus* v. *Board of Education,* 342 U.S. 429 (1952).

31. 24 Pa. Stat. 15–1516.

32. *Schempp* v. *Abington School District,* 177 F. Supp. 398 (1959).

33. *Ibid.,* p. 404.

34. *Ibid.*

35. *Ibid.,* p. 405.

36. *Ibid.,* p. 406.

37. *Ibid.*

38. *Ibid.,* p. 407.

39. *Ibid.*

40. Act No. 700 of the laws of the General Assembly of the Commonwealth of Pennsylvania 1959 session.

41. *School District of Abington* v. *Schempp,* 364 U.S. 298 (1960).

42. *Schempp* v. *School District of Abington,* 201 F. Supp. 815 (1962).

43. *Ibid.,* p. 819.

44. *Ibid.*

45. *Ibid.*

46. *Ibid.*

47. *Ibid.*

48. *The New York Times,* July 19, 1960, p. 24.

49. *Engel* v. *Vitale,* 191 N.Y. Supp. 2d 453 (1959); 10 N.Y. 2d 174 (1961); 370 U.S. 421 (1962).

50. *Engel* v. *Vitale,* 191 N.Y. Supp. 2d 453 (1959).

51. *Ibid.,* p. 491.

52. *Engel* v. *Vitale,* 10 N.Y. 2d 174 (1961).

53. *Ibid.,* p. 180.

54. *Ibid.,* p. 189.

55. The Supreme Court granted review on December 4, 1961. *Engel* v. *Vitale,* 368 U.S. 924 (1961).

56. *Engel* v. *Vitale,* 370 U.S. 421 (1962). Justice Frankfurter, who was ill, and Justice White, who was appointed to the Court after the oral arguments, did not participate in the decision.

57. *Ibid.,* p. 425.

58. *Ibid.,* p. 430.

59. *Ibid.*

60. *Ibid.,* p. 431.

61. *Ibid.,* p. 435.

62. *Ibid.*

63. *Ibid.,* p. 437.

64. *Ibid.,* pp. 439–440.

65. *Ibid.,* p. 441.

66. *Ibid.,* p. 443.

67. *Ibid.,* p. 444.

68. *Ibid.,* p. 445.

69. See *The New York Times,* June 27, 1962, p. 1.

70. *Engel* v. *Vitale,* 191 N.Y. Supp. 2d 453, 495 (1959).

71. U.S. Code, Title 36, Chap. X, Sec. 172.

72. *Lewis* v. *Allen,* 159 N.Y. Supp. 2d 807 (1957).

73. *Ibid.,* p. 813.

7

Sunday Laws
and
Religious Freedom

SUNDAY LAWS BEFORE THE COURT

When citizens disagree on an issue involving both conscience and pocketbook, a quickening of community tensions is a double certainty. And when a majority writes into legislation a religious and economic point of view, a tangled skein of judicial controversy is equally predictable. Such is the case with current efforts to restrict retail sales on Sunday.

Forty-nine states make illegal on Sunday some form of conduct which would be lawful if performed on weekdays.[1] Fifteen states forbid only one or several activities, while thirty-four have enacted a comprehensive ban on Sunday labor and sales. Of the latter states, twenty-one make an exception from the ban against

Sunday labor for conscientious Sabbatarians, but only ten extend the exemption to Sunday sales.[2] In all, thirty-eight states maintain some form of restrictive legislation on Sunday labor or sales or both without exempting conscientious Sabbatarians.

Sunday laws affect both religious conscience and economic commerce. The issue divides America's religious communities into two rival camps similar to those which form over the place of religious instruction in public education. Orthodox Christians, for the most part, stand among the advocates of the laws, while Orthodox Jews and Seventh-Day Adventists are the principal religious opponents. But many secular humanists, on whom claimants to religious liberty can usually rely, here join hands with those who defend at least the constitutionality of Sunday laws. What probably makes the difference is the fact that Sunday laws have a secular purpose, and the issue, as many secular humanists are likely to see it, is the supremacy of the state in matters of secular competence. The issue of Sunday laws is not peculiarly "Catholic," of course, but Catholic opinion has involved itself prominently in the defense of the laws. A partial explanation for this involvement is the deep anxiety of the Catholic lest the least concession to the dissenter lead to the state establishment of the secularist creed. In the interest of the conscientious Sabbatarian whose dilemma under Sunday laws is quite real, in the interest of harmony among citizens of different religious beliefs, and in the interest of the sound interpretation of the political principles of the First Amendment's religious guarantees, Catholics and all Americans should re-examine the case for and against Sunday laws.

Though Sunday laws date from colonial times, expanding commerce at highway shopping centers in the decade of the fifties presented a new challenge to enforcement of the Sunday rest. Despite condemnation by Christian groups and economic loss to local merchants, the easy convenience of the shopping centers combined with the traditional Sunday leisure to send Sunday sales soaring. In many instances the new shopping centers were beyond the jurisdiction of local ordinances, and ancient statutes did not provide for an effective state-wide regulation of Sunday sales. Many states responded to the challenge by enacting new, more specific legislation and by enforcing old Sunday laws more energetically. In turn, opponents of Sunday laws looked to the courts for relief, and their efforts were climaxed when the United States Supreme Court on April 25, 1960, agreed to review on appeal the constitutionality of these laws.[3]

Actually the Supreme Court had been asked in 1951 to review New York's Sunday law. Two orthodox Jewish retailers were convicted of violating the Sunday law, and the New York Court of Appeals, though admitting that "the so-called Sunday laws may be said to have had a religious origin," upheld the law as a valid exercise of the state's power to provide for health and welfare.[4] The defendants appealed to the United States Supreme Court, where they claimed that the New York Sunday law constituted a religious establishment, violated religious freedom, and employed an arbitrary system of classifying prohibited occupations. Nonetheless, "for want of a substantial federal question," the Supreme Court refused to review the convictions.[5] Three subsequent appeals on similar grounds from the Sunday laws of other states were made to the Court and were refused for the same reason.[6]

Why, then, did the Supreme Court decide in 1960 to review the constitutionality of Sunday laws? The answer lies in the conflicting decisions the previous year by the federal courts of the First and Third Circuits. On May 18, 1959, in a split decision a three-judge federal court of the First Circuit declared the Massachusetts Sunday legislation unconstitutional, whereas on December 1, 1959, a three-judge federal court of the Third Circuit affirmed the constitutionality of similar Pennsylvania legislation.[7] In addition to the two divergent circuit court decisions from Massachusetts and Pennsylvania which occasioned the review, two other cases involving Sunday legislation were appealed to the Supreme Court at that time and were granted review, one from a federal district court in Pennsylvania and the other from the Court of Appeals of Maryland.[8] This conflict had significance far beyond Massachusetts, Pennsylvania, and Maryland because slightly better than three-fourths of the states (thirty-eight) maintain, as we have noted, some restriction on Sunday labor or sales without exempting Sabbatarians.

SUNDAY LAWS AND THE "ESTABLISHMENT OF RELIGION": THE MAJORITY VIEW

The most serious attack on the validity of Sunday laws is based on the religious guarantees of the First and Fourteenth Amendments, namely, that Sunday laws violate the prohibition of a religious establishment and the guarantee of free religious exercise. In the Massachusetts case, the operators of the Crown Kosher Supermarket of Springfield asked the federal district court to prohibit enforcement of the Sunday law because it offered special protection to Christian orthodoxy and thereby constituted a religious establishment prohibited by the First and Fourteenth Amendments. They further complained that by obeying the Sunday law they were economically penalized for their religious beliefs, and were thus deprived of the freedom of religious exercise guaranteed by the same Amendments.

Sunday laws of the colonial period reflected an exclusive concern for fostering Christian observance of the Lord's Day. The Massachusetts law, similar to the laws of many other states both in religious wording and in religious origin, prohibited employment or business on the Lord's Day except works of necessity or charity. First adopted in 1653 for the "observance of the Lord's Day," the law represented an effort by the Bay Colony's theocracy to uplift the religious observance of second-generation Puritans.[9]

Judge Calvert Magruder, speaking for two of the three judges of the First Circuit Court case, concluded that the Massachusetts law offered special protection to the dominant Christian sects which observed Sunday as the Lord's Day without furnishing such protection to those who observe Saturday as the Sabbath. Although the Supreme Judicial Court of Massachusetts had interpreted the Sunday law as a "day of rest" statute in 1877 and as recently as 1957, Judge Magruder rejected the "characterization" and emphasized the religious purpose of the law.[10] The religious character of the statute, Magruder also maintained, distinguished it from the New York law which the United States Supreme Court had refused to review.

Like Massachusetts, Pennsylvania had a Sunday law of long standing which prohibited worldly employment or business on the Lord's Day.[11] Unlike Massachusetts, Pennsylvania felt obliged to amend her Sunday law in 1959 to provide more effective penalties for the sale of enumerated items.[12] Two Guys From Harrison, a discount house operating a highway shopping center near Allentown, asked the federal district court to declare the Pennsylvania Sunday law, as amended in 1959, unconstitutional on the basis of the religious guarantees of the First and Fourteenth Amendments.

Judge William Hastie, speaking for the Third Circuit Court, refused to upset the Pennsylvania Sunday law on the controlling authority of the United States Supreme Court's refusal in 1951 to review the New York Sunday law. That case, Judge Hastie felt, presented the Supreme Court squarely with the opportunity to rule on the question. The "historical religious connection is so clear in both statutes [New York and Pennsylvania] as to be obvious and indisputable."[13] Since the Supreme Court had denied the presence of a substantial federal question in the case of the New York statute, Judge Hastie concluded that the Pennsylvania law was constitutional. Obviously puzzled by Judge Magruder's rejection of the New York precedent, Judge Hastie found the Massachusetts opinion "not elaborate enough to make the court's reasoning clear to us."[14]

On May 29, 1961, the Supreme Court of the United States ruled on the Sunday laws of Massachusetts, Pennsylvania, and Maryland.[15] Chief Justice Warren, speaking for the majority, rejected the contention that the Sunday laws in dispute were religious legislation. These laws, the Chief Justice conceded, "are undeniably religious in origin" and "still contain references to the Lord's Day."[16] Now, were fostering Christian observance of the Lord's Day the exclusive basis today for Sunday laws, they could not be sustained in face of the religious establishment injunction of the First Amendment. In *Zorach* v. *Clauson* the Supreme Court did indeed approve a measure of "accommodation" by the state to the spiritual needs of the American people, but the Court did not contemplate the preferential hallowing by legal sanction of the holidays of all or some religious groups.

The Chief Justice found, however, that the basis for the Sunday legislation before the Court was no longer exclusively or even primarily religious. Under review here by the Supreme Court were not simply the Sunday laws of the colonial era but Sunday laws which came with a modern gloss to the Court in 1960. Human laws are not empty formulae but are the living expressions of human creativity. Like all of human life, they are subject to change. Today the legislative basis for restriction of work and sales on Sunday, the Court held, was economic and recreational, namely, to preserve salutary conditions of employment and competition as well as to safeguard a common day of rest and recreation. The highest courts of the states whose Sunday laws were involved—the Supreme Judicial Court of Massachusetts, the Supreme Court of Pennsylvania, and the Court of Appeals of Maryland—have passed on the constitutionality of the laws and have authoritatively interpreted them on a secular basis.[17]

The Court did not go so far as to say that there was no objectionable language in the Sunday legislation or its judicial interpretation. What the Court did conclude was that the statutes' purpose "was no longer solely religious" and that, "for the most part, they have been divorced from the religious orientation of their predecessors."[18] In short, the Court found that the religious purpose of the Sunday laws in dispute was at the present time neither exclusive nor primary and that the secular purpose of the laws was sufficient to provide a legitimate legislative basis.

Since the Court had determined that the Sunday legislation under consideration was not primarily religious in intention, the Court did not have to consider a case in which the religious purpose, though not exclusive, was at least as important as the secular purpose. Suppose that the Sunday legislation of a state was based *equally* on religious and secular motives. Would such legislation constitute a "religious establishment"? The Court did not say, but there is no reason why the logic of the Court's argument would not apply to that case. The religious basis of the legislation is objectionable, but the secular basis is legitimate. Therefore Sunday laws would appear to be valid as long as the objectionable religious basis was neither exclusive nor primary.

What is the secular basis commonly alleged in favor of Sunday laws? Sunday laws provide a periodic respite from work for all citizens and simultaneously ensure fair conditions of retail competition. Of course, the day-of-rest purpose would be fulfilled adequately by a regulation which prescribed a one-day-in-seven rest, leaving the choice of the day to the individual. But, the Chief Justice observed, "it seems plain that the problems involved in enforcing such a provision would be exceedingly more difficult than those in enforcing a common day-of-rest provision."[19] Important, too, was the Chief Justice's finding that:

. . . the State's purpose is not merely to provide a one-day-in-seven work stoppage. In addition to this, the State seeks to set one day apart from all others as a day of rest, repose, recreation and tranquility—a day which all members of the family and community have the opportunity to spend and enjoy together. . . .[20]

No doubt many advocates of Sunday laws are motivated by religious conviction, but the basis of legislative action must be the power of the state to protect the health, safety, and welfare of its citizens. The legislature may recognize as harmful the economic conditions which tend to promote work and competition seven days a week, and may institute a common day of rest and recreation. If the legislature may do this, may it not accommodate its legislation to the day of rest desired by the majority of its citizens? One effect of the legislation, of course, is to prefer the orthodox Christian day of rest, but this does not make the legislation religious legislation. On this point Chief Justice Warren remarked cogently that "it would seem unrealistic for enforcement purposes and perhaps detrimental to the general welfare to require a state to choose a common day-of-rest other than that which most persons would select of their own accord."[21]

SUNDAY LAWS AND THE "FREE EXERCISE OF RELIGION": THE MAJORITY VIEW

But many religious individuals and groups find Sunday laws, however economically based, a violation of their religious freedom. Quite obviously, there is no direct violation of the Sabbatarian's conscience by Sunday laws: no Sabbatarian is forced to stay open on Saturday. There is, however, an economic consequence if the Sabbatarian retailer both obeys the Sunday law and keeps the Sabbath according to the dictates of his conscience. Because of the paramount importance of religious freedom, it is urged, we should not hesitate to consider even economic consequences safeguarded by the constitutional principle of religious freedom.

Now, the principle of religious freedom is demanded by a form of government which rests on participation by citizens as equals in the decision-making process. A loss of religious liberty would introduce an inequality among citizens in the one value which is paramount to every other value in their lives. Religious liberty, then, is not a theological doctrine but a political principle based on the exigencies of a pluralistic, democratic mode of government. Being a political principle, freedom of religious exercise is not absolute with respect to social action but is conditioned by the effects of that exercise on other individuals and on the polity itself. The freedom to hold religious beliefs is absolute, but, as Chief Justice Warren indicated, "the freedom to act, even when the action is in accord with one's religious convictions, is not totally free from legislative restrictions."[22]

The Court noted that the Sunday laws in dispute did not make any religious practice unlawful. The Sunday law "simply regulates a secular activity and . . . operates to make the practice of their [Sabbatarian] religious beliefs more expensive."[23] The Court refused to strike down legislation which imposed only an indirect burden on the exercise of religion without "the most critical scrutiny."[24] Of course not all legislation which imposes an indirect burden on religious observance is unassailable.

But if the State regulates conduct by enacting a general law within its power, the purpose and effect of which is to advance the State's secular goals, the statute is valid despite its indirect burden on religious observance unless the State may accomplish its purpose by means which do not impose such a burden.[25]

The Sabbatarians before the Court contended that states with Sunday legislation are obliged at least to exempt from the Sunday labor and sales ban those who conscientiously observe another day of the week as a day of rest. Such an exemption, they argue, would achieve the state's interest in a day of rest for all citizens and simultaneously relieve Sabbatarians of the economic burden imposed by the Sunday laws. If a state can achieve the secular purposes of Sunday laws without imposing an indirect burden on the religious observance of Sabbatarians, the application of the Sunday laws to them is invidiously discriminatory and constitutionally invalid.

The central question is whether the state can in fact achieve the secular goals of Sunday legislation if it extends exemptions to conscientious Sabbatarians. Chief Justice Warren pointed out several ways in which exemptions might adversely affect the secular aims of the Sunday laws. First, enforcement problems would be more difficult, since there would be two or more days to enforce rather than one. Moreover, to "allow only people who rest on a day other than Sunday to keep their businesses open on that day might well provide these people with an economic advantage over their competitors who must remain closed on that day."[26] Because of the potential competitive advantage, unscrupulous entrepreneurs might assert that religious convictions compelled them to close on a less profitable day, and a state might object to conducting an inquiry into the sincerity of merchants' religious beliefs. Exempted employers might hire only employees whose religious beliefs qualified them for the exemption, and a state might legitimately oppose the injection of a religious factor into the employment picture. Finally, if exemptions for conscientious Sabbatarians did indeed assure a day of rest for all citizens without upsetting the balance of competition or creating other problems, still they would undermine the common day of rest and recreation which the Sunday laws were also designed to provide.

States without exemptions, to be sure, might be wise to imitate the ten states which do exempt from Sunday laws retailers who conscientiously observe the seventh or another day of the week as the Sabbath. Perhaps they would fulfill more or less adequately the community's interest in preserving salutary conditions of employment, competition, and recreation while likewise relieving conscientious Sabbatarians of the economic consequences of the Sunday laws. Perhaps for our pluralistic society this would have been, as Chief Justice Warren suggested, "the wiser solution to the problem."[27] But the Court could not say that Massachusetts, Pennsylvania, Maryland, and states with similar laws arbitrarily choose to restrict uniformly certain sales on the traditional day of rest, Sunday.

Here is operative the classic distinction between legislative determination of a statute's wisdom and judicial review of a statute's constitutionality. Unwise legislation does not in itself violate the United States Constitution. The sole question to be determined judicially is whether Sunday laws violate the religious guarantees of the Constitution. The legislation, so the Court concluded in the cases under consideration, was based on the power of the state to protect citizens against the evils of un-interrupted labor and unequal competition as well as to promote an opportunity for common rest and recreation. The legislation was not religious legislation, hence not an "establishment of religion." Nor did the legislation prohibit free exercise of religion: Massachusetts, Pennsylvania, Maryland, and their sister states did not command the performance of any act contrary to the conscience of the Sabbatarian. What the legislature had determined was that Sunday closings were an efficacious means to preserve healthy conditions of employment and competition as well as to promote the opportunity for common rest and recreation. If economic consequences fall on the conscientious Sabbatarian as a result of the operation of the statute, they remain, nonetheless, economic consequences of a statute based on the police power of the state. Free religious exercise, however constitutionally preferred in a democracy, is not absolutely guaranteed beyond the sanctuary of conscience. On balance the legislation in dispute did not appear to the Court a constitutionally unreasonable restriction of religious freedom, however preferred.

SUNDAY LAWS AND THE CLASSIFICATION OF PROHIBITED OCCUPATIONS

Opponents of Sunday laws also objected that the legislative classifications of permissible and prohibited occupations were arbitrary and thus violated the Fourteenth Amendment's guarantee of "the equal protection of the laws." Classifications of and exceptions from prohibited occupations have been subject to pressure from almost every lobby. For this reason Judge Magruder considered the result in Massachusetts "prolix and irrational."[28] Yet the general rationale of Sunday laws, including those of Massachusetts, Pennsylvania, and Maryland, is fairly clear. The legislatures wished to establish a day of rest by more or less comprehensively forbidding unnecessary business on Sunday. If we take into account the recreational opportunities proper to a day of rest, many of the apparent anomalies of classification dissolve.

But even if there remain substantial anomalies of classification, legislatures may recognize degrees of harm and act accordingly. To exercise discretion in the choice of means to combat the evils of uninterrupted labor or to express belief concerning the degree of harm in certain business activities is part and parcel of the legislative function of classification. For these reasons, as Judge Hastie observed, the Supreme Court is reluctant to interfere with even "near whimsical" classifications when these are part of a scheme of economic legislation.[29] Justice Holmes once remarked with no little legal insight that objection to the reasonable basis of legislative classification is the "usual last refuge of constitutional arguments." And Chief Justice Warren concluded that "on the record before us we cannot say that these statutes do not provide equal protection of the laws."[30]

THE DISSENTERS' VIEW

Justice Douglas dissented from the decision of the Court in all four cases.[31] In his view the Sunday laws in dispute constituted religious legislation, and hence a religious establishment prohibited by the First and Fourteenth Amendments. Moreover, Sunday laws "put an economic penalty on those who observe Saturday rather than Sunday as the Sabbath," and hence constituted state interference with the free exercise of religion.[32] The American ideal of religious liberty, in Justice Douglas' view, demands absolute respect for the "religious regime of every group . . . unless it crosses the line of criminal conduct."[33] And Sunday labor or sales are intrinsically "wholesome and not antisocial."[34]

Justices Brennan and Stewart dissented only in the two cases in which Sabbatarians complained of an infringement of the free exercise of their religious beliefs. Justice Brennan admitted that Sunday laws do not compel overt affirmation of a repugnant belief, that the effect of Sunday laws on the religious observance of Sabbatarians is indirect, that the granting of exemptions for Sabbatarians would "make Sundays a little noisier and the task of the police . . . a little more difficult," and that the exempted "non-Sunday observers might get an unfair [competitive] advantage."[35] But the mere convenience of having everyone rest on the same day cannot justify making one or more religions economically disadvantageous. The free exercise of religion is a "preferred" freedom and may be infringed—even indirectly—only to prevent the grave and imminent dangers of criminal actions or substantive evils.

But Chief Justice Warren pointed out a sound reason why not every indirect burden on the freedom of religious exercise can be protected to the same broad degree as direct burdens:

To strike down, without the most critical scrutiny, legislation which imposes only an indirect burden on the exercise of religion, i. e., legislation which does not make unlawful the religious practice itself, would radically restrict the operating latitude of the legislature.[36]

The Chief Justice mentioned specifically the indirect burdens which limited tax deductions for religious contributions imposed on those whose religion required larger donations and the indirect burden which the closing of the courts on Saturday and Sunday imposed on lawyers who observed another day of the week as their day of rest. Still, the argument of Justices Brennan and Stewart might have been persuasive if provision for a common day of rest were the *sole* basis for the denial of exemption to conscientious Sabbatarians. The interest of common recreation by itself, perhaps, is not imperative enough to warrant even the indirect economic burden imposed on the religious observance of the conscientious Sabbatarian. The additional factor, however, that exemptions from Sunday laws for conscientious Sabbatarians might also confer on them a distinct economic advantage rather than merely equalize their economic position with respect to the non-Sabbatarian merchant is a more convincing reason to justify the permissibility of legislative discretion in the grant of exemptions.

THE QUESTION OF POLICY

These are the constitutional issues concerning Sunday laws which the Supreme Court has determined with finality. Only a future decision could reverse the result. Yet the question of the practical wisdom of Sunday laws involves more than the Constitution. Wise legislators in a democratic polity will probe for ways of accommodating schemes of economic and recreational legislation, where feasible, to the realities of religious pluralism. Comity among citizens, after all, is both a goal and a condition of societal organization. And the fact that conscientious Sabbatarians are relatively numerous in particular areas further underscores the value of seeking to achieve the economic and recreational objectives of Sunday laws without at the same time occasioning economic loss to conscientious Sabbatarians.

As previously indicated, ten states employ a more liberal policy to promote the economic and recreational objectives of Sunday laws. These states grant exemptions from the Sunday sales ban to persons who conscientiously observe the seventh day of the week as the Sabbath and abstain from work thereon. Careful study should show whether, particularly in the case of the self-employed merchant, these exemptions can more or less adequately guarantee the social objectives of a common day of rest while preserving a fair balance of competition. At any rate, simply to prefer the interest in common recreation—"the interest of enforced Sunday togetherness," as Justice Stewart felicitously put it—to the interest of conscientious Sabbatarians in the economic consequences of their religious observance does not appear to be the wiser course of legislative action for a pluralistic polity.[37]

As we look back over the bitter controversy which has led to the present climax we can only note with sadness how explosive has been the mixture of religious belief and economic interest. These deep-seated tensions are not likely to have been relieved by the verdict of the United States Supreme Court.

NOTES

1. Alaska is the only state with no Sunday legislation. See Appendix II to the concurring opinion of Justice Frankfurter, *McGowan* v. *Maryland,* 366 U.S. 420, 551 (1961).

2. One state with a selective sales ban, Wisconsin, also provides exemptions for conscientious Sabbatarians.

3. *McGowan* v. *Maryland,* 362 U.S. 959 (1960); *Gallagher* v. *Crown Kosher Supermarket,* 362 U.S. 960 (1960); *Two Guys From Harrison* v. *McGinley,* 362 U.S. 960 (1960); and *Braunfeld* v. *Brown,* 362 U.S. 987 (1960).

4. *Friedman* v. *People of New York,* 302 N.Y. 75, 79 (1950).

5. *Friedman* v. *New York,* 341 U.S. 907 (1951).

6. *McGee* v. *North Carolina,* 346 U.S. 802 (1953); *Ullner* v. *Ohio,* 358 U.S. 131 (1958); and *Kidd* v. *Ohio,* 358 U.S. 132 (1958).

7. *Crown Kosher Supermarket* v. *Gallagher,* 176 F. Supp. 466 (1959); *Two Guys From Harrison* v. *McGinley,* 179 F. Supp. 944 (1959).

8. *McGowan* v. *State,* 220

Maryland 117 (1958); *Braunfeld* v. *Brown,* 184 F. Supp. 352 (1960). See note 3, *supra,* for the citations of the granting of review.

9. Mass. Stat., Ch. 136.

10. *Commonwealth* v. *Has,* 122 Mass. 40 (1877); *Commonwealth* v. *Chernock,* 336 Mass. 384 (1957).

11. 18 Pa. Stat. 4699.4.

12. 18 Pa. Stat. 4699.10.

13. *Two Guys From Harrison* v. *McGinley,* 179 F. Supp. 944, 951 (1959).

14. *Ibid.*

15. *McGowan* v. *Maryland,* 366 U.S. 420 (1961); *Two Guys From Harrison* v. *McGinley,* 366 U.S. 582 (1961); *Braunfeld* v. *Brown,* 366 U.S. 599 (1961); *Gallagher* v. *Crown Kosher Supermarket,* 366 U.S. 617 (1961).

16. *McGowan* v. *Maryland,* p. 446; *Gallagher* v. *Crown Kosher Supermarket,* p. 626.

17. See note 10, *supra,* for the citation of the Massachusetts decisions; *Sprecht* v. *Commonwealth,* 8 Pa. 312 (1848), which was relied on specifically in the recent case of *Commonwealth* v.

Bauder, 188 Pa. Super. 424 (1958); *Hiller* v. *State*, 124 Maryland 385 (1914); and *McGowan* v. *State*, 220 Maryland 117 (1958).

18. *Gallagher* v. *Crown Kosher Supermarket*, p. 626.
19. *McGowan* v. *Maryland*, p. 451.
20. *Ibid.*, p. 450.
21. *Ibid.*, p. 452.
22. *Braunfeld* v. *Brown*, p. 603.
23. *Ibid.*, p. 605.
24. *Ibid.*, p. 606.
25. *Ibid.*, p. 607.
26. *Ibid.*, pp. 608–609.

27. *Ibid.*, p. 608.
28. *Crown Kosher Supermarket* v. *Gallagher*, 176 F. Supp. 466, 476 [n. 5] (1959).
29. *Two Guys From Harrison* v. *McGinley*, 179 F. Supp. 944, 952 (1959).
30. *McGowan* v. *Maryland*, p. 428.
31. *Ibid.*, p. 561.
32. *Ibid.*, p. 577.
33. *Ibid.*, p. 575.
34. *Ibid.*
35. *Braunfeld* v. *Brown*, pp. 614, 615.
36. *Ibid.*, p. 606.
37. *Ibid.*, p. 616.

8

The Natural Law
and
American Pluralism

When Americans awakened to the twentieth century sixty years
ago, both the Catholic and the non-Catholic, for the most part,
eyed the religious beliefs of the other with suspicion and even
hostility. By dint of vast changes in the structures of American
society and the singular action of divine grace the situation
today is quite different. In America today the Catholic and
the non-Catholic share a sincere and sympathetic interest in
the religious consciousness of their fellow citizens. Many old
prejudices have crumbled and many old tensions have dissipated.

Yet it would be foolish indeed to think that all tensions between the Catholic and the non-Catholic have ceased or even
eased. In fact, the vast changes in American society over the
past sixty years have also created new foci of discord among

citizens of different religious creeds. Foremost among the forces operating at present to divide the community is the growing tension which one senses over divergent standards of moral behavior. Sixty years ago the Catholic and the non-Catholic were scarcely distinguishable in their code of personal and familial morals. Today, of course, they are far apart on many moral questions.

Why have differences in moral codes stirred increasing tension at a time when differences in religious belief have so notably declined as a divisive force in American life? The answer must lie partly in the Catholic's conception of the natural law and the non-Catholic's fear of it, especially its political implications. On the one hand, the Catholic seems to judge that the influence of moral principle is ebbing in American society, and to regard this as a matter of public concern.[1] On the other hand, the non-Catholic uneasily wonders whether a concept of morals somehow both for the Catholic and for the general public does not imperil the freedom of a pluralistic society.[2]

The problem of divergent moral codes is, of course, an ecumenical problem. But it is also a genuine problem for the political scientist and the philosopher. We shall limit our immediate concern in this chapter to the general social and political significance of the Catholic's concept of the natural law for a pluralistic society. The purpose of the chapter is twofold: first, that a rather conventional but still salutary clarification of the Catholic's understanding of natural law and particularly of its implications for American society will help in some measure to ease the anxiety of non-Catholics and perhaps advise Catholics better of the depth of their own tradition; and, secondly, that Americans will renew their covenant in what Walter Lippmann has called the "public philosophy" and will undertake in a serious way the task of elaborating the moral principles to energize social action.[3] The present chapter, then, is intended both as a clarification and as an invitation.

It is impossible, of course, to articulate in any detail here the specific prescriptions of the natural law since such an attempt would envelop the whole of the science of ethics. But we can trace in outline the more important facets of the philosophical analysis on which the specifics of the natural law rest. Indeed, we must do at least this much if we are to explore the implications of natural law for American society.

THE NATURAL LAW: THE THOMISTIC MODEL

Perused cursorily from the outside, the concept of natural law may appear a vast complication of metaphysical abstractions and Aristotelian terminology. Yet the concept of natural law is at once both simple and complex. The concept is simple insofar as its basic outline is etched in the hearts of men; it is complex insofar as its metaphysical principles mirror the complexity of the world of which it is the expression. Nor does the Catholic conceive the natural law as a bloodless abstraction or as the outmoded product of a bygone cosmological age. Rather, the Catholic envisions the natural law as the living response of reflective intellects of any age to the implications of human experience.

In the first place, natural law rests on the rockbed of a realistic epistemology.[4] Unless reality is the measure of consciousness and consciousness the reflection of reality, a freewheeling and autonomous ego will be the only and the absolute norm of human conduct. Yet, the realist insists, the capacity of the human mind to know the real is given in the actuality of knowing the real. In the transparency of actual experience man knows that his consciousness opens on a real world of material objects and human subjects, that his consciousness does not construct or posit, but rather absorbs and responds to, the real. Thus the realist rejects the so-called "principle of immanence," which, while purporting to be faithful to the immanent, perfective, and possessive properties of human knowledge, arbitrarily decrees that human consciousness cannot have for its object a reality which transcends the act.

Natural law also presupposes the dynamic relationship of action to being which reflective intelligence discovers in the data of human experience. Activity develops, fulfills, and perfects a being; hence the structure of the being which acts determines the structure of the being's activity. An activity (e.g., photosynthesis) which perfects one type of being (e.g., plants) need not perfect another type of being (e.g., animals). Now, Aristotle and his followers use the term "nature" to describe the structure of a being considered as the dynamic, immanent principle of a being's determined and perfective activity. And they use the term "human nature" to describe the common structure of being which members of the human family share and which is the principle of human activity.

The objective goal of human activity, then, is to develop, fulfill, and perfect man's being. This fulfillment of man's being clearly depends on the manner of being which man is and, though uncompleted by the performance of any single act, progressively unfolds in the dynamic continuum which constitutes the life of man. The philosophy of natural law presupposes from the psychology of human nature that man is both rational and animal, both social and individual, both psychic and physical, both unique person and participant in a common structure. Man's activity, therefore, if it is truly to develop man's personality, must be responsive to the demands of his *total* being.

Unique among the beings of experience, man is endowed with the freedom of self-position and its prerequisite, reflective intelligence. By reflective intelligence man understands in some measure the real structure of himself and his world; by freedom of self-position man is free to determine whether to act or not to act, whether to act in this way or that with respect to himself and his world. This intelligence and this freedom open to man the richness of the life of human subjectivity which achieves perfect fulfillment only through the friendship and love of other human subjects. Without social dimensions even man's individual exercise of intelligence and freedom will remain radically truncated and incomplete. These are the unique characteristics of the nature which man must develop by his activity.

By using the word "must" we have arrived almost at the point where we may speak of law. But first we shall look to the last general presupposition of natural law—the Author of nature. At the crown of a realistic metaphysic is the Supreme Being, God, whose causal influence is constitutive of the very actuality of the contingent beings of experience. Correlatively, man and all creation are totally, essentially, and permanently dependent on God for existence. God not only causes the beings of experience to be, He causes them to be in the way in which they are and, consequently, with the specific goal for the sake of which they act. In short, God is the Author of being and nature.

As the Author of nature God is in a certain sense a legislator. With infinite intelligence He orders beings to their goals. By the very act of creating a specific being God imprints His law in the natural exigencies of the being which He creates. This "natural law" is found no less in man. Man is not so free that he may appoint his own specific goal or determine his own structure of being. As in other beings, so in man the exigencies of nature are not self-defined.

Creatures other than man have no freedom in placing actions conducive to their proper perfection. But in the case of man God did not physically necessitate obedience to the law of human nature. Man is an intelligent and free creature. By his reflective intelligence man can discern the being he is and the relation of prospective actions to his proper perfection; by freedom of choice man can ratify or reject actions which are proper means to achieve this goal.

The natural law for man, then, is the entire set of commands and prohibitions imposed by nature on human action. These commands and prohibitions are derived not from the will of man but from the exigencies of man's total and integrally constituted nature. Because man is an intelligent and free creature, the natural law for man is a *moral law*, that is, a law which he discerns and freely ratifies or rejects. If he ratifies the law, he fulfills his nature and thus satisfies himself; if he rejects the law, he suffers the penalty of deformity of nature and thus frustrates himself. Canon Albert Dondeyne has reminded us of the personalist originality of moral conduct. "In a general way," he observed, "it may be said that our conduct can be described as good or bad morally to the extent that it appears as an effective, concrete recognition of the dignity of the human person."[5]

Existentialist philosophers have made us quite conscious that there is more to personal fulfillment than merely "action conformed to nature." No doubt men can obey the commands and prohibitions of the natural law without fulfilling higher and richer exigencies of the human subject. Not by law alone does man live but by the friendship and love which supplies the third dimension of existential fulfillment to the human person. And so, in the minds of many the natural law is the ethical symbol of a discredited essentialism. Yet, if it be true that actions conformed to the nature of man do not by the mere fact of conformity assure the existential fulfillment of friendship and love, it does not follow that existential fulfillment is unrelated to the structure of human nature. The plain truth, often passed over by existentialist philosophers, is that human existence is not a pure existence but a structured existence. Hence the richest activities flowing from the activity of the human subject, if they are genuinely to fulfill man's personality and existence, must be proportioned to the structure of the human person. Love offers the maximum opportunity for man's activity to be plentifully human, but we must never forget that the natural law imposes the minimum standard for man's conduct to be human at all.

THE NATURAL LAW: THE LOCKEAN MODEL

By an accident of historical homonymy the Thomistic tradition of natural law became confused in America with the static Lockean model. As a result, the term "natural law" today is distasteful to many Americans, for the Lockean "law of nature" and its fellow-traveling *laissez-faire* economics, frightfully obstinate to the requirements of social justice, colored the whole cloth of the post-Appomattox American political, social, and economic system. Even when the ravages of the Great Depression gave sharp impetus to new experiments, Justices of the United States Supreme Court ignored Justice Holmes' disclaimer and continued to ensure that the Constitution enacted Mr. Herbert Spencer's *Social Statics*.

John Locke postulated a mythical and imaginary "state of nature" which never actually existed but which functioned as a laboratory model for elaborating the natural rights of man. In this imaginary but functional state each man was "free, equal and independent."[6] There man lived "without asking leave, or depending upon the will of any other man," with "all the power

and jurisdiction . . . reciprocal, no one having more than another," and as "absolute lord of his person and possessions, equal
to the greatest, and subject to nobody."[7] In such solitary splendor
each man enjoyed his natural rights to life, liberty, and property.
The only limitation on the individual "lord" was the equal right
of every other "lord" to his life, liberty, and property.

Nonetheless, according to Locke, men were driven by weak-
nesses in the "state of nature" to form a society through consent
or compact. Why, "if man in the state of nature be so free,"
would an "absolute lord" wish to amend his life of innocent
delight by entering a society?[8] Locke explained that men, "being
biased by their interest, as well as ignorant for want of study
of it [the law of nature], are not apt to allow of it as a law
binding to them in application of it to their particular case."[9]
They needed an impartial judge "with authority to determine
all differences according to the established law" and with "power
to back and support the sentence when right."[10]

How did all these little islands of rugged individualism unite
to form a society? Locke answered that "men being, as has been
said, by nature free, equal and independent, no one can be put
out of this estate and subjected to the political power of another
without his own consent."[11] Thus men entered society on the
basis of a contract, and the single purpose of the Lockean
society was to preserve the natural rights of the individuals
who entered the society. Hence, while the majority might judge
and execute the "law of nature," the scope of action was precisely
limited by the compact to those functions. The compact was
binding on the members, but if the sovereign violated the terms
of the compact, then revolution was justified.

This framework was made to serve in post-Civil War America
as the philosophical underpinning of *laissez-faire* economics. To
be sure, the Darwinian hypothesis superimposed a vertical
dynamism on Locke's two-dimensional view of man and nature.
New language about the "survival of the fittest," sounding more
like Hobbes than like Locke, was added to the "law of nature"
vocabulary. Individualism was now still more "rugged." But
the basic framework of the "law of nature," sanctified in the
Declaration of Independence and to a less extent in the Constitution, remained Lockean in concept and language. Small

wonder, then, that many social reformers of the twentieth century rejected *in toto* the concept of a natural law when their efforts were frustrated by appeals to the "law of nature."

Today, we may assume, no refutation of Locke's theory of the "law of nature" is necessary. The centuries have made transparent the aprioristic rationalism, so foreign to the older tradition, of Locke's theory of the "law of nature." Unfounded on the rockbed of human experience, underived from the totality of man's being, the "law of nature" was an abstract deduction from a postulated "state of nature." Unquestionably, the worst single result was the radical individualism which the "law of nature" reflected and to which it contributed. Modern psychology, economics, and philosophy have made abundantly clear that man is no island and that society is no artifice. In this the modern view is at one with the traditional scholastic metaphysic which asserted that the individual fulfills his personality in and through society. Man cannot even reach the natural perfection of his individuality without participation in society.

Paradoxically enough, however, Locke's radical opposition between individual and society paved the way for the Marxian reduction of the individual to a function of society. In fact, Marx assumed the same disjunction between the individual and society as did Locke, but he opted for society as natural and relegated the individual to the realm of artifice. Against Marx the traditional scholastic metaphysic contended that society was meaningful only in terms of the individual members whose perfection society supplied. This the scholastic was able to maintain because he rejected the exaggerated antithesis between individual and society which both Locke and Marx accepted.

At the beginning of this century the social reformers confused the tenacious opposition of an intransigent and asocial "law of nature" with the whole tradition of natural law. Quite reasonably the reformers anathematized the "law of nature" and all its works. They welcomed support from any quarter, and near at hand they found a theoretical buttress in the tenets of positivism. If the field of knowledge were restricted to sensible experience, as the positivists claimed, then man could never attain any knowledge of an elusive abstraction like "human nature." And if there were no "nature" accessible to human understanding, then neither could a man of science believe that a "law of nature" brooded omnipresently over the affairs of man. Of course, the positivist considered all human activity "natural" in the sense that it took place in the world of nature. Or, in another sense, the positivist would admit that certain human activities were "natural" as conventionally accepted modes of behavior. But the fact that men in a given society agreed on certain standards of behavior did not by any means establish those norms as absolute. This is the philosophy which many social reformers welcomed for its openness to change and progress.

The philosophy of legal positivism as expressed by men like the prestigious Oliver Wendell Holmes, Jr., had gained the ascendancy in this country by the 1930s. Law, said Holmes succinctly, is nothing more nor less than "what the courts will do in fact," and the first requirement of sound law is "that it should correspond with the actual feelings and demands of the community, whether right or wrong."[12] Yet, as the history of totalitarianism evidences, such a philosophy could be just as much at home with absolutism and injustice as with democracy and reform. Positivism rendered no ultimate intelligibility to the ideal of social reform.

Despite the prognostications of the doctors of positivism, the patient, though weakened by the pretensions of radical individualism, refused to die. In fact, natural law experienced a remarkable revitalization in the United States after World War II. Revelation of the extensive atrocities against humanity perpetrated by the Hitler regime, whose legitimacy in terms of German law was open to little question, startled even the most cynical. The positivist's complacent explanation that morality was a matter of convention paled before the reality of moral evil so fully visible in the remains of Dachau and Buchenwald. Nor did the succession of Soviet brutalities culminating in Hungary diminish the renewed conviction that positive law is not its own end but, rather, is subordinate to the claims of a higher law.

Walter Lippmann, a keen observer of social and political institutions, caused a furor in the intellectual world when he called for a return to the "public philosophy" based on the natural law.[13] (We shall have occasion later to analyze the public consensus or public philosophy which Lippmann so cogently advocated.) And the eminent political scientist George Catlin asserted:

Properly stated, *the theory of natural law is not only defensible but essential,* and is the meeting ground between law and fundamental politics, sociology and, I would add, psychology.[14]

Both Lippmann and Catlin, of course, are careful to distinguish the natural-law tradition of integral personalism from the "law of nature" gospel of radical individualism.

Modern revivalists like Lippmann and Catlin well realize that the natural law must ever develop new applications and generate new solutions to meet the challenge of change in the physical, social, and cultural environment of man. Opening on a ceaselessly changing universe, natural law can be wedded permanently to no social or cultural structure of a moment of history. In short, far from opposing change, natural law develops with man in history; far from being deduced by pure reason alone, natural law depends for its discovery and application on the experience of the concrete world in which man is engaged. The natural law is no finished product of pure reason, the efforts of Locke and eighteenth-century rationalists at inflexibility notwithstanding.

RECOGNITION OF THE NATURAL LAW

The central problem, to be sure, with respect to the natural law—both from the personal and the social point of view—is epistemological. How do we as individuals or as society ascertain what the natural law commands or prohibits? Certain of our responsibilities we have no difficulty recognizing in elementary life situations. Even without articulate reflection we grasp implicitly the fundamental or, in the words of St. Thomas, the "first" principles of the natural law which govern human action;[15] for example, "Act according to reason" and "Do good and avoid evil." Moreover, when we recognize—as recognize we do and must—that murder, theft, and disrespect of parents are evils to be avoided, then we arrive at the "second" principles; for example, "Do not kill," "Do not steal," and "Respect parents." But in "quite a few cases," as St. Thomas put it, individuals or even entire peoples can be ignorant of secondary principles of the natural law or their application.[16] In some cases, especially in those involving the labyrinths of the economic order, the complexity of human experience and industrial organization requires the labor of experts, "wisemen" in the language of St. Thomas, to unravel concrete moral imperatives. In other cases, the force of custom or habit or even prejudice makes difficult the recognition of the claims of natural morality. No one can minimize or deny the magnitude of the problem. But clearly one beacon of hope lies in tapping whatever resources human intelligence posesses, especially the human intelligence of the wise among us. Man cannot abdicate responsibility because the task is difficult.

Yet reflective intelligence operates to discover the mandates of the natural law not in a vacuum of individual effort but within the collective framework of man's concrete and continuous historical experience. We must recognize both the social and the historical dimensions of the operation. As man's collective perspective on the breadth of human existence is enlarged, so too is his perspective on the implications of the natural law. A most significant case in point is the growth in the course of Western history of man's sensitivity to the value of his own unique personality and of the bonds of spiritual communion which link him to his fellow men. Man's collective discovery of the implications of the natural law develops with the unfolding of history.

Not that man's collective consciousness of the mandates of the natural law is always on the track of progressive discovery. The process of learning, after all, is matched by the process of forgetting. And so, especially in the area of personal and family integrity, the Catholic sees evidence that man has disavowed dictates of the natural law which he once acknowledged. Yet, for all the reality of collective "forgetting" of certain implications of the natural law once professed, articulate voices can still be heard to remind their fellows of these implications. In this sense, at least, we can say that man has accessible to him now more of the implications of the natural law than at any previous moment of history.

THE NATURAL LAW AND
THE POLITICAL ORDER

We have already outlined in Chapter II the specific structure and purposes of political organization which nature itself, not human convention, has specified.[17] We indicated there how the state, as the chief instrument of political society, is limited according to the principle of subsidiarity: the state should do for the citizens only what the citizens through their responsible organizations cannot conveniently do for themselves.

What, then, does the natural law require of the state in the exercise of political authority? First of all, the natural law requires that no political authority command what the natural law forbids or forbid what the natural law commands. This is implied in the very concept of the natural law as higher law. From the days of the Stoics and especially their Roman interpreters such as Cicero and Seneca, political philosophers have refused to accredit as true laws binding the consciences of men what did not accord with the universal and immanent rational principles of things. In this way the absolute values of Plato became constitutive of human laws as well as criteriological. St. Thomas summarized the tradition in the dictum:

Thus, every human law possesses the character of law only insofar as it derives from the natural law. But if it should not accord with the natural law in some respect, then it will not be law but a corruption of law.[18]

On November 26, 1960, Dr. Martin Luther King, in a televised discussion with James J. Kilpatrick, editor of the *Richmond News-Leader*, appealed to this principle to justify the crusade against racial segregation.[19] Dr. King acknowledged that, even if the courts were to uphold legislation favorable to racial segregation, he would not feel bound by such decisions to obey unjust

laws. Dr. King's statement was no call to anarchy. Americans
will recall similar sentiments about unalienable rights superior
to human law in the Declaration of Independence. It is not
anarchy to refuse obedience to an unjust law; rather, as Dr. King
said, "an unjust law is no law."

As the state may not command what the natural law forbids,
so the state may not directly promote, foster, or facilitate immoral activities. The specific goal of the state is to provide those
common conditions conductive to man's self-development, perfection, and happiness. Since activities prohibited by the natural
law lead away from rather than toward this goal, to promote
such activities would violate the state's own finality. If, for
example, the natural law forbids the practice of eugenic sterilization, then the natural law also prohibits the state and the federal
government from directly promoting the practice at home or
abroad.

Thus the natural law acts negatively to limit state action. The
state may neither command nor directly promote what the
natural law forbids. But the moral order has a much more intimate relationship to the political order than merely to function as a negative norm, for the state is entrusted with the
specific function of developing the good of the whole body
politic. Now, the good of the whole body politic which the
state seeks dynamically and positively to promote includes not
merely the citizens' material well-being but also their moral
perfection. Man perfects, develops, and fulfills himself not simply
by physical activity but specifically by the moral character of his
free acts. The state, as the specific instrument of the body politic,
therefore, must provide in a general way a public climate which
facilitates man's self-development, moral as well as physical.
Aristotle expressed this formative function of legislation in the
moral development of citizens thus:

. . . Lawgivers make citizens good by developing in them habits of
right action—this is the goal of all legislation, and if it fails to do this
it is a failure. . . .[20]

Unfortunately, many modern heirs of classical liberalism interpret political freedom as an absolute freedom of the autonomous
individual save what the individual must surrender to the state

in order to forestall the "warre of every man against every man."[21] Thus human law becomes simply the power to ensure peace, not virtue. Political freedom becomes divorced from moral virtue and political liberty from moral rectitude. There is no room in this scheme of things for legislative participation in the moral development of citizens.

It is a surprising and sad irony of history and dialectic that the classical liberal's inchoative identification of human law with physical power and his divorce of politics from morality unwittingly moved the Western world a giant step in the direction of the omnipotent state. In fact, at the end of the eighteenth century a great liberal, Immanuel Kant, would admit that:

. . . even if the Supreme Power [in the state], or the Sovereign as its agent, were to violate the original contract, and thereby in the judgment of the subject to lose the right of making laws, yet as the Government has been empowered to proceed even thus tyrannically, no right of resistance can be allowed to the subject as a power antagonistic to the state.[22]

For Kant this was so because conscience ruled only the inner sphere of morality, relinquishing to the state undisputed control of the outer sphere of legality. Modern liberals who accept Kant's premise on the antinomy of conscience and law should consider whether they are also willing to accept his total obedience to the state.

Modern minds, which for a generation now have renounced the exaggerated individualism of classical liberalism as applied to the economic and social spheres of human activity, still cling to the anarchic atomism of eighteenth-century political philosophy in the sphere of morality. The evident moral character of so many social and political crises in the twentieth century makes the more inexplicable and anachronistic the refusal to accept the public and social relevance of moral activity. Hopefully, a future generation will find today's atomism in matters moral as outmoded as moderns find yesterday's individualism in matters economic. Indeed, even today's ideal of economic and social justice rests on an incompletely articulated moral commitment.

There are two basic ways of misconceiving the nature of the political order. The first error, the error of the doctrinaire pragmatist, is to attempt to substitute practical policy for moral principle; the second error, the error of the moral simplist, is to attempt to substitute moral principle for practical policy. Against both the tradition of natural law affirms the genuine roles which both moral judgment and practical wisdom must play in the order of politics. Moral principle is the wellspring of political action, but practical wisdom must be exercised in the selection of means to implement objectives based on moral principle. Thus not only must statesmen assent to the moral objectives of peace and justice, but they must with all prudence determine how best to defend the commonwealth, how best to conduct foreign policy, how best to administer justice, how best to ensure an equitable social order, and so forth.

THE NATURAL LAW AND THE PUBLIC CONSENSUS

With respect to the role of moral principle as the wellspring of social action, Fr. John Courtney Murray has spoken of the "tradition of reason," Sir Ernest Barker of the "tradition of civility," and Walter Lippmann of the "public philosophy."[23] All refer to the same reality—the widespread agreement of citizens on the basic principles expressive of the natural law which should govern social action. This public consensus is a pre-political energy, an inchoative law, and an ultimate criterion which impels or restrains political, economic, social, and cultural activity. These distinguished authors by no means suggest that the consensus constitutes the truth of the principles subscribed. The principles are not true because the public holds them; rather the public holds them (or should hold them) because they are true. The public can consent because the subscribed principles express the more general aspects of the natural law which are accessible to the light of each man's reason. In this sense, public consensus can be a sign—if not an infallible one —of the principles of the natural law.

The public consensus, then, as Fr. Murray and the others envision it, is not just agreement but agreement on a basic set of moral principles governing social action and accessible to human intelligence. Yet an overprotective zeal for liberty has led many to deny that such a consensus is necessary, desirable, or even possible in a pluralistic society. For these libertarians the only absolutely immutable principle in the American consensus is the commitment to an "open" or "free" society. Americans, in a word, agree only on the right to disagree.

But how justified are these fears? First of all, it must be noted that no advocate of a public consensus based on the natural law in any way challenges the political wisdom of American democracy or American freedom. In fact, quite the contrary is true. Advocates of the public consensus regard the democratic process of decision making and the freedoms which are its indispensable conditions as ideal for a maturely developed body politic. They regard the democratic process as fully articulating in the political order the natural-law truths of man's common intelligence and unique personality.

But the democratic process, however vital and appropriate for a mature society, is the means and not the goal of human activity. The process of making decisions is not to be confused with the content of the decisions made. The goal of political organization is to foster conditions conducive to man's proper self-development; the democratic process and its associated freedoms are only means to achieve that goal. Now, to speak of "man's proper self-development" is at once to speak of the natural law. This is why the public consensus, as a pre-political energy based on the natural law, should inform the whole process of decision making and the exercise of freedom.

Moreover, agreement on the democratic process by itself will scarcely ensure enough unity of mind and heart to transform a collection of autonomous individuals into a politically organized society. A society is a society only insofar as the members share common goals and aspirations. In another connection Justice Frankfurter had occasion to speak felicitously of the "agencies of mind and spirit which may serve to gather up the traditions of a people, transmit them from generation to generation, and thereby create that continuity of a treasured common life which constitutes a civilization."²⁴ The public consensus proposes to serve as such an agent and to function as such a binding tie of cohesive sentiment.

The public consensus is a body of practical, not speculative, truths. As such the public consensus is designed not for the speculative intellect to contemplate but for the practical reason to acknowledge as a sound basis for social action. Fortunately, then, Americans do not need to create the public consensus *ab ovo* as an exercise of abstract reason or pure speculation. Nor do Americans of each generation need to debate anew the basic principles of social concourse. Present and future generations of Americans are fortunate enough to be heirs to the "tradition of reason" which, though it is older than America herself, our forefathers adapted and energized into a living reality. This "tradition of reason" has itself been generated and invigorated by the "tradition of faith." Dr. John C. Bennett has pertinently observed:

The fact that all three of our [religious] communities have the Old Testament in common is of vast importance for American life. . . . [T]he prophets of Israel are masters of us all in our interpretation of public morality.²⁵

In these traditions is recapitulated a wealth of human wisdom which is necessary and accessible for constituting the public consensus. Tradition must, of course, be open to change but not on the level of basic principles nor on the level of "national purpose." Truly the life of a political society is experience and not logic; the task of the political wisemen is to articulate what is already active, if implicit, in the wisdom of the nation's experience.

The immovable forces of inertia and prejudice, of course, will resist the impulse to restore the public consensus to a place of honor. This is not surprising in view of the widespread emphasis on the differences among Americans in matters moral. But the spiritual crises of the twentieth century should serve to unite Americans in reasserting the community of moral principle which such an emphasis on differences has tended to obscure. In this Americans have the hopeful example of the flourishing interfaith dialogues among Protestants, Catholics, and Jews. These, without any attempt to ignore or minimize real differences of belief, have successfully overcome obstacles at least analogous in some respects to those which now confront the public consensus.

Religious-minded citizens of the Protestant tradition may be inclined to a distaste for the theory of natural law which forms the basis of the public consensus. From the Protestant point of view the theory of natural law may seem to endow vitiated nature with too much virtue, to entrust fallible reason with too much strength, and to assign too small a role to the divine initiative. On the other hand, St. Paul, in his Epistle to the Romans, claimed that God had revealed himself and the law of his creation clearly enough to the pagans to hold them responsible for their actions.[26] Thus, according to Paul, God took the initiative by making moral demands on mankind through the law which He inscribed in their hearts. This is not the place to analyze the theological aspects of Protestant belief. But we do ask here whether the Protestant point of view must exclude the natural law as the basis of the public consensus. Dr. Bennett, in his own excellent way and within the Protestant tradition, has answered this question in the negative:

Surely there is a moral order which human laws do not create. . . . There are differences here [among the religious communities] but they should not obscure what is common to our traditions in contrast to secular moral relativism. . . . I do believe that the objective moral order does press upon us even when we do not recognize it.[27]

Fr. Gregory Baum has indicated the division of Protestant opinion on the issue of natural law:

There is an interesting formulation of the controversy going on within the Protestant community between those who uphold, in one form or another, the ancient idea of natural law and those who do not believe that the divine imperative is expressed in the structure of God's universe and of the human heart.[28]

We can only hope that the former view will prevail among Protestants. Otherwise Protestants would risk having nothing of relevance to say in moral matters to the millions of men without faith in Jesus Christ. The paradoxical result would be that Protestants who opposed the natural law in defense of the divine transcendence would actually strengthen the hand of the doctrinaire positivists.

THE CATHOLIC, THE PUBLIC, AND THE
SPECIFICS OF THE NATURAL LAW

The public consensus, of course, refers specifically to basic principles of the natural law operating as a social energy. But the potentialities of the public consensus are greater to the extent to which public consensus is alive and energetic to the more particular dictates of the natural law. How operative are specifics of the natural law in America today? Pessimists are wont to speak in this regard of a "descending curve" of public morality.[29] And in many areas, indeed, agreement on specific principles of public morality has visibly contracted; the public today is more indifferent than in the past to the moral imperatives of such issues as premarital sexual behavior, divorce, abortion, and euthanasia. Yet in many other areas agreement on specific principles of public morality is expanding; the public today is more concerned than in the past with the moral imperatives of such issues as racial segregation, social injustice, business ethics, union corruption, and the venality of public officials. The resulting status of the public consensus on specific principles of the natural law—at least as the Catholic sees it— may be described summarily as weakening in the area of personal and family responsibility and consolidating in the area of economic and social morality.

There is therefore occasion for both concern and hope over the present vitality and future prospects in America of public agreement on specific moral imperatives. The task before the American people, as the Catholic sees it, is to defend—more accurately, perhaps, to recover—the personal and familial territory of the consensus while continuing to advance its social and economic frontiers. Yet such a specific task can be entered

upon only if there is first a general acceptance of the value of
the public consensus and a general commitment to a dialogue
on the problematics of the consensus. By definition the "tradition of reason" can be elaborated only if a people, and particularly its wisemen, accept the role of reason in human society
and engage themselves concretely in the discussion.

Quite often Catholic and non-Catholic alike misconstrue the
role of the Catholic in any discussion of specific moral imperatives. The source of this misconstruction lies in the Catholic's
dual recognition of natural reason and supernatural authority.
In moral matters the Catholic appears, on the one hand, to
appeal to the principle of the natural law and, on the other
hand, to acknowledge the supremacy of the Church's teaching
authority. Understandably the non-Catholic may feel that the
Catholic is attempting to have his cake and eat it too. Is the
Catholic invoking reason or authority in the discussion? If he
wishes to invoke the authority of the Church, then the non-
Catholic can readily understand why the Catholic holds the
view he does. But often the non-Catholic will be unable to accept the conclusion because the non-Catholic does not share the
Catholic's recognition of the Church's authority. And if the Catholic wishes to invoke reason, then often the non-Catholic will be
unable to accept on rational grounds the certainty or at least
the universality of the Catholic's conclusion.

The truth of the matter is that the Catholic's role in any
discussion on the public consensus is complex. It is but another
phase of the Catholic's age-old problem of relating faith to reason. The Catholic does not invoke the power of reason alone
in the formation of moral principles. The Catholic recognizes
the primacy of the teaching authority of the Church in moral
matters, and he recognizes that the Church has in fact spoken
authoritatively on many specific questions of the natural law
(e.g., birth control, divorce, artificial insemination, etc.). Therefore, even if the Catholic in such a case feels his reasoning
persuasive rather than conclusive, his conclusion probable rather
than certain on rational grounds, he will rely on the teaching
authority of the Church for the certainty of his conclusion. Or
even if the Catholic feels his reasoning conclusive and his conclusion certain on rational grounds, still he must acknowledge

both the potential activity of grace in the operation of his intellect and the direction of faith which the Church has imparted
to his search for rational evidence.

The theory of natural law, to be sure, is *ex professo* a philosophical doctrine, a doctrine based on natural reason and not on
the supernatural gift of faith. Yet the Church must propose and
promote not only the observance of those obligations of the moral
law which flow uniquely from the positive legislation by God and
the Church to execute the special designs of the salvific dispensation but also those obligations of the moral law which flow specifically from man's human nature. This the Church must do both
because man's reason, darkened by original sin, requires as a
practical certainty an authoritative guide to the natural law and
because the Church has the task of instructing the faithful in
all that pertains to the integrally constituted moral order.

The Catholic is ever mindful in forming moral principles of the
thought which Pius XII expressed in the encyclical *Humani Generis* and which echoed the words of the First Vatican Council:

We have to admit, then, the moral necessity of a revelation from God.
Without that, religious and moral truths, which of their own nature lie
within the scope of human reason, cannot be apprehended promptly,
with full certainty and without some alloy of error, in the present state
of mankind.[30]

The Catholic should be equally mindful of the significance of that
principle in the context of the public consensus. The Catholic
may and should offer to the non-Catholic the wisdom of the
Church. Simply as a human institution the Church has witnessed
two thousand years of man's progress and regress. She has not
kept all these things carefully in her heart without storing up
much wisdom. But the Catholic should not, however, expect that
non-Catholics will agree with the Catholic's judgments or ana-
lyzes in all areas of morality. The Church surely does not expect
this.

In one way the Catholic's reliance on the Church in moral matters is not really unique. All religious-minded people believe that
the divine action is the sustaining force in the recognition and
observance of even natural morality. And cultural anthropologists

confirm the fact that religion has operated through the ages as the cohesive and invigorating element in the maintenance of a people's moral code. In America, too, our religious traditions are responsible in great part for the extent to which the public consensus is an effective force. The important task facing the religious communities at present is to elaborate and elevate the status of that consensus.

We have observed that the Catholic does not invoke the power of reason *alone* in the formation of moral principles, but he does recognize the power of reason. True, the Catholic acknowledges the teaching authority of the Church in moral matters, but he also recognizes that the Church herself invokes her authority to support the natural law and invites him to exercise his own reasoning powers to understand the principles of natural law. As best he can, the Catholic, especially the expert, attempts to grasp and organize the rational evidence for moral judgments. The evidence accessible to reason is what the Catholic strives to contribute to any discussion looking to an elaboration of the public consensus. This is all fair-minded men ask.

THE CATHOLIC, THE NATURAL LAW, AND POLITICAL COERCION

It is all well and good to speak of public agreement on basic principles of the natural law and of the operation of the public consensus as a pre-political energy. But to what extent does the Catholic judge that coercion by political authority is required for the specific mandates of the natural law which the Catholic articulates under the aegis of the teaching authority of the Church? Is the concept of the natural law a Trojan horse which will betray the whole political order to the jurisdiction of the Roman Catholic spiritual authority? In short, are the political implications of the natural law compatible with the ethical pluralism of American democracy? This is a problem which occasions grave concern to many non-Catholics today.

Focus of excessive attention on the place of governmental coercion in matters of public morals may serve, unfortunately, to obscure the true function of the state as a subsidiary of the whole body politic. The first function of the state is to encourage other responsible organizations of the body politic—familial, religious, and cultural—to exercise their partial tasks regarding the protection and promotion of the moral good of the whole community. Yet, as the highest subsidiary of political society, the state alone has such a specific function, and when other organizations prove inadequate to the task, the state may be required to take the initiative, even to invoke its coercive power, to cope with public problems of a moral nature. We shall consider here to what extent a democratic state as ethically pluralistic as America should enforce the natural law code of public morals.

What makes this problem so pertinent at present is the general change within living memory in the public's code of personal and family responsibility. Today the public in large part accepts birth control and divorce; tomorrow the public may more widely accept abortion and euthanasia. As a result of such changes in the climate of public morality many urge the legislature to relax the present enforcement of public morals.[31] Others, on the contrary, urge the legislature to maintain or even strengthen present enforcement. How should Catholics and others react to these forces? Under what conditions is state enforcement of public morals desirable or even possible?

Of course, the state is not concerned with private or individual morality. The area of the state's legitimate competency, whether in moral or other matters, is restricted to the public and social dimensions of human behavior, to what concerns the community as a whole. Yet human activities are so interwoven that scarcely any are without some measure of social significance. We live in a human beehive, and by our behavior each of us affects others and the whole. It is an exercise of human prudence to determine to what degree and with what result individual activities affect the public interest. This judgment will depend on how widespread is the activity and how bad is the effect.

The general motive for all coercive legislation in this field is to control the evils, both moral and physical, which would result to society from violation of the moral order. The individual who violates the law of his nature incurs the natural sanctions of self-deformity and self-dissatisfaction. So, too, the society which disregards the public climate of morality reaps the natural sanctions of social deformity and social dissatisfaction. Society is designed to fulfill and satisfy man; it should not help to disorder and frustrate him. The state, therefore, as specifically entrusted with the protection and promotion of the welfare of the community, seeks to foster social conditions conducive to a sound moral order. This is why not even the democratic state which establishes the equality of all citizens before the law in the sphere of religious belief can permit so full an equality in the sphere of moral action.

Few are foolish enough to deny the propriety of coercion by the state to restrain actions which would physically harm others or violate their rights. Indeed, few would deny the propriety of restraining behavior which would corrupt the morals of the young or take advantage of the mentally deficient for immoral purposes. But why should the state otherwise be concerned with the moral activities of adults enjoying the full exercise of their powers to reason and choose? What harm can these actions inflict on anyone else? Unable to give any positive answer to these questions, many suggest that a "free society" has no rationale for forbidding to its citizens such activities as voluntary euthanasia.

First of all, even immoral actions which do not directly inflict physical harm on others may, when practiced more or less widely, result in physical harm to the whole community. Thus, for example, obscene literature could lead to delinquency and violence. But beyond the possibilities of physical harm stands the moral danger to the whole community from immoral activities. Citizens cannot isolate themselves from the public climate which results from the moral character of individual actions any more than they can escape the public effects of individual actions in economic affairs. After all, citizens dwell in one and the same society.

Yet legislation which seeks to advance the welfare of the community in one respect often adversely affects the community in another. This is especially true in the case of legislation enforcing public morals. Balance and prudent judgment will be necessary to ensure the wise exercise of the coercive power of the state. Human law, as a determination of practical reason, must take full measure of the conditions of possibility, the weakness of human nature, and the living traditions of a people. Hence, St.

Thomas sagely concluded seven centuries ago, "human law cannot prohibit everything which the natural law prohibits."[32] "Political hypermoralism," as Professor Maritain remarked, "is no better than political amoralism."[33]

Tolerance of public moral evil by the state is always for the sake of a greater good. In this St. Thomas observed the basic analogy between human and divine government:

. . . human government is derived from and should imitate divine government. Now God, although all powerful and supremely good, nonetheless permits some evil to occur in the universe which He could prevent. He does so lest the removal of these evils entail the loss of greater goods or even cause worse evils. By the same token those charged with the government of human affairs rightly tolerate some evil to promote good or even to prevent worse evil.[34]

Pius XII similarly remarked in an allocution to the Italian jurists on December 6, 1953, that the duty of repressing moral error cannot be an ultimate norm of action.[35] "It must be subordinate to *higher and more general* norms, which *in some circumstances permit,* and even perhaps seem to indicate as the better policy, toleration of error in order to promote a *greater good.*"[36]

What concretely are the "higher and more general norms" to which the enforcement of public morals is subordinate? One such norm is the possibility of effective enforcement. A law which cannot effect what it is designed to effect is a foolish law indeed. Yet often enough the state simply cannot enforce legislative prescriptions of public morals or at least not without odious police intrusion into the intimate lives of ordinary citizens. Take, for example, the Connecticut ban on the practice of birth control. Since contraceptives are easily accessible in neighboring states, the Connecticut legislation is, if only from this point of view, a monument to folly. At best, unenforceable legislation like the Connecticut birth-control ban serves only as a declaration of public policy, and at worst, legislation so widely disobeyed encourages disrespect for all law. In this matter Americans readily recall the legacy of national prohibition.

Another norm to which enforcement of public morals is subordinated stems from the pluralistic character of the American polity. Some accommodation among citizens of different ethical convictions on the state's role in matters of public morals is a necessary part of political wisdom. Harmony among citizens, after all, is both a goal and a condition of societal organization. Such accommodation by the nature of things is relative to time, place, and subject matter. Yet surely legislators would be unwise to enforce without grave justification a matter of public morals on which the community was widely and deeply divided. If libertarians often judge erroneously that tranquillity is the only essential goal of a political society, traditionalists may also err if they fail to esteem properly the paramount value of internal harmony among citizens.

A third "higher and more general" norm for legislation in matters of public morals derives from the peculiar exigencies of a democratic form of government. Democracy, which rests on participation of citizens as equals in the decision-making process, must institutionalize a maximum liberty of self-direction. This liberty of action, of course, is not absolute but is conditioned on the effects of action on other individuals and on the polity itself. Yet, simply as a political principle, maximum individual liberty remains a condition of democratic government. St. Thomas recognized this characteristic and its consequences:

. . . in a democratic polity, where the whole people choose to rule, . . . all citizens share equal liberty. . . . Therefore, the ordinances of a democratic regime are not just because they achieve justice absolutely but because they achieve justice according to the nature of the polity.[37]

Lastly, coercive legislation in the area of public expression, however successful it might appear in attaining certain moral objectives, runs the special risks of stultifying artistic initiative and inhibiting scientific development. More fearsome still is the political specter of arbitrary and despotic rule—the very antithesis of the moral finality of government—which such censorship raises. This is not to deny that a state may with reason restrict some forms of expression—no nation should protect libel or pornography, for instance—but to restrict freedom of expression in a democracy demands the most compelling reasons. The "free marketplace of ideas" is an indispensable condition for the democratic community to exercise intelligently the role of making necessary and prudent political decisions.

On the other side of the equation, legislators—and ultimately in a democracy the citizens—must weigh the magnitude of the dangers which prompt coercive action. The state will be especially zealous to prohibit acts which deprive other citizens of what is rightfully theirs. Thus the state will protect the rights of each citizen to his life, liberty, and property. Further, the state must act dynamically to ensure conditions such that no citizen is deprived of his right to obtain for himself and his family as the fruit of his labor the support, security, and leisure which is worthy of his human dignity. Just how much beyond this the state goes will depend. Some restrictions, of course, will be required of actions which prove seriously harmful to the commonwealth even when the actions do not necessarily deprive others of their rights, for example, restrictions on the consumption of alcohol, on divorce, on polygamy. But what restrictions of which activities will depend in large part on how widespread the activity is and how bad the results are. No magic formula will offer a ready substitute for the painstaking exercise of human prudence.

Perhaps the best we can do in this whole matter by way of summary is to cite the advice of St. Thomas:

. . . human law does not prohibit all vices from which the virtuous abstain but only the more serious ones from which the greater part of the people can abstain. Especially does human law forbid vices harmful to others which, if not prohibited, would destroy human society. E. g., murder, theft and so forth.[38]

CONCLUSION

In general, such is the role which the Catholic conceives that the natural law should play in American political life. He does not, of course, mistake the natural law for the whole, or even the principal, ingredient in the Christian conception of the world.

The generosity of love always colors the Christian's world picture more than the exactitude of justice. In fact, the Christian hopes to effect the justice of men through the charity of Christ. But the order of justice, natural law, and natural rights remains, nonetheless, a real and essential element of this picture.

Nor should Catholics and non-Catholics lose perspective on what constitute the chief concerns of public morality today. Different concepts of individual and family ethics should not deter Americans from articulating and implementing their common moral obligations in the matters of race relations, economic development of underdeveloped nations, and nuclear war. It is the latter rather than the former concerns which are the most critical politico-moral problems of our generation.

Yet the political problem of the natural law and American pluralism is only one phenomenon, one level of a much larger concern which is basically ecumenical. Matters of morality are not simply problems for the political society but genuine concerns for the religious communities. The ultimate key to solving even the political and social dimensions of moral issues may well lie with the vitality of present and future discussions among the faiths. In this the aspirations of the religious communities and the political society are one.

NOTES

1. See, for example, Donald McDonald, "The Declining Curve," *America*, August 27, 1960, pp. 575–576.

2. See, for example, R. McA. Brown (and G. Weigel, S.J.), *op. cit.*, pp. 58–62.

3. Walter Lippmann, *The Public Philosophy* (Boston: Little, Brown & Co., 1955).

4. Critics are quite sensitive to the epistemological presupposition of natural law. See Felix E. Oppenheim, "The Natural Law Thesis: Affirmation or Denial?"

American Political Science Review, Vol. LI (1957), pp. 41-53.

5. Canon Albert Dondeyne, "Toleration and Collaboration," in *Toleration and the Catholic*, p. 84.

6. John Locke, *Two Treatises on Government*, ed. Thomas I. Cook (New York: Hafner Publishing Co., Inc., 1947), 2d treatise, Ch. VIII, sec. 95, p. 168.

7. *Ibid.*, Ch. II, sec. 4, p. 122, and Ch. IX, sec. 123, p. 184.

8. *Ibid.*, Ch. IX, sec. 123, p. 184.

9. *Ibid.*, Ch. IX, sec. 124, p. 184.

10. *Ibid.*, Ch. IX, secs. 125, 126, pp. 184, 185.

11. *Ibid.*, Ch. VIII, sec. 95, p. 168.

12. Oliver Wendell Holmes, Jr., "The Path of the Law," *Collected Legal Papers* (New York: Harcourt, Brace and Co., 1920), p. 173, and *The Common Law* (Boston: Little, Brown & Co., 1881), p. 57.

13. Lippmann, *op. cit.* For an adverse reaction see Morton G. White, "Original Sin, Natural Law and Politics," *Partisan Review*, Vol. XXIII (1956), pp. 218–236.

14. George E. Catlin, "Political Theory: What Is It?" *Political Science Quarterly*, Vol. LXXII (1957), p. 21.

15. St. Thomas, *Summa Theologica*, I-IIae, q. 94, a. 2.

16. *Ibid.*

17. *Supra*, Ch . II, pp. 17–18, 20–21.

18. St. Thomas, *Summa Theologica*, I-IIae, q. 95, a. 2.

19. *The New York Times*, November 27, 1960, p. 95.

20. Aristotle, *Nicomachean Ethics*, 1103b, 3–5.

21. Thomas Hobbes, *Leviathan* (London: J. M. Dent & Sons, Ltd., 1914), Part I, Ch. XIII, p. 66.

22. Immanuel Kant, "The Principles of Political Right Considered in Connection with the Relation of Theory to Practice in the Right of the State," *Kant's Principles of Politics*, ed. and trans. by William Hastie (Edinburgh: T. & T. Clark, 1891), p. 50. Kant, of course, would cen-sure the tyrannical action as immoral.

23. J. C. Murray, S.J., *We Hold These Truths;* Sir Ernest Barker, *Traditions of Civility* (Cambridge University Press, 1948); and Walter Lippmann, *op. cit.*

24. *Minersville School District v. Gobitis*, 310 U.S. 586, 596 (1940).

25. John C. Bennett, "Cultural Pluralism: The Religious Dimension," *Social Order*, February, 1961, p. 56.

26. *Epistle to the Romans*, 1:19–21 and 2:14–15.

27. Bennett, *art. cit.*, p. 57.

28. Gregory Baum, O.S.A., "Protestants and the Natural Law," *The Commonweal*, January 20, 1961, p. 428.

29. McDonald, *art. cit.*

30. "Humani Generis," *Acta Apostolicae Sedis*, Vol. XLII (1950), p. 562. The translation is by the late Msgr. R. A. Knox, *The Tablet*, September 2, 1950, p. 187.

31. Norman St. John-Stevas has attempted in two recent works to strike a reasonable note on the issue of law and public morality: *Obscenity and the Law* (London: Secker and Warburg, 1956) and *Life, Death and the Law* (Bloomington: Indiana University Press, 1961). But not all petitions for relaxation of the present enforcement of public morals are so balanced or so understanding of moral perspectives. See, for example, Llewelyn Glanville Williams, *The Sanctity of Life and the Criminal Law* (New York: Alfred A. Knopf, Inc., 1957).

32. St. Thomas, *Summa Theologica*, I-IIae, q. 96, a. 2, ad 3.

33. Jacques Maritain, *Man and the State* (Chicago: University of Chicago Press, 1951), pp. 61–62.

34. *Ibid.*, II-IIae, q. 10, a. 11.

35. Pius XII, "Religion in the Community of Nations," *The Catholic Mind*, April, 1954, p.

248. The italics are supplied from the original: *Acta Apostolicae Sedis*, Vol. XLV (1953), p. 799.

36. *Ibid.*

37. St. Thomas, *Commentarium X Libros Ethicorum ad Nicomachum*, V, lect. 2.

38. St. Thomas, *Summa Theologica*, I-IIae, q. 96, a. 2.

9

Catholics,
Birth Control,
and Public Policy

The moral stance of Catholics toward the practice of artificial birth control isolates them today almost completely from the opinion of their Protestant, Jewish, and secular fellow citizens. In fact, very few non-Catholics even feel much sympathy for the moral teaching of the Church on birth control. The current divergence in Catholic and non-Catholic concepts of family morality was not always so. Sixty years ago Catholics, Protestants, and Jews would have agreed rather generally on a code of family morality, including the matter of artificial birth control. But today the cleavage of moral judgment in this area is a vital fact which poses genuine political as well as religious problems. Indeed, artificial birth control is the single area of Catholic moral teaching in which non-Catholics are most sensitive and apprehensive of the political consequences.

Our interest is with the political rather than with the religious consequences of this divergence of moral judgment. We shall not attempt, therefore, to explain here why Catholics regard artificial birth control as immoral. Discussion of the subject is highly desirable and contributes indirectly, though importantly, to political harmony. But such a discussion is outside the focus of public policy with which we are now concerned. Our concern is to seek out the proper role of the public authority toward birth control precisely in view of the deep division of moral judgment which currently exists within the American community. The question is actually a double one: (1) Should the public authority prohibit or regulate the practice? and (2) Should the public authority promote or support the practice? The former aspect, for the most part, is an issue of the domestic policy of state and local governments, while the latter aspect, for the most part, is an issue of the national policy of the United States foreign-aid program and the international policy of the United Nations. We shall consider each aspect in turn.

DOMESTIC REGULATION OF BIRTH CONTROL

Federal law on its face restricts the distribution of contraceptives in several ways. First, the use of the mails for the transportation of contraceptives or of any information on where to buy or how to use contraceptive devices is forbidden.[1] Secondly, the use of common interstate carriers other than the mails for the transportation of contraceptives or of any information on where to buy or how to use contraceptive devices also constitutes a federal felony.[2] Thirdly, federal law prohibits the importation of contraceptives from abroad.[3] These restrictions, when read literally, appear quite far-reaching, but, in fact, the federal courts have interpreted the statutes otherwise. They have ruled that information on contraception is not necessarily to be considered "obscene."[4] More importantly, they have ruled that the statutes require an intent to use the contraceptive articles for illegal and immoral purposes and do not prohibit an intent to use them for the health or welfare of married couples.[5] Judge Augustus Hand, in one of the leading cases on the subject, concluded that Congress did not intend to prohibit the distribution of contraceptives "which might intelligently be employed by conscientious and competent physicians for the purpose of saving life or promoting the welfare of their patients."[6] It is highly unlikely, however, that those responsible for the Comstock Act of 1873 or the Tariff of 1930 had any such frame of mind. Their language was absolute, and all attempts to modify the legislation in a liberal direction antecedent to the rulings of the federal courts failed. At any rate, federal law as judicially interpreted since the 1930s offers no restraint of any practical significance to the distribution of contraceptives for the practice of birth control by married couples.

The law of the states varies from no regulation at all to the total prohibition of contraceptive practices.[7] Twenty states and the District of Columbia have no legislation on the matter. Seventeen states prohibit the sale of contraceptives but except doctors, pharmacists, and special licensees. Five states prohibit the sale and advertisement of contraceptives without exception. Eight states restrict or prohibit only the advertisement of contraceptives. One state, Connecticut, prohibits the use of contraceptives. Of the five states which purport to prohibit absolutely the sale and advertisement of contraceptives, in only two—Connecticut and Massachusetts—do the laws have practical effect. Even in the latter two states the practical effects are limited, since the authorities make no attempt to enforce the laws except with respect to the operation of birth-control clinics. Thus the Connecticut and Massachusetts laws certainly do not touch the rich and the educated although the Planned Parenthood League asserts that the laws are effective enough with the poor and uneducated.

THE CONSTITUTIONAL QUESTION:
POE v. *ULLMAN*

Many advocates of birth control question the constitutionality of restrictive state statutes as applied to married couples. They argue that the statutes restrict or deny to married people their right to sexual relations at the time and manner of their choosing. The Fourteenth Amendment, they claim, protects this fundamental right against arbitrary state action. The Connecticut birth-control legislation—the most extreme in all American jurisdiction—offered the best target, and a test case was instituted in the state courts. The case eventually reached the United States Supreme Court, and a consideration of the opinions expressed there, especially the dissenting opinion of Justice Harlan, will allow us the opportunity to explore and weigh many of the substantive constitutional issues.[8]

In 1958 Dr. C. Lee Buxton and several of his patients, residents of New Haven, petitioned the courts of Connecticut to declare void the legislative ban against the sale, prescription, or use of contraceptives. When the case reached the Supreme Court of Connecticut, Chief Justice Raymond E. Baldwin, speaking for a unanimous court on December 8, 1959, rejected the plea of Dr. Buxton and his patients.[9] Immediately following this decision the plaintiffs appealed to the United States Supreme Court, and on May 23, 1960, the Court agreed to review the case.[10]

Dr. Buxton, Chairman of the Department of Obstetrics and Gynecology at the Yale University School of Medicine, claimed that the general statutes of Connecticut prevented him from giving his patients counsel on contraceptives and thus from fulfilling his professional duty of imparting to his patients the safest and best-founded prescriptions of medical science.[11] Sixty-six deans and doctors from the nation's medical schools filed a brief in support of Dr. Buxton's plea. Joined with Dr. Buxton in the action before the Supreme Court were several of his patients, who for the sake of anonymity employed fictitious names. Mrs. Jane Doe, twenty-five years old, barely survived a difficult pregnancy. The result was a stillborn child and partial paralysis for Mrs. Doe, who sought from Dr. Buxton advice on how to lead a "normal married life" without seriously endangering her health. She claimed that the Connecticut law prevented Dr. Buxton from giving the requisite advice and that the law unreasonably abridged her right to marital relations without serious risk to life. Another patient, Mrs. Pauline Poe, twenty-six years old, had given birth to three abnormal children. Although the underlying mechanism was as yet unclear, Dr. Buxton and other consultant specialists suspected a genetic cause. Mr. and Mrs. Poe were upset at their prospects for future children and sought advice from Dr. Buxton on how to enjoy marital relations without fear of conceiving abnormal children. Mr. and Mrs. Poe claimed that the Connecticut law prevented Dr. Buxton from giving the necessary advice and that the law unreasonably restricted their right to marital intercourse without fear of conceiving abnormal children.

The question put before the Court by the plaintiffs was whether the Connecticut birth-control legislation was a reasonable exercise of the state police power over the health, safety, morals, and welfare of citizens. Does the Connecticut legislation unreasonably restrict the rights of Mrs. Doe and Mrs. Poe to marital relations and the professional right of Dr. Buxton to counsel his patients? The key words, of course, are "reasonable" and "unreasonable."

On June 19, 1961, Justice Frankfurter delivered the opinion of a closely divided Court. He found no case or controversy, no justiciable issue, within the meaning of Article III, section 2 of the Constitution:

It is clear that the mere existence of a state penal statute would constitute insufficient grounds to support a federal court's adjudication of its constitutionality in proceedings brought against the state's prosecuting officials if real threat of enforcement is wanting.[12]

And Justice Frankfurter saw "no real threat of enforcement:"

The fact that Connecticut has not chosen to press the enforcement of this statute deprives these controversies of the immediacy which is an indispensable condition of constitutional adjudication. This Court cannot be umpire to debates concerning harmless, empty shadows.[13]

Therefore Justice Frankfurter declined to rule on the substantive constitutional issues. Justice Brennan, in a concurring opinion, added that "the true controversy in this case is over the opening of birth-control clinics on a large scale. . . ." and the Court will have the opportunity to decide the "true controversy" when the facts of another case impose this necessity.[14]

The majority no doubt was keenly aware of the practical state of affairs in Connecticut. Resident doctors who simply disclose the findings of medical science on contraceptives as a matter of information rather than counsel their use as a matter of prescription cannot be considered accessories to subsequent violations of the law on their patients' own initiative. Nor is it clear just how many residents find the Connecticut legislation a barrier to the practice of birth control. As a matter of common knowledge the dominant pattern of contemporary American sexual mores does not change abruptly at the borders of the state of Connecticut. There is no indication that Connecticut enforces, or even could enforce, the ban on the use of contraceptives. Married couples can purchase contraceptives in or from neighboring states. In fact, Connecticut permits the prescription, sale, and use of contraceptives for prophylactic purposes. Thus the Court concluded that the plea of Dr. Buxton and his patients was in large measure symbolic.

Yet very often controversies over symbols are fought more bitterly than are controversies over realities. Despite almost yearly attempts in the last twenty years to induce the legislature to modify the ban, the practice of artifical birth control in Connecticut by married couples remains a criminal act. Those who believe the practice morally justified resent the criminal stigma attached to the practice by the Connecticut law even though actually unenforced. Frustrated by the legislature's repeated refusal to modify the law, they have turned to the courts in the hope of relief. The climax of the appeal to the courts was the decision of the Supreme Court.

For their part, the four dissenters—Justices Black, Douglas, Harlan, and Stewart—felt that the plight of Dr. Buxton and his patients was real enough to constitute a justiciable controversy. Justice Douglas argued that the Connecticut statute was effectively enforced to exclude the operation of birth-control clinics and that the issue of Dr. Buxton and his patients "would not be changed one iota had a dozen doctors representing a dozen birth-control clinics sued for remedial action."[15] Furthermore, the fact that married couples and the physicians advising them had not been prosecuted in the past gave no assurance for the future. Justice Harlan made the point that the Connecticut courts had heard the case and, thus, had acknowledged the existence of a genuine legal controversy. The appellants' professed fear of prosecution, he felt, must be taken as bona fide: "I think that it is unjustifiably stretching things to assume that appellants are not deterred by the threat of prosecution. . . ."[16] Nor did Justice Harlan think it a safe assumption that Connecticut would not prosecute known violators of the law. The state's attorney indicated in argument before the Court that he would prosecute whenever he had sufficient evidence. Thus Justice Harlan found it difficult to believe "that doctors generally—and not just those operating specialized clinics—would continue openly to disseminate advice about contraceptives . . . in reliance on the State's supposed unwillingness to prosecute. . . ."[17]

The majority looked beyond the formalities of the case to weigh the concrete situation in Connecticut, while the minority restricted their sights to the evidence presented to the Court in the judicial process and refused to assume the falsity of the appellants' professed fear of prosecution. But whatever the judgment on the genuineness of the controversy which Dr. Buxton and his patients urged the Court to review—and the dissenters make a strong argument for the justiciability of the appellants' suit— only Justices Douglas and Harlan went on to discuss the substantive constitutional issue raised by the case.

Justice Douglas held that the First Amendment afforded an absolute protection of Dr. Buxton's right to advise his patients on contraceptives. Yet surely the First Amendment does not give a doctor the right by reason of professional privilege to advise or counsel the commission of a crime. A doctor cannot advise or counsel his patients, for example, to the commission of a criminal abortion. The First Amendment protects the right of a doctor to impart information but not to incite or abet the criminal act itself. In this matter there is essentially no difference in the nature of the rights claimed by the doctor and his patients. The doctor's right to counsel contraceptives is clearly dependent on the patients' right to follow the counsel. Justice Douglas' contention that the First Amendment affords absolute protection to the speech of physicians has confused the right to speak with the abettance of a criminal act. It is a further question, of course, whether a state may constitutionally make the use of contraceptives by married couples a crime.

With respect to the married couples themselves, Justice Douglas argued that the state may not constitutionally prohibit their use of contraceptives. To do so would involve an intrusion by the state into the most intimate relationship of husband and wife, and would necessitate recourse to repugnant methods of enforcement. Justice Harlan developed the same points at greater length and with greater precision. His thoughtful analysis deserves a detailed consideration.

Although Justice Harlan reached the conclusion that the Connecticut statute was an "intolerable and unjustifiable invasion of privacy in the conduct of the intimate concerns of an individual's personal life," he made it clear that he found it "difficult and unnecessary at this juncture to accept appellants' other argument that the judgment of policy behind the statute, so applied, is so arbitrary and unreasonable as to render the enactment invalid for that reason alone."[18] Justice Harlan found difficulty in accepting the "other argument" because the state traditionally has concerned itself with the moral soundness of its people:

Yet, the very including of the category of morality among state concerns indicates that society is not limited in its objects only to the physical well-being of the community, but has traditionally concerned itself with the moral soundness of its people as well.[19]

Moreover:

It is in this area of sexual morality, which contains many prescriptions of consentual behavior having little or no direct impact on others, that the State of Connecticut has expressed its moral judgment that all use of contraceptives is wrong.[20]

The moral judgment which Connecticut expressed on the use of contraceptives, Justice Harlan observed, was no different qua moral judgment from that expressed on divorce, adultery, homosexuality, abortion, sterilization, or euthanasia. Hence Justice Harlan felt in no postion to say that the moral judgment of Connecticut was incorrect.

Justice Harlan, in effect, enunciated two important principles concerning the power of a state over public morals: (1) that a state may prohibit actions simply because they seriously and adversely affect community *morals,* independently of any physical injury to another or the danger of physical evil to society; and (2) that the Court cannot say that the moral judgment of a state is incorrect in areas of traditional concern with human behavior. Both of these principles are wise. The first reaffirms the classic understanding that public morals as such are part of the public concern, and the second restates the traditional concept that the primacy of judgment on the nature and extent of the protection of public morals resides with the legislature, not with the Court. The first expresses the moral component of the police powers of the state, and the second applies the doctrine of the separation of powers to the field of public morals.

But, Justice Harlan continued, not just the state's moral judgment on overt actions but also the state's *"choice of means* becomes relevent to any constitutional judgment on what is done."[21] What is involved here is that "the state is asserting the right to enforce its moral judgment by intruding upon the most intimate details of the marital relations with the full power of the criminal law."[22] Harlan recognized, however, that the objection raised here against the Connecticut statute appeared equally applicable to the crimes of adultery and homosexuality. The Justice suggested the distinction that the latter crimes were "sexual intimacies which the State forbids altogether, but the intimacy of husband and wife is necessarily an essential and accepted feature of the institution of marriage, an institution which the State . . . in every age . . . has fostered and protected."[23] Thus, according to Justice Harlan, it is one thing to forbid extramarital sexuality altogether, but it is another to regulate the details of marital intimacies which the state must and does recognize.

Justice Harlan was surely correct in his contention that any determination of the constitutionality of state action in the field of public morals must weigh not only the state's declaratory moral judgment but also its choice of legal means to give effect to the moral judgment. His contention that Connecticut chose constitutionally repugnant means is less evident. Any prohibition of sexual relations, whether adulterous, homosexual, or contraceptive, would appear to involve the same degree of intrusion into the intimate sphere of personal activity. It is difficult to see, at least on a logical basis, precisely what makes public intrusion into contraceptive relations between husband and wife more odious than intrusions into other sexual relations. No doubt public opinion is more favorable to birth control than to adultery or homosexuality, but this is not a satisfactory norm of judicial discernment of the constitutional issue. Nor is Justice Harlan's explanation entirely convincing that marital sexual intimacies are constitutionally protected because the state allows and fosters marriage, whereas extramarital sexual intimacies are not so protected because the state may prohibit these intimacies altogether. In fact, it may be argued that legislation which prohibits the use of contraceptives to married couples interferes less with the intimate details of personal relationships than the total prohibition of extramarital relationships. Justice Harlan appears to have confused the legislation which regulates personal relationships with the odious enforcement of such legislation. It is not the legislation which intrudes on the actual intimacy of personal relationships but rather the odious methods of enforcement. Justice Harlan should have concluded more properly that the latter in all cases are forbidden to the state.

There is another objection, more technical and procedural, to Justice Harlan's *ad horrendum* portrayal of the intrusion of the Connecticut legislation into the intimacies of married life. Granted that enforcement of the legislation would be a constitutionally prohibited means of giving effect to the state's moral judgment against the use of contraceptives, were the appellants in a position to raise the issue? Connecticut made no effort to intrude itself into the lives of Dr. Buxton's patients by an odious enforcement of the law. The state had indeed expressed its moral judgment on the use of contraceptives but had not enforced its judgment by the methods which Justice Harlan found repugnant. Here, perhaps, the view of the majority was relevant. The dissenters may have been correct in their contention that the appellants had a genuine controversy to submit to the Court's decision, but the dissenters had less reason to accept the appellants' *ad horrendum* picture of the methods of enforcement said to be inherent in the Connecticut statute when that state had never resorted to the repugnant methods either with respect to the appellants or anyone else. In the absence of *any* enforcement by the state the Court was in a poor position to say that a repugnant intrusion by the public authority was inherent in the statute. After all, if Connecticut does not employ odious methods of enforcement, the statute remains only a declaration of moral judgment, which Justice Harlan admitted to lie within the compass of legislative authority.

THE CONSTITUTIONAL QUESTION: ANALYSIS AND SUMMARY

There is no record of any opposition on the basis of the federal Constitution (1) to the legislation of the seventeen states which prohibit the sale or dispensing of contraceptives but provide an exemption for doctors, pharmacists, and special licensees; (2) to the legislation of the eight states which do not prohibit the sale or dispensing of contraceptives but which restrict or prohibit their advertisement; or (3) to the legislation of the three states which in form prohibit the sale, dispensing, or advertisement of contraceptives but which contradict the prohibitory language by other public enactments and practices. The reason for the lack of recorded opposition is clear enough. All of the cited legislation freely permits the operation of birth-control clinics by qualified personnel, the prescription of contraceptives by doctors, their sale by pharmacists, and their use by married couples. Hence there is little chance of any challenge to the legislation or of any success if the legislation were challenged.

Only the statutes of Massachusetts and Connecticut have been opposed on constitutional grounds. Both states prohibit the advertisement, prescription, sale, or dispensing of contraceptives, and Connecticut in addition prohibits the use of contraceptives. Opponents challenge the constitutionality of applying the legislation of the two states to married couples. In 1938 a physician appealed to the United States Supreme Court from a Massachusetts decision which rejected his claim to an exemption from the operation of the state statute in order to counsel married patients, but the Supreme Court dismissed the appeal in a *per curiam* opinion "for want of a substantial federal question."[24] In 1961 Dr. Buxton and his patients appealed to the Court from the Connecticut decision against the use of contraceptives by married couples or their prescription by doctors, but the Court by the bare margin of five to four found no real controversy for adjudication. The opinions expressed in the Poe case, however, gave some indication of what several members of the Court were thinking on the substantive constitutional issues raised by Dr. Buxton and his patients.

The majority's views are difficult to discern in detail. This is understandable since the majority found no real controversy properly before the Court for adjudication. But even a casual reading of the Frankfurter opinion reveals that the majority bloc was no more kindly disposed than the dissenters toward the Connecticut statute. Had the state enforced the statute, the majority justices gave every indication that they would have joined the minority and struck the statute down. While unfavorably disposed toward state intrusion on marital intimacy or the doctor-patient relationship, the majority justices did not reveal their state of mind on the right of married couples to purchase, or of pharmacists to sell, contraceptives. One may argue that the latter rights are implicit in the asserted right of married couples to use contraceptives. But one may also argue that the prohibition of the purchase and sale of contraceptives does not involve that intrusion by the state into the intimate relations of husband and wife or of doctor and patient which seemed to constitute the principal objection to the Connecticut statute.

Justice Douglas' views are more evident. He acknowledged the constitutional right of doctors to give any counsel to their clients which they considered to be medically indicated, and to this right corresponded the constitutional right of married couples to use contraceptives when prescribed. Justice Douglas did not directly indicate what he thought about the right to purchase or sell contraceptives, but it is likely that he would consider these rights to be ancillary to the right of doctors to prescribe, and of married couples to use, contraceptives. Justice Harlan acknowledged that married couples had a constitutional right to use contraceptives, or at least that the state had no right to intrude on marital intimacy. The Justice is much less specific about the right of married couples to purchase, or of pharmacists to sell, contraceptives. The close logic of Justice Harlan's opinion need not lead him to assert the latter as constitutional rights, since the prohibition of the purchase and sale of contraceptives does not involve the odious intrusion which was the heart of his objection to the Connecticut statute.

The right to operate birth-control clinics, which Justice Brennan called the "true controversy" in the Poe case, constitutes a further constitutional question. Only Justice Douglas explicitly equated the right of many doctors to operate a birth-control clinic with the right of individual doctors to prescribe contraceptives for married couples. But to operate a birth-control clinic would seem a far more public affair than the individual prescription of contraceptives. An individual physician privately counsels contraception to those who seek his counsel, but a birth-control clinic solicits patients for the purpose of counseling contraceptives and thus actively promotes birth control by means of the public forum. Whether or not Justice Douglas' view is shared by a majority of the justices may be decided in the near future, for Dr. Buxton initiated a new test of the Connecticut statute by opening a birth-control clinic in New Haven on November 1, 1961, which the state forced to close ten days later.[25]

This entire constitutional question shows how slippery is the slope on which judges must determine the "reasonableness" of state restrictions, especially in matter of public morality. If and when Connecticut employed odious methods to enforce its legislation against the use of contraceptives by married couples or their prescription by doctors, then the Court could declare the legislation a violation of due process of law. On the other hand, the legislative prohibition of the purchase or sale of contraceptives does not involve the objectionable intrusion of the state into personal relationships which is inherent in the enforcement of the peculiar feature of the Connecticut law. Nor does the operation of birth-control clinics seem equivalent to the private prescription and use of contraceptives. Here the Court should defer broadly to the judgment of the legislature.

THE QUESTION OF POLICY

Whatever the resolution of the constitutional question, there remains the question of prudence. This is the question which

Catholics, who comprise a majority or near-majority of the voters of Massachusetts and Connecticut, must ask themselves with exacting scrutiny. The Catholic tradition of jurisprudence has always acknowledged the impossibility of comprehensive public enforcement of the natural law. The virtue of prudence, we suggest, requires as a better policy that Catholics in this country, particularly the Catholics of Massachusetts and Connecticut, support the legal right of married couples to the prescription, sale, and use of contraceptives. Catholics should restrict their legislative goals to those which command the general approval of the community, such as the prohibition of the sale of contraceptives from slot machines or to unmarried minors. Catholics might also weigh the possibility of legislation which would prohibit the sale of contraceptives without a doctor's prescription as a means to prevent their accessibility to the unmarried. But Catholics would violate the virtue of prudence if they sought to obtain or to maintain the prohibition of the sale of contraceptives to, or their use by, married couples.

The first reason for these conclusions is the impossibility of effective enforcement. A law must be capable of accomplishing what it is designed to accomplish. But no state can enforce the prohibition of the use of contraceptives by married couples, not at least without an odious police intrusion into the intimate lives of ordinary citizens. And if such a statute is not enforced, then the widespread disobedience of the particular law breeds contempt for all law. Nor, in the current context, is the prohibition of contraceptive sales to married couples in Massachusetts and Connecticut much better able to accomplish its purpose since contraceptives are easily accessible in neighboring states or even within those states as prophylactics.

A more fundamental objection to the application of contraceptive legislation to married couples stems from the necessity of consensus in law, especially the law of a pluralist society. Legislation, especially in the area of public morals, should enjoy the general approval of the community. But it is quite obvious that the morality of artificial birth control is a matter on which the community is widely and deeply divided. Moreover, the pluralistic character of the American polity makes some accommodation among citizens of different ethical convictions a necessary part of political wisdom. So many conscientious non-Catholics believe the practice of artificial birth control morally licit that the present legislation in Massachusetts and Connecticut, without any compensating hope of enforcement, unjustifiably increases hostility among citizens of different religious beliefs and moral codes.

We conclude, therefore, that the virtue of prudence in the American context requires as a better policy that Catholics support the legal right of married couples to the prescription, sale, and use of contraceptives. Catholic citizens of Massachusetts and Connecticut could and should make a genuine contribution to good politics and good law by supporting reasonable modifications of the contraceptive legislation of their states. Of course, Catholics should also make clear that they advocate such action on strictly political and legal grounds which in no way affect their theological and moral opposition to the practice of artificial birth control.

PUBLIC HOSPITALS AND BIRTH CONTROL

In July, 1958, an incident in New York City focused national attention on the propriety of contraceptive advice in tax-supported hospitals. The New York City hospitals adhered at the time to the policy that physicians on hospital duty should not give advice on contraceptives. A non-Catholic physician wished to fit a non-Catholic patient with a contraceptive device, but the Commissioner of Hospitals refused to allow him to do so. Non-Catholic spokesmen generally argued in favor of the physician and his patient, while Catholic authorities spoke in favor of the Commissioner. The non-Catholics claimed that a physician should not be prevented from prescribing a method which both he and his patient judge morally licit. Catholics, on the other hand, contended that tax-supported institutions should not be employed to further immoral practices.

After several months of public controversy the Hospital Board voted in September to reverse the Commissioner's ban and to permit physicians in the municipal hospitals to provide contraceptive medical advice and devices for their female patients.[26] The Board laid down the following restrictive conditions, however: (1) The health of the patient, in the opinion of at least two physicians of the medical staff, must be in danger from a future pregnancy; (2) the patient must wish to avail herself of the contraceptive advice and device; (3) if possible, the consent of the husband should be obtained; (4) a conference of the patient with her spiritual adviser was recommended; and (5) physicians, nurses, or hospital employees with moral objections were free not to participate in the program.

The problem of public policy faced by New York City in 1958 is by no means unique. In many cities in the North, public hospitals forbid physicians from offering any contraceptive advice or devices to willing patients. The resolution of this problem achieved by New York City is a compromise which aimed at the neutrality of the public hospitals in the matter of birth control. On the one hand, general contraceptive advice was left to voluntary agencies, and, on the other, non-Catholics have access to contraceptive medicine where pregnancy would be a danger to life or health.

The compromise, however, may not be really necessary: voluntary agencies or private birth-control clinics can adequately provide for patients in danger from a future pregnancy who wish contraceptive advice. More important, the compromise does not truly assure the neutrality of the public hospitals: institutions supported by the public are committed to provide both contraceptive advice and devices. It is one thing for the state not to prohibit contraception to married couples but another for the state to promote the practice through prescription and supply at public expense. Indeed, under the new New York City policy, hospital physicians who favor artificial birth control may persuade indifferent patients to the practice. Catholics may wonder at the logic by which non-Catholics object to the prohibition of contraception by the public authority on the grounds of religious pluralism but demand the prescription and supply of contraceptives by public institutions without regard for the moral susceptibilities of Catholics. On the practical side of the problem, however, we should note that the New York City compromise does not affect too large a number of patients and certainly will not make birth-control clinics of the public hospitals. The compromise is, in fact, closely restricted to those cases where the willing patient would be in danger of life or health from a future pregnancy.

POPULATION CONTROL: FACTS AND ARGUMENTS

The regulation or prohibition of artificial birth control within the nation is no longer a pressing problem of public policy. The problem of policy which today rather concerns the public is whether the United States and the United Nations should sponsor or support artificial birth control outside the nation in an effort to control the "population explosion." Any intelligent discussion of the proper public policy toward population control must begin by understanding and appreciating, at least in a general way, the best scientific estimates of the magnitude and consequences of the present and prospective growth in world population.

In 1950 the estimated world population was two and a half billion. This was twice the estimated world population of 1850 and four times that of 1650. Thus the world population has successively doubled since 1650 in one-half the time. It is not the past, however, but the future which causes concern to the experts, since the world population is expected to double again before the turn of the century.[27] The annual rate of population increase in the world is over three times that of 1650, fifteen to thirty times that of the preceding Christian era and is still going higher. Moreover, the fastest rates of population growth exist in the countries of Asia, Africa, and Latin America, where resources are least developed to provide for the enormous increases in population. If the world fertility rate simply maintains the current high level and if the world mortality rate simply remains at the present low level (it is likely, barring a nuclear holocaust, to decline still further), the net world rate of population growth will stay at the present level, and in one hundred years the world population will total fifteen billion people. Since the primary cause of the increased rate of population growth over the last several centuries has been the decline in the mortality rate, especially in the infant mortality rate, the likely prospect of a further decline in the mortality rate will push the population growth rate still higher if the fertility rate remains the same.

The world "population explosion" is a social problem, however, only insofar as the growth in population exceeds the development of the resources required to support it. How adequate is the balance of world resources to world population? Catholic and non-Catholic authorities have tended, for the most part, to disagree. Catholic demographers point out the following optimistic facts: that the world food production since the end of World War II has increased faster than the world population; that the total land under cultivation can be increased at least 25 per cent and perhaps more; that the application of modern agricultural technology to underdeveloped nations can vastly multiply the food production per unit area; that new technological breakthroughs, such as the industrial conversion of sea water to fresh water, will revolutionize the potentialities of world food production; that the cooperation and aid of developed to underdeveloped nations can resolve present and future imbalances between resources and population; and that freer immigration policies on the part of nations with resources and room can ease local problems of overpopulation in underdeveloped and crowded nations.

Non-Catholic demographers, on the other hand, point out the following pessimistic facts: that the per capita food consumption in underdeveloped countries is less than before World War II; that the food consumption of some one-half to two-thirds of the world's population is on a subsistence or below-subsistence level; that underdeveloped peoples aspire to more than mere subsistence; that the conflict between the aspirations and the achievements of underdeveloped nations will lead to instability, even to war or to communism; that the magnitude of the population growth exceeds any real prospects for the commensurate development of resources in the emerging nations; and that the wealthy nations are not likely to provide the long-term, massive help which is required to develop the resources of the poorer nations.

The Catholic contribution to the argument is to dispel the unrealistic predictions of disaster which can easily characterize overenthusiastic descriptions of the population problem. But the non-Catholic may legitimately ask why a problem as serious as that of population growth should not be attacked both from the aspect of increased resources *and* from the aspect of population control, for even if all the Catholic claims for the potentialities of the world resources were realized, the result would be only to maintain a level of subsistence for the mass of mankind which can scarcely be called a truly human existence. In all honesty, Catholics must admit that, if artificial birth control were morally licit and practically feasible, they would favor public sponsorship and support of such a program in underdeveloped countries. It must not be forgotten, therefore, that the basic objection of Catholics to the practice of artificial birth control and to a policy of public sponsorship or support for the practice is moral and not economic.

POPULATION CONTROL: ARTIFICIAL BIRTH CONTROL AND PUBLIC POLICY

Non-Catholic authorities on the population problem generally favor United States and United Nations sponsorship and support of a program of artificial birth control for Asia, Africa, and Latin America. Such an opinion involves a double assumption: (1) that artificial birth control is a necessary and efficient means of population control, and (2) that United States and the United Nations support is a necessary and desirable means of promoting artificial birth control. Whether artificial birth control is a necessary or efficient means of population control—and we shall consider the merits of this assertion in the section immediately following—Catholics can never approve the direct use of any public funds to promote or support the practice of artificial birth control. Catholics cannot endorse public support of a practice which they regard as immoral, and this attitude should not cause non-Catholics the least surprise. Yet, in the furor which ensued over the Draper report, some non-Catholic spokesmen indicated not only surprise but even indignation at the fidelity of Catholics to conscience.

On July 23, 1959, the committee appointed by President Eisenhower to study the foreign-aid program submitted its third interim report.[28] The committee, under the chairmanship of William Draper, Jr., recommended cooperation with underdeveloped countries "in the formulation of . . . plans designed to deal with the problem of population growth." As explained by Mr. Draper in a letter to *America*, the report did not mean that the committee was "advocating any birth control program" but rather that the committee was calling attention to the population problem.[29] Catholics and non-Catholics alike, unfortunately, did not take so detached a view of the Draper report. On November 25, 1959, the Catholic bishops of the United States announced that they would oppose any attempt to use foreign-aid funds to promote programs of artificial birth control.[30] The "logical answer," according to the bishops, was to increase the food supply, which is "almost unlimited in potential." James A. Pike, Protestant Episcopal Bishop of California, condemned the bishops' statement and asked whether the statement would be binding on a Catholic President.[31] The fat was now in the fire, and all the major candidates for president as well as President Eisenhower felt obliged to comment. President Eisenhower unequivocally opposed the incorporation of any birth-control design into the foreign-aid program, and the then Senator Kennedy, at whom Bishop Pike's query was obviously aimed, replied obliquely that the United States should not impose birth control on other nations.[32] But other aspirants indicated their endorsement of some form of public support for artificial birth control through the foreign-aid program.[33]

Both the Catholic bishops and President Eisenhower were correct in their unequivocal opposition to any use of foreign-aid funds for programs of artificial birth control. In a pluralistic society public funds should not be employed to sponsor or support programs which are morally unacceptable to one religious group if this is at all compatible with the goals of organized society. As Catholics would display a gross lack of political wisdom if they were to maintain or press for legislation prohibitive of the practice of artificial birth control at home, so non-Catholics would display an equal lack of political wisdom if they were to press for the implementation of artificial birth control in foreign lands through the use of federal funds.[34] In short, the government should adhere to a strict neutrality on the issue of birth control. Besides disturbing the harmony of a pluralistic body politic, an attempt to gain the use of public funds for artificial birth control would risk the demise of the entire foreign-aid program. Disaffected Catholics, unwisely but no less effectively, might join the ranks of the opposition to the foreign-assistance program. This result would be unfortunate for the free world and to the sole advantage of the Communists.

A similar controversy developed over the role of the United Nations with respect to population control. At the 1954 World Population Conference the nations agreed to a policy of neutrality on the subject of artificial birth control out of respect for differing religious and ethical values. As in the case of American foreign aid, and perhaps more so due to the confederate nature of the United Nations, the condition of pluralism requires a policy acceptable to the creeds of all the nations represented. Some non-Catholics have complained of this restriction, but it is difficult to see how else Catholics could be expected to participate at all in the efforts of the international organization to deal with the population program. If the world organization were committed to a method of population control repugnant to Catholics, the latter could hardly be expected to cooperate with the program.

Voluntary, private non-Catholic organizations, however, are free to continue to finance research and to support programs of artificial birth control in those underdeveloped countries willing to accept them. Whether even the ample resources of private funds in the United States could support much more than research and small-scale experiments is, of course, doubtful.

POPULATION CONTROL: PERIODIC CONTINENCE AND PUBLIC POLICY

United States and United Nations support for artificial birth control is morally unacceptable to Catholics and therefore politically unwise. This does not mean, however, that national and international agencies are entirely powerless with respect to population control. These agencies may promote and support public programs of population control based on periodic continence, which is the only method morally acceptable both to Catholics and non-Catholics. Whether such programs are desirable will depend, of course, on how easily the method could be introduced into underdeveloped areas, on how economical the cost of public promotion would be, and on how effective the method would prove when introduced.

The dimensions of the population problem do not permit complacency with the prospects for a vast development of food production or other world resources. To mobilize the productive resources of the world, if successful, may do little more than win a race for survival rather than raise the level of most men's existence to a truly human level. At least on the basis of our present knowledge, the population problem is so pressing that no man or society can reasonably be satisfied solely with efforts to increase food production and develop the world's other resources if an acceptable and effective method of population control is available. Catholics and non-Catholics, therefore, should cooperate to see that the public authorities undertake to promote periodic continence if that method offers any hope as an effective population control.

Periodic continence is morally acceptable both to Catholics and non-Catholics at least where there exists sufficient reason to justify its use. The magnitude of the world-wide and regional population problem, as described by competent demographers, presents more than a sufficient reason for married couples to practice periodic continence in the countries affected. In fact, the gravity of the problem may require couples to limit births for the physical, intellectual, and moral good of their own children as well as for the good of the whole community. Catholics may have to admit a serious failure in this matter; opposition to the practice of artificial birth control may have induced a blindness to the positive respect which married couples owe to their own children and to the whole community in areas severely threatened by the consequences of overpopulation.

Periodic continence is the only method of population control which the public agencies of a pluralistic national or international society can promote if they respect sound political principles. Because periodic continence is the only method morally acceptable both to Catholics and non-Catholics, it is the only politically acceptable method which the United States foreign-aid program and the United Nations can directly sponsor or support. Moreover, periodic continence is also the only method of population control politically acceptable to many recipient nations, particularly in Latin America.

But is periodic continence a method of population control effective enough to justify the expenditure of public funds and public effort?[35] There are two well-known difficulties with the successful application of the method: the complicated nature of computing the infertile period and the necessity of restraint by the married couple during the fertile period. The chief advantages of the method are economy and universal moral acceptability. Even if the rhythm method were adopted by only 20 per cent of the married population of underdeveloped countries, this would make a significant contribution to restricting population growth. Moreover, the development of a pill which would cheaply and effectively regularize an abnormal menstrual cycle in a morally acceptable way would make the method of periodic continence easier to practice and, consequently, to promote. The cooperation of the Church in Latin America with the public authorities in the sponsorship of such a program might help to secure wider adoption of periodic continence there. In connection with the question of the efficiency of periodic continence we should also recall that the claims made for artificial birth control are usually exaggerated and frequently unchallenged. Artificial birth control, by the present standards of underdeveloped nations, is quite expensive, difficult in many places to teach, and never completely effective.

The plain truth is that *no* program of population control is a panacea. All forms of birth limitation depend on the will of married couples to limit the number of their children. In non-Western countries the existing system of values does not encourage or, in some instances, even tolerate such an attitude. Obviously, re-education on a vast scale is necessary before any method of population control would be successful in these countries, and the time lag before the effects of the educational effort were realized would be considerable. Moreover, both periodic continence and artificial birth control have their own peculiar liabilities. Catholics and non-Catholics alike had best recognize that there is no simple, quick, and inexpensive solution to the problem of population expansion. They had best recognize also the urgency of the problem. Citizens and governments must work with all deliberate speed and dedication, therefore, to the development of world resources and to the control of world population through means which are morally acceptable to all and hold some promise of success.

Catholics in developed and underdeveloped nations have failed, for the most part, to sense the urgency of the population problem. They have not grasped the necessity for the rapid expansion of the world's productive resources and for the control of the world's population growth. If non-Catholics have demonstrated more recognition of the urgency of the population problem, they have dissipated much of their effort in attempts to gain public sponsorship and support for programs of artificial birth control which are morally unacceptable to Catholics and, therefore, politically unwise for that reason alone. Non-Catholics must redirect their efforts toward public programs to expand world resources and to control population growth through methods morally acceptable to all. The double failure of Catholics and non-Catholics need not endure if men of intelligence and good will cooperate to provide the necessary leadership and response.

NOTES

1. 18 U.S.C.A. 1461.

2. 18 U.S.C.A. 1462.

3. *Ibid.* and 19 U.S.C.A. 1305.

4. *U.S.* v. *One Book Entitled "Contraception,"* 51 F. 2d 525 (1931).

5. *Davis* v. *U.S.*, 62 F. 2d 473 (1933) and *U.S.* v. *One Package,* 86 F. 2d 737 (1936).

6. *U.S.* v. *One Package,* p. 739.

7. See St. John-Stevas, *Life, Death and the Law,* p. 63.

8. *Poe* et al. v. *Ullman*, 367 U.S. 497 (1961).

9. *Buxton* et al. v. *Ullman*, 147 Conn. 48 (1959).

10. *Buxton* et al. v. *Ullman*, 362 U.S. 987 (1960).

11. Conn. Gen. Stat. §53-32 and 54-196 (1958).

12. *Poe* et al. v. *Ullman*, 367 U.S. 497, 507 (1961).

13. *Ibid.*, p. 508.

14. *Ibid.*, p. 509.

15. *Ibid.*, p. 513.

16. *Ibid.*, p. 529.

17. *Ibid.*, p. 533.

18. *Ibid.*, p. 539.

19. *Ibid.*, pp. 545–546.

20. *Ibid.*, p. 546.

21. *Ibid.*, p. 547.

22. *Ibid.*, p. 548.

23. *Ibid.*, p. 553.

24. *Gardner* v. *Mass.*, 305 U.S. 559 (1938).

25. For an account of the opening and closing of the birth control clinic, see *The New York Times*, November 3, 1961, p. 37, and November 11, 1961, p. 25.

26. For an account of the policy reversal of the New York City Board see *The New York Times*, September 18, 1958, p. 1

27. For population and resources estimates see *World Population and Resources: A Report* (London: Political and Economic Planning, 1955); *The Determinants and Consequences of Population Trends* (New York: U. N. Publications, St/SOA/Series A, No. 17, 1954); *The Future Growth of World Population* (New York: U. N. Publications, St/SOA/Series A, No. 28, 1958).

28. *The New York Times*, July 24, 1959, p. 1.

29. Cited in an editorial comment, *America*, August 8, 1959, p. 583.

30. *The New York Times*, November 26, 1959, pp. 1, 43.

31. *Ibid.*, p. 1.

32. For President Eisenhower's statement see *The New York Times*, December 3, 1959, p. 1; for the then Senator Kennedy's statement see *The New York Times*, November 28, 1959, p. 12.

33. For Governor Rockefeller's position see *The New York Times*, November 30, 1959, p. 17; for the positions of Senator Humphrey, Senator Symington, and former Governor Stevenson see *The New York Times*, November 29, 1959, p. 43.

34. If Congress did authorize foreign aid funds for the implementation of artificial birth control programs in underdeveloped nations, a prominent Catholic moralist has concluded that a Catholic president could licitly permit the congressional action to become law without his signature and administer the program when enacted. This analysis is based largely on the nature of the American constitutional system of separation of powers which invests the legislature rather than the executive with the responsibility of making laws. Fr. John R. Connery, S.J., "May a Catholic President Sign . . ."? *America*, December 12, 1959, pp. 353–354.

Catholic moral principles would also permit Congress to appropriate funds whose specific use foreign countries could determine. The difficulty with such an arrangement would not be moral, since Congress would not directly sponsor or support any program of artificial birth control to which the foreign government might commit the funds. The real difficulty with such an arrangement would be economic, since the United States would have no way of ensuring the sound use of the funds appropriated.

35. Estimates differ radically on the percentage of married couples that can learn and will use periodic continence. Several experiments in India led to reported success rates ranging from 5 to 65 per cent. *World Population and Resources,* p. 219, and *The New York Times,* October 20, 1951, p. 17. If the average success rate were to run over 20 per cent, the results would be significant.

10

Catholics
and
Censorship

Controls on the communications media constitute a unique area in the regulation of public morals. Here Catholic principles and Catholic power are particularly suspect to the liberal mind, since the liberal recognizes that no abuse of public or private power would more threaten the structure of the democratic process than restrictions on free speech. Other regulations of public morals may be repugnant to a minority, but as long as the channels of communication remain open, these regulations can be changed. The chief objection to censorship is that it threatens to close the channels of communication themselves and thus to amputate the most vital organ of the democratic process. What worries the liberal is the apparent willingness of the Catholic to support, almost as a matter of principle and often without critical judgment, efforts at public and private censorship. It is significant that a current series of books which seeks to explain "Catholic viewpoints" has included one on censorship.[1] This bears witness to the fact that reflective Catholics recognize the need to articulate principles which not only will provide security for the common moral order but which also will be consistent with democratic practice, principles which not only will be theologically and philosophically acceptable to the Catholic but which also will accord with the dictates of political realism in a pluralistic society.

The problem of censorship is more comprehensive than merely what restrictions the public authority may impose on the communications media. The family and the church also act as censors for their members; they too share within their societal structures and for the sake of their own proper goals the problem of balancing liberty and restraint. But what is more politically significant is the fact that private groups within the community may attempt to persuade others to accept their moral judgment on books, plays, movies, or television. As long as this persuasion is limited to the rational expression of their views no political problem, to be sure, arises. The use of economic pressure to force those in control of the communications media to accept the moral judgment of a particular group, however, does create questions concerning the sound functioning of a pluralistic polity. There are therefore two related though distinct aspects of the censorship problem which political analysts must evaluate. The first is to what extent, if any, the public authorities under a democratic constitution may or should censor the communications media. The second is to what extent, if any, private groups within a pluralistic society may or should attempt to coerce the communications media to accept their particular moral judgments. We shall take up each aspect of the problem in turn.

GOVERNMENT CENSORSHIP OF THE COMMUNICATIONS MEDIA

The classical liberal position has been to emphasize the chasm between thought and action. Jimmy Walker's celebrated remark that no woman was ever raped by a book epitomizes the attitude of the liberal mind toward censorship as a projected protection of public morality. Action is external and accessible to responsible public control, while thought belongs to the internal and utterly inviolable sanctuary of the individual conscience. The former is subject to the legitimately exercised police power of the state, but the latter is not. The liberal points to the inherent dangers basic to any censorship: the threat of authoritarianism, the stifling of literary, scientific, or artistic productivity, and the impossibility of setting an acceptable standard in a pluralistic society. These dangers are sufficient for the liberal to condemn without reservation the use of censorship as an instrument of public policy.

The classical conservative position, on the other hand, has been to stress the bridge between thought and action. The conservative might take as his own the Aristotelian maxim that no action is willed unless it is first known. Thought is certainly internal and, as such, inviolable, but thought, when expressed and communicated, is as external and accessible to public control as any other type of activity. The conservative does not deny, but he tends to minimize the dangers of censorship. He insists that a reasonable and controlled censorship is both necessary and feasible. Absolute freedom to propagate ideas can undermine society quite as effectively as other activities; as a consequence, society has the right and even the duty to defend itself from corruptive influences. On balance the dangers from corruption in the absence of public censorship outweigh the well-publicized dangers attributed to restraints on free communication.

Both the liberal and the conservative score some solid points in their opposing contentions. The conservative has a much surer instinct for the integral workings both of the human personality and of human society. The conservative has a more realistic recognition of how closely thought and action are interrelated, a more realistic appraisal of how much the wide dissemination of ideas can affect the social fabric, a more realistic sensitivity to the existence and importance of the common moral good, and a more realistic fear of the potency of morally corruptive influences. In short, the conservative has a better grasp of the substantive motives for censorship. But the liberal has a much deeper insight into political processes and literary complexities. The liberal is more realistic in his skepticism of the effectiveness of censorship, in his recognition of the role of free communication in the democratic process, in his fear of the political dangers latent in censorship, in his sympathy for emerging literary, scientific, artistic, or cultural values, and in his sensitivity to the pluralistic value structure of American democracy. In short, the liberal has a better grasp of the procedural implications of censorship.

How are we to evaluate the merits of the case for and against government censorship? How are we to reconcile the conflicting arguments? Let us begin with the observation against the doctrinaire members of both camps that any decision with respect to the role of government censorship is political in nature, that any decision will necessarily have disadvantages, and that any decision will necessarily involve risks. The United States Supreme Court in recent years has given a fairly sharp outline to the course of action which both the federal and state governments must follow in the matter of censorship. Perhaps it could have reached other results, and certainly the results which the Court has reached do pose definite risks. But the Court has achieved a highly reasonable synthesis and in some cases the only reasonable solution. The Court has tended in general to adopt the liberal analysis, but on pragmatic rather than on doctrinaire grounds. What has proved most telling with the Supreme Court has been the close affinity of free communication with the democratic process and literary expression. Only in the area of obscenity has the Court permitted any sizable opening in the constitutional wall against government censorship.

GOVERNMENT CENSORSHIP OF "IDEAS"

Three important cases of the last fifteen years offer a reliable index of the Court's rather broad agreement, despite dissent on particular applications, concerning the role of the government in the censorship of "ideas" to safeguard public morality.[2] In *Burstyn* v. *Wilson* the Court unanimously struck down a New

York statute which banned "sacrilegious" motion pictures. The occasion for the decision was the film *The Miracle*, for which Joseph Burstyn, Inc., was the American distributor. The heroine of the story was a simple-minded woman named Mary who delusively took a bearded stranger for St. Joseph and was seduced by him. She became pregnant, was mocked by the townspeople, bore her child, and eventually regained sanity. Cardinal Spellman and others protested that *The Miracle* made a mockery of Christian belief and the sacred relationship of Jesus, Mary, and Joseph. After a review the New York Board of Regents judged that the film was "sacrilegious" and revoked its license. The highest court in New York, the Court of Appeals, upheld the Board's action and found nothing repugnant about the statutory provision against "sacrilegious" motion pictures: "It is simply this: that no religion, as that word is understood by the ordinary, reasonable person, shall be treated with contempt, mockery, scorn, and ridicule."[3]

The defendants appealed to the United States Supreme Court, which, speaking through Justice Clark on May 26, 1952, found the proscription of "sacrilegious" films unconstitutional:

. . . the state has no legitimate interest in protecting any or all religions from views distasteful to them. . . . It is not the business of government in our nation to suppress real or imagined attacks upon a particular religious doctrine whether they appear in publications, speeches, or motion pictures.[4]

Justice Clark was careful to make clear, however, that it did "not follow that the Constitution requires absolute freedom to exhibit every motion picture of every kind at all times and all places. . . ."[5] Justices Frankfurter, Jackson, and Burton concurred on the ground that the term "sacrilegious" was too vague. Justice Reed concurred because the particular film in question did not seem to him "to be of a character that the First Amendment permits a state to exclude from public view."[6]

The substantive merits of the Burstyn decision are unassailable. In a pluralistic society the government cannot protect any religion from criticism or caricature. That such criticism or caricature may be distasteful or blasphemous to the orthodox is not

enough to justify governmental supervision and suppression. The
mere fact that a communication is distasteful is not constitutionally sufficient by itself to justify restrictions on the freedom
of speech. The irreligious and the unorthodox in our political
system have the right to express their views as trenchantly as
they choose—short of individual or, perhaps, group libel. The
believer may find the result quite distasteful, but the believer
must recall the strictly political implications of democratic government.

Four years before the Burstyn decision the Supreme Court
passed on another and more difficult subject area of governmental censorship: the lurid portrayal of crime and violence.
Murray Winters, a New York bookseller, was convicted in 1941
of selling magazines in violation of the state law. The magazine
was *Headquarters Detective,* and the crime alleged was the possession with intent to sell of magazines "principally made up of
criminal news, police reports or accounts of criminal deeds, or
pictures, or stories of deeds of bloodshed, lust or crime." The
New York Court of Appeals interpreted the statute to prohibit
the publication of criminal deeds of bloodshed and lust "so
massed as to become vehicles for inciting violent and depraved
crimes against the person . . ." and upheld Winters' conviction.[7]
Winters then appealed to the United States Supreme Court.

Justice Reed, speaking for a six-man majority, found the New
York law, even when considered with the gloss put on the literal
meaning by the Court of Appeals, "too uncertain and indefinite"
in the specification of what publications were prohibited:

Even though all detective tales and treatises on criminology are not
forbidden, and though publications made up of criminal deeds not
characterized by bloodshed or lust are omitted from the interpretation
of the Court of Appeals, we think fair use of collections of pictures
and stories would be interdicted because of the utter impossibility of
the actor or trier to know where this new standard of guilt would
draw the line between the allowable and the forbidden publications.[8]

To propose to punish the portrayal of deeds of bloodshed or lust
when so "massed" as to incite to crime, the Court judged too
vague to be constitutionally permissible. "Though we see noth-

ing of any possible value to society in these magazines," Justice Reed observed, "they are as much entitled to the protection of free speech as the best of literature."[9] Yet, like Justice Clark in the Burstyn case, Justice Reed here was careful to make clear that the requirement of specificity did not prevent the states and Congress "from carrying out their duty of eliminating evils to which, in their judgment, such publications give rise."[10]

Justice Frankfurter, joined by Justices Jackson and Burton, vigorously dissented. The New York law, in his view, represented an attempt by the legislature to solve "the problem of crime and, more particularly, of its prevention."[11] The result of the majority's decision, Justice Frankfurter continued, is "that it gives publications which have 'nothing of any possible value to society' constitutional protection but denies to the state the power to prevent the gross evils to which, in their rational judgment, such publications give rise."[12] New York had not sought to restrict publications merely because they are devoted to, or are principally made up of, criminal news or police reports. Rather, the proscribed publications must so mass pictures and stories of criminal deeds of bloodshed or lust as to incite readers to similar deeds. In the dissenters' view, New York was entitled to believe that such publications as *Headquarters Detective* could become vehicles for inciting violent and depraved crimes. Justice Frankfurter then met head on the majority's charge that the law was too indefinite:

Suppose then that the New York legislature now wishes to meet the objection of the Court. What standard of definiteness does the Court furnish the New York legislature in finding indefiniteness in the present law? . . . What is there in the condemned law which leaves men in the dark as to what is meant by publications that exploit "criminal deeds of bloodshed or lust," thereby "inciting violent and depraved crimes"?[13]

"Insofar as there is uncertainty," Justice Frankfurter concluded, "the uncertainty derives not from the terms of condemnation, but from the application of a standard of conduct to the varying circumstances of different cases."[14]

It would be difficult to underestimate the practical effects which the Winters decision has had on the whole area of publications exploiting crime and violence. The New York legislature made two subsequent efforts in 1949 and in 1952 to rectify the law, but both were vetoed by Governor Dewey because they failed to cure the basic defect of the original statutory language. The Winters decision has ended, for all practical purposes, efforts by New York in this area of public censorship, and there is no indication that other localities are actively enforcing similar regulations. Moreover, the influence of the so-called "uncomic non-books" which luridly exploit crime and violence is matched today by some recent developments in television, whose potential as a communication medium was not envisioned at the time of the Winters decision. The Federal Communications Commission, like New York, would find the Winters ruling a barrier to any attempt at direct government regulation of the current television fare.

The criticisms of the minority speaking through Justice Frankfurter also have strength beyond a consideration of practical effect. The New York statute appeared to be as definite and specific as is consistent with regulation in the area desired. The majority in no way indicated what New York could or should do to remedy the defective statute. Yet, as a matter of constitutional principle, the Winters majority did not rule out censorship under a certain and definite standard of publications exploiting criminal deeds of bloodshed or lust where these might reasonably be construed as incitements to crimes against the person. The Winters majority simply insisted on the principle that a criminal statute in this area must be certain and definite enough to protect legitimate publications of criminal news or police reports, whether literarily worthwhile or not. The formula found constitutionally acceptable nine years later in the Roth-Alberts cases as a test for the constitutionally permissible censorship of obscenity may prove helpful here, *mutatis mutandis*. In fact, the majority in the Roth-Alberts cases explicitly rejected the application of the Winters ruling to the regulation of obscene publications.[15] Closely following the Roth-Alberts formula for obscenity, therefore, we suggest this test: whether to the average person, applying contemporary community standards, the dominant theme of the material portraying criminal deeds of bloodshed and lust when taken as a whole incites to the commission of crimes against the person. This test, we submit, is at least as certain and definite as the approved test for obscenity and can equally meet constitutional objections on that score.

The majority and minority in the Winters case disagreed not on any constitutional principle but rather on the application of principle to the particular statute at hand. The New York statute, as interpreted by the Court of Appeals, sought to proscribe not the abstract advocacy of an "idea" but the concrete incitement to crime. The New York specification that the "idea" must incite to criminal action is consistent with the accepted permissibility of restricting free speech where there is a "clear and present danger" of substantive evil. Both the majority and the minority indicated no unwillingness to permit a properly framed restriction of this type. But a state should not expect to accomplish too much through action against publications of criminal deeds of bloodshed or lust which incite to the commission of crimes against the person. It is not easy to demonstrate that a publication does in fact incite readers to the commission of crimes against the person, and any doubt would have to be resolved in favor of the defendant publisher, distributor, or seller.

What about the regulation of "immoral ideas" themselves, irrespective of any immediate prospect of criminal action? On June 29, 1959, the Supreme Court made known its views on this question.[16] The New York Board of Regents had banned *Lady Chatterley's Lover*, a motion picture based on the D. H. Lawrence novel, because the film portrayed adultery "as a desirable, acceptable and proper pattern of behavior." Both the Regents and the New York Court of Appeals conceded that the film was not obscene. The sole basis for the ban on the film was that it portrayed sexual immorality, specifically adultery, in a favorable light. The United States Supreme Court on review unanimously upset the ban, although it took six opinions to do so. Justice Stewart, speaking for five members of the Court, argued:

What New York has done, therefore, is to prevent the exhibition of a motion picture because that picture advocates an idea—that adultery under certain circumstances may be proper behavior. Yet the First

Amendment's basic guarantee is of freedom to advocate ideas. The state, quite simply, has thus struck at the very heart of constitutionally protected liberty.[17]

Justice Stewart considered the contention that "the state's action was justified because the motion picture attractively portrays a relationship which is contrary to the moral standards, the religious precepts, and the legal code of its citizenry."[18] But Justice Stewart held that this argument misconceived the nature of the constitutional guarantee of free speech which "protects advocacy of the opinion that adultery may sometimes be proper, no less than advocacy of socialism or the single tax."[19] New York sought to ban the film for the mere abstract advocacy of an idea, not for the concrete incitement to criminal action; the statute and its application to *Lady Chatterley's Lover*, therefore, were unconstitutional.

Three justices—Frankfurter, Harlan, and Whittaker—agreed with the result reached by Justice Stewart. They felt, however, that the New York statute should have been read in a light favorable to its constitutionality, and that only the application of the statute to the film in question should have been set aside. Justice Harlan observed:

. . . I cannot regard this film as depicting anything more than a somewhat unusual, and rather pathetic, "love triangle," lacking in anything that could properly be termed obscene or corruptive of the public morals by inciting the commission of adultery.[20]

Justice Clark also concurred in the result, but he reached his conclusion on the ground that the New York statute gave the censors a roving commission to indulge their individual impressions.[21] That three justices of the Supreme Court considered *Lady Chatterley's Lover* a "pathetic love triangle" while four judges of the New York Court of Appeals held the film "immoral" well illustrated the weakness of the statute. Justices Black and Douglas added concurring opinions which voiced objections to all prior censorship.[22] This, of course, has been their consistent view in many cases, and Justice Douglas summed up his basic position on the First Amendment thus: "Judges sometimes try to read the word 'reasonable' into the First Amendment. . . . But its language, in terms that are absolute, is utterly at war with censorship."[23]

The decision on *Lady Chatterley's Lover* is a matter of utmost constitutional importance. Despite the proliferation of opinions the Court was in rather general agreement against any ban on motion pictures which advocate an idea, even an idea of sexual immorality. Now, the contention of the Court is not beyond criticism. First of all, a motion picture does not present an idea abstractly or propositionally; a motion picture is rather a concrete dramatic form with an impact on the emotions and imagination far beyond that of a logic handbook. In this connection, to equate the communication of ideas which treat of sexual immorality with the communication of ideas which espouse a political program can be misleading. Ideas favorable to sexual immorality are not presented by a motion picture to the human mind in any rational and abstract way even relatively comparable to speeches and writings on politics and economics. Unfortunately, ideas favorable to sexual immorality can exercise wide influence more subtly without formal or explicit ideological articulation. Standards of sexual morality are difficult enough to sustain, and in an age of mass media the best of citizens are moved all too easily by a cumulus of psychological and social influences to accept those lower norms of behavior which are more amenable to human weakness. Justice Stewart notwithstanding, the attraction to adultery is far less a matter of pure ideology than the attraction to the single tax. Moreover, the "idea" of adultery, when attractively presented, can undermine the social fabric no less effectively because its influence is indirect and long-term. Ideas have consequences beyond their direct and immediate results, and the "idea" of sexual immorality in particular has effects far less susceptible than other ideas to the charms of rational counterargument.

Yet, for all the criticisms that may be brought against the Court's decision in the case of *Lady Chatterley's Lover*, there are more convincing arguments in its favor. Justice Clark made an effort to demonstrate the difficulties attendant on the censorship of motion pictures which portray sexual immorality "as a desirable, acceptable and proper pattern of behavior." He appealed to the difficulty of determining whether a film does in fact advocate adultery or other sexual immorality. Did *Lady Chatterley's Lover* portray "a rather pathetic 'love triangle,'" as Justice Harlan and two other justices thought, or did the film advocate adultery, as four judges of the New York Court of Appeals concluded? Justice Frankfurter pointed out that the New York censorship would tend to limit the literary and artistic presentation of the theme of illicit love "except by way of sermonizing condemnation."[24] Moreover, governmental proscription of ideas favoring immorality could lead step by step to governmental proscription of ideas favoring political, economic, or even religious unorthodoxy. The Court's decision need not rest on the questionable libertarian dogmas that the motion picture is a medium of propositional logic, that ideas favorable to sexual immorality are the same as political ideas, and that such ideas have negligible social consequences. The Court's decision should rather be understood as a piece of rational and balanced calculation of the risks to literary expression and political process from this type of censorship when weighed against the risks to the moral and physical good of society from the favorable portrayal of sexual immorality. To protect potential literary values, the Court has restricted the scope of permissible censorship to the favorable portrayal of sexual immorality which incites to its commission. The censorship is tightly controlled by the immediate and direct effect of the portrayal on antisocial activity. Since the effect of a motion picture on activity is difficult to establish, the Court's decision for all practical purposes may have put an end to all censorship of "ideas" favorable to sexual immorality. Yet the Court conspicuously left open another and more practical area of censorship to safeguard sexual morality: obscene materials whose dominant or exclusive appeal is to prurient interest.

The case of *Lady Chatterley's Lover* also presented the recurring issue of prior censorship. Blackstone described the historical meaning of liberty of the press in a now classical remark: "The liberty of the press is indeed essential to the nature of a free state; but this consists in laying no *previous* restraints upon publications, and not in freedom from censures for criminal matters when published."[25] But this remark is at least too narrow and perhaps too broad. It is too narrow because liberty of the press must also include protection against unreasonable subsequent punishment of individuals for harmless publications. It is too broad, in the view of some commentators, because prior restraints should be permissible under rigid controls in certain types of cases. The reason usually advanced in favor of prior censorship in certain situations is the possibility of irreparable damage to individuals or to society from the communication. But the reasons why courts and jurists are so strongly averse to prior censorship are much more persuasive. The potentiality of abuse is higher in prior censorship than in subsequent punishment; the burden would be on the communication to prove its legitimacy rather than on the censor to demonstrate its illegitimacy; the time consumed before judicial review might cut the public off from important information or artistic values; and the economic penalties involved in the time-consuming adjudicative process would pressure commercial enterprises to capitulate to the censors. The Western tradition has long held that freedom should be the rule and restraint the exception, that a man is presumed to act responsibly until he gives proof of an irresponsibility in need of legal correction. Recently the Supreme Court refused only by the narrow margin of five to four to state as a matter of abstract constitutional principle that no circumstances would justify prior restraints on allegedly obscene motion pictures.[26] With the single exception of a limited injunctive remedy against the distribution or sale of already published obscene material, however, the Court has consistently disapproved of every instance of prior censorship in which a concrete form has been litigated before it.[27]

There can be little doubt that the Court has accorded a wide protection to "ideas." Only when ideas incite to criminal action may they constitutionally be censored. This attitude, of course, rests on the latitude accorded freedom of communication in a democracy and the necessity of protecting "all ideas having even the slightest redeeming social importance." The attitude is also a strong affirmation of that human reasonableness which is the underlying assumption of a democracy and of what Holmes colorfully called the "free marketplace of ideas." The worthwhile idea will establish itself by rational persuasion and in free competition, whereas the unworthy idea will be discarded. No one can deny that the view represents an ideal which it is the task of the citizen to make real. But, as Holmes also once remarked, "every idea is an incitement to action," and abstract advocacy of an idea is a matter of degree. Moreover, some "ideas," some media of communication, some circumstances do not enshrine the calm of the academy or the detachment of the drawing room. To think that the option for almost unfettered communication of ideas involves no serious risks would be foolish dogmatism and a sad confusion of the ideal with the real. The true basis for the option in favor of almost unlimited freedom for the communication of ideas is not that such freedom is without risks but that censorship would involve still greater risks. Realistic judgment and pragmatic appraisal rather than a pure idealism or a pure dogmatism serve as the sound political foundation for the broad rejection of governmental censorship of ideas.

GOVERNMENT CENSORSHIP OF OBSCENITY

The notable exception to the constitutional prohibition against government censorship is the area of obscene materials. Not that the Court looks with an uncritical eye on obscenity statutes or that the exemption of obscenity from constitutional protection has gone unchallenged before the Court. The Roth and Alberts decisions of June 24, 1957, settled whatever doubts had existed on the permissibility of federal or state statutes against publishers, distributors, and sellers of obscene materials as a result of other rulings. In so doing the Supreme Court not only excluded obscene materials from the constitutionally protected freedom of communication but also offered a test for obscenity.

Samuel Roth's troubles with the United States postal and other authorities had a long history, but the particular case which led to the epoch-making Supreme Court decision began in 1955. Roth was indicted in New York on twenty-six counts for mailing obscene pictures, magazines, and books in violation of federal law. When the jury convicted him on four counts, the judge fined him five thousand dollars and sentenced him to five years in prison. The Court of Appeals for the Second Circuit upheld the conviction in a split decision, and the United States Supreme Court granted certiorari. At the same time on the West Coast Los Angeles authorities were prosecuting David Alberts for keeping for sale obscene and indecent books in violation of the California criminal code. Alberts was fined five hundred dollars and sentenced to sixty days in prison. He challenged the constitutionality of the state law and, like Roth, asked the Supreme Court to review his conviction.

Both cases reached the Supreme Court in a high degree of abstraction. On the issue of free speech and free press the Court was asked only to rule whether obscenity was within the area of constitutional protection. There was no question raised, at least in the view of the majority, concerning the actual obscenity of the materials on which the convictions were based. Justice Brennan responded for five members of the Court that obscenity is "utterly without redeeming social importance" and, therefore, "not within the area of constitutionally protected speech of press."[28] From this it followed that those responsible for obscene materials might be punished if the materials incited to impure sexual thoughts even though "not shown to be related to any overt antisocial conduct."[29] Like libel, obscenity is simply outside the constitutional protection of free speech, and there need be no presence of a "clear and present danger" of impending criminal action.

But "sex and obscenity are not synonymous."[30] Therefore it is vital to set forth standards for judging obscenity in order to protect the legitimate protrayal of sex in art or literature. The early Hicklin test judged whether material was obscene "merely by the effect of an isolated excerpt upon particularly susceptible persons."[31] Justice Brennan rejected the Hicklin test and substituted his own: "whether to the average person, applying contemporary community standards, the dominant theme of the material taken as a whole appeals to prurient interest."[32] Lastly, Justice Brennan found that the term "obscene" had a sufficiently certain and definite content to avoid the objection of unconstitutional vagueness which would fail to give citizens adequate warning of what was prohibited.

Chief Justice Warren concurred in the result but not in the

majority's reasoning: "It is not the book that is on trial; it is a person. The conduct of the defendant is the controlling issue, not the obscenity of a book or picture."[33] The circumstances in which Roth and Alberts purveyed erotic material were sufficient to establish that the materials were obscene in the context and that those responsible could be punished. Justice Harlan concurred in the Alberts case and dissented in the Roth case.[34] For him, the decisive factor was the nature of the federal structure which permitted more latitude to state than to federal action in the field of censorship. However, Justice Harlan did indicate that the so-called "hard-core" pornography could be subjected to regulation through the federal postal power. Justice Douglas, joined by Justice Black, dissented in both cases.[35] He insisted that obscene materials were entitled to the same constitutional protection as other communications. It is not enough that obscene materials excite lustful thoughts; they must present a "clear and present danger" of criminal action. Censorship of obscenity merely because of a tendency to excite lustful thoughts "creates a regime where, in the battle between the literati and the Philistines, the Philistines are certain to win."[36]

Insofar as the Brennan opinion excepted obscene publications as "utterly without redeeming social importance" from the constitutional protection of the First Amendment, it was on strong historical, legal, and political grounds. But the key problem is to define obscenity in a way calculated to safeguard literary and artistic values which do have redeeming social importance. The definition set forth by the Brennan opinion is not without difficulties. How can the "average person" be the standard of obscenity when the primary threat of obscenity is to the sexually immature or even the psychologically disturbed? Are local or national "contemporary community standards" to be applied? How is the "dominant theme of the material" to be determined with any degree of certitude or consistency? What is the "whole" work to be evaluated for obscenity? What is the precise meaning of "appeal to prurient interest"? Does the literary or artistic value of a work play any role in determining whether or not material is obscene? Lastly, are the defendant's motives a factor in the evaluation of obscenity?

The test outlined by the Roth-Alberts majority is presented in context as a reaction against two defective features of the Hicklin rule: the effect of "isolated excerpts" on "particularly susceptible persons." The majority's effort at definition was primarily a negative formulation designed to deny that allegedly obscene material may be censored on the basis of random passages or censored for the total public on the basis of the effect on the weakest and perhaps most insignificant portion of the reading public. In fact, earlier in the year 1957 a unanimous Court had struck down a Michigan statute precisely because the statute made it a misdemeanor to sell a book to the general public if the book tended to incite minors to violent or depraved acts. "Surely," Justice Frankfurter observed succinctly, "this is to burn the house to roast the pig":

We have before us legislation not reasonably restricted to the evil with which it is said to deal. The incidence of this enactment is to reduce the adult population of Michigan to reading only what is fit for children.[37]

With the primarily negative character of the Roth-Alberts test for obscenity in mind, we may attempt a few clarifying remarks. To say that obscenity must be determined by the reaction of the "average person" means that material may not be proscribed for the entire reading public on the basis of the effect on particularly susceptible persons. Prurient materials, of course, make their greatest appeal to immature individuals, but material should not be judged prurient for all because of the effect on a few. "Contemporary community standards" are included in the test because obscenity is in part a relative concept. Whether a particular material does actually appeal to the prurient interest of concrete human subjects depends to a large extent on the prevailing attitudes and accepted practices of a society. Material prurient to the Victorians need not be so today. The phrase "dominant theme of the material" is designed, as indicated above, to exclude the determination of obscenity on the basis of isolated passages. It does not, therefore, give any guidelines on just how the "dominant theme" is discovered in a particular work or how the norm is consistently applied to many works. Nor is it easy to say in many cases what constitutes the "whole" work on which the determination of obscenity is made. An explicit representation of the sexual act in an otherwise innocuous collection of photographs unquestionably would be taken by itself to constitute a "whole" and would be judged separately from the rest of the material. Anthologies raise a similar problem of what constitutes the whole work to be evaluated.

The most important element in the test for obscenity is the "appeal to prurient interest," and Justice Brennan indicated that he considered it a paraphrase for the excitation of lustful thoughts and desires. But many insist that the terms "prurient" and "lustful" are no less indefinable and vague than the term "obscene." Two distinguished experts, William Lockhart and Robert McClure, have suggested that the "constant" concept of obscenity, on which the Court appeared to rely in the Roth-Alberts cases, was the concept of pornography.[38] Lockhart and McClure have followed Dr. Margaret Mead in defining pornography as "words or acts or representations that are calculated to stimulate sex feelings independent of the presence of another loved and chosen human being."[39] In the case of photographs, Lockhart and McClure offered the added qualification that the material must be "shocking" in order to fall within the area of permissible censorship.

The Supreme Court gave an indication in a series of *per curiam* opinions in the term following the Roth-Alberts decisions that the Court did consider "obscene" to mean "pornography," as Lockhart and McClure suggested.[40] The Court summarily reversed three lower court rulings against allegedly obscene materials. In reversing the rulings the Supreme Court gave final disposition to the three cases and thus determined that the material in question was beyond constitutionally permissible censorship. Since there were ample grounds for considering the material obscene if obscenity signified more than pornography, the Court appears to have identified obscenity with pornography for all practical purposes.

Lockhart and McClure have also elaborated a "variable" concept of obscenity as an alternative or supplement to the "constant" concept. In their view of the variable concept, material would be judged obscene if it appealed to the craving for erotic

fantasy of the typical representative of the primary audience
for whom the material was intended. Here the nature of the
publisher, distributor, and seller's appeal would help to decide
not only what audience was intended but also whether the
material itself in such circumstances was obscene. The variable
concept would permit the same material to be considered obscene
when directed to one audience (e. g., the sexually immature)
and acceptable when directed to another (e. g., the literati).
The Lockhart and McClure variable formula gives attention to
the specific designs of the defendants and in this respect in-
corporates a portion of the position of Chief Justice Warren.
To date, however, there is no indication that such a formula
would commend itself to a majority of the Court.

Since the presupposition of the majority opinion in the Roth-
Alberts cases was that obscene material is "utterly without
redeeming social importance," the literary and artistic features
of the work are highly relevant to the determination of obscenity.
If the material appeals *solely* to prurient interest, of course, it is
simply beyond social redemption. But if there is question whether
the presence of objectionable material vitiates the entire work,
literary or artistic considerations will be integral to the determination whether the work as a whole is obscene. A judge or
jury must study them in order to establish whether it is in fact
the dominant theme of a work with allegedly objectional material to appeal to prurient interest.

On December 14, 1959, in a corollary to the Roth-Alberts
ruling, the Supreme Court unanimously agreed that the element
of *scienter*, or knowledge, was constitutionally required to sustain the conviction of a bookdealer for the possession of obscene
material.[41] Eleazar Smith had been convicted under a Los
Angeles city ordinance which made it unlawful "for any person
to have in his possession any obscene or indecent writing [or]
book . . . in any place of business where . . . books . . . are sold
or kept for sale." The Court reversed the conviction because the
ordinance failed to require *scienter*, or knowing possession, as
an element of the criminal offense. Justice Brennan again spoke
for the Court. The Roth-Alberts decisions established that obscene writings were not protected by the constitutional guarantees of free speech and free press. But the Constitution does

not "recognize any state power to restrict the dissemination of books which are not obscene; and we think that this ordinance's strict liability feature would tend seriously to have that effect. . . ."[42] If "the bookseller is criminally liable without knowledge of the contents, and the ordinance fulfils its purpose, he will tend to restrict the books he sells to those he has inspected."[43] Thus "the bookseller's burden would become the public's burden," and the constitutional guarantees of free speech and free press would be adversely affected.[44] The majority opinion cautiously noted, however, that "circumstances may warrant the inference that he [the defendant bookdealer] was aware of what a book contained despite his denial."[45]

Several states have instituted a limited injunctive remedy against obscene material on the model of an American Law Institute recommendation. This type of statute does not seek to punish the sale or possession for sale of obscene works. Rather, it provides for an injunction against the sale or distribution of the obscene material itself and for an order to confiscate the condemned publications. The subsequent violation of the injunction or order, of course, would lead to criminal prosecution for contempt of court. Kingsley Books, Inc., were the publishers of a piece of pornography, appropriately entitled *Nights of Horror*, which had been offered for sale in the Times Square area. Operating under section 22a of the New York Code of Criminal Procedure as amended in 1954, the corporation counsel for New York City in 1955 petitioned for an injunction against the booklet. Supreme Court Justice Matthew Levi, before whom the petition was laid, gave the defendants four days to show cause why the injunction should not be granted *pendente lite*. Kingsley Books agreed to the injunction *pendente lite* and did not press for a prompt trial as they were entitled to under subsection 2 of section 22a. (The subsection authorized a trial within one day after the issue was joined and a court decision within two days after the close of trial.) Trial by the presiding justice as provided by the statute resulted in a finding of obscenity, and the injunction against the defendants was made permanent. The New York Court of Appeals affirmed the decision.

The booksellers appealed to the United States Supreme Court. They did not challenge the finding that *Nights of Horror* was obscene. They objected to the entire statutory provision as an unconstitutional prior censorship. The Supreme Court on the same day as the Roth-Alberts decisions upheld the injunction against Kingsley Books by the bare margin of five to four.[46] Justice Frankfurter, speaking for the five-man majority, defended the New York statute as a constitutionally valid weapon in the state's armory against obscenity. If a state chooses to proceed against obscenity by injunctive relief, "it is not for us to gainsay its selection of remedies."[47] The New York injunctive proceedings accorded full protection to the bookseller: the bookseller was assured a prompt trial on the merits of the publication, and the proceeding was directed against the specific book and not against the person of the bookseller. Under the New York statute, the enforcement machinery moved against Kingsley at exactly the same time as the California statute permitted the enforce-ment machinery to move against Alberts—after publication and before sale. Only material actually published and found to be obscene in a fair hearing fell under the penalty of injunction.

Chief Justice Warren objected to placing a book and not the bookseller on trial. "In my judgment, the same object may have wholly different impact depending upon the setting in which it is placed. Under this statute the setting is irrelevant."[48] This, concluded the Chief Justice, "savors too much of book burn-ing."[49] Justice Douglas, joined by Justice Black, leveled several telling criticisms against the New York statute. In his view, the statute enabled courts to restrain publications even before a hearing was held, which was "prior restraint and censorship at its worst."[50] Although the defendant was assured a prompt hearing and a prompt decision on the issue of obscenity, still the statute authorized a temporary injunction to be issued before the hearing began and before the substantive merits had been determined. If the material were ultimately judged not to be obscene, the bookseller would have been deprived of the right to sell and the public would have lost the opportunity to read the work. The time might be short, but the principle is of no little importance. Justice Douglas also objected to the entire idea of an injunctive proceeding against a book where the effect would be to ban permanently the sale of the book throughout the entire state. Audiences separated by time and space may react differently to the same material. What is obscene to one audience may not be so to another: "The audience . . . that hissed yesterday may applaud today, even for the same performance."[51] Justice Brennan dissented solely on the ground that the defendants were constitutionally entitled to a trial by jury on the obscenity issue, while the New York statute prescribed trial by the presiding justice.[52]

The New York statute has several advantages both for the facilitation of law enforcement and for the protection of honest booksellers. On the one hand, law enforcement officers can move against an obscene material in a single proceeding rather than by piecemeal prosecution of the publisher, distributor, and seller. On the other, the publisher, distributor, or seller can have a judicial determination of the issue of obscenity without the personal risk or stigma of a criminal prosecution. The injunction issues against material which is found in a judicial action to be obscene. If the material would not be obscene for another audience at a different time or place, then the injunction could be lifted at that time or modified for that locality. But the statute, unfortunately, permits a temporary injunction to be issued even before a judicial hearing on the obscenity of the material has begun. This provision is both unwise and unnecessary. It is unwise because material is proscribed without a hearing for howsoever brief a period of time; it is unnecessary because the seller of obscene material prior to the issuance of an injunction would still be liable for criminal prosecution as the seller of obscene material. On this point Justice Douglas had the better of the argument.

GOVERNMENT CENSORSHIP: A SUMMARY

In the cases involving *The Miracle, Headquarters Detective,* and *Lady Chatterley's Lover* the Supreme Court accorded an unfettered freedom to the communication of ideas which do not concretely incite to criminal action. The Roth-Alberts decisions, however, established that obscenity was beyond the constitutional protection of the First Amendment freedoms and outlined a legal test of obscenity. The test needs further judicial interpretation, but for the present it may be understood at least to reject evaluation of material for alleged obscenity on the basis of isolated passages or the effect exercised on particularly susceptible persons. A series of summary, *per curiam* reversals of the censorship of particular materials alleged to be obscene indicated that the Court adhered to a "constant" concept of obscenity based on pornography, and that the Court was slow to sanction censorship where there was the possibility of redeeming social value. There is no indication to date that the Court accepts or will accept as a substitute or a supplement the "variable" concept of obscenity based on the nature of the primary audience which Professors Lockhart and McClure suggested. In the Smith case the Court insisted that knowledge was a necessary element in the criminal prosecution of a defendant bookseller on the charge of possession of obscene materials. Lastly, the Court has upheld by a narrow margin an injunctive remedy against obscene material, even extending on a limited and temporary basis to pretrial and trial phases of the action.

Catholics and others often indicate their impatience with the reticence of the Court to approve government action against what seems to them patently pernicious material masquerading as literature. It has always been the strength of religious men to recognize the dangers of moral evil; it has always been their weakness to look indiscriminately to the government for action against it. Responsible citizens will both recognize the grave though subtle risks inherent in governmental censorship and doubt the capacity of coercive action to deliver a moral utopia, especially in sexual matters. Censorship is an essentially negative weapon and leaves fundamental factors in the moral climate untouched. Those who on all moral problems cry "there oughta be a law" reflect the instinct of human frustration rather than the imperative of a sound jurisprudence. Good law demands the exercise of balanced and prudent judgment.

The Court, for its part, has moved judiciously and circumspectly. It has prohibited the censorship of abstract ideas but permitted government regulation in the closely circumscribed area of obscenity. Even in the area of obscenity, however, government censorship cannot and should not be expected to accomplish all that decent citizens may wish. As a result, citizens may seek to effect by private action what is wisely prohibited to the government. But the vast potentialities of private action in turn raise another problem of censorship for a pluralistically structured democracy.

NON-GOVERNMENT CENSORSHIP:
PRIVATE ACTION

In October, 1956, John Fischer, editor of *Harper's Magazine*, leveled a series of strong accusations against the National Organization for Decent Literature (NODL), which had been founded in 1938 by the Catholic bishops of the United States to fight against the publication and sale of obscene magazines and pocket books.[53] In his sharp essay "The Harm Good People Do" editor Fischer charged the group with engaging in techniques which constituted a "shocking attack on the rights of their follow citizens."[54] Msgr. Thomas Fitzgerald, national director of the NODL, denied in rebuttal that the group recommended its lists of objectionable material for purposes of economic boycott or police coercion.[55] If there were abuses, he insisted, they were due to overzealous local units operating beyond the instructions of the national office.

Whatever the merits of the particular charges against the NODL (there were local incidents to provide a basis for editor Fischer's attack) or the mode of their presentation (the indictment of the NODL was overdrawn), the issue served to focus public attention and discussion on the subject of censorship by private groups, which is a vital one for a democracy. Private action to influence the communications media is not a new problem, however, as those old enough to recall the New York Society for the Suppression of Vice and the New England Watch and Ward Society will bear witness. We shall attempt to elaborate here only a few basic principles concerning private efforts in this field.[56]

There is, of course, no political problem when an individual acts to control his own reading or viewing. Self-control according to the norms of prudent judgment is not even censorship as that term is ordinarily employed. Censorship refers rather to control of the approach of other individuals to the avenues of communication. Nor is there any political problem in family censorship. Parents in the execution of their responsibilities and as a matter of prudent judgment exercise authority over their children's reading or viewing. The children may complain of overseverity, but others cannot. The political problem begins only at the point where many citizens form a group which by reason of its persuasion or power can influence or control the access of the general public to the avenues of communication. Citizens as individuals undoubtedly have as much legal right not to buy as to buy, even for the worst of motives. Citizens in combination undoubtedly have as much legal right to communicate their views against as for specific books, dramas, films, or television programs. And, at least as the law is presently constituted, citizens in combination have as much legal right to oppose the circulation of certain materials by boycott against the distributors or sellers as others have to favor them by purchase.

Yet unrestrained private group action to influence the communications media, if legal, remains a genuine political problem. The common law suspicion of combined action, which frustrated the union movement for so long, was not without foundation. Uncontrolled power of united activity can create dangers for the commonweal, and in the matter of communication the danger to a democratic polity would be singularly grave. If a single group could, through the economic power of numbers, control the access of the entire public to the avenues of communication, it would threaten the public's right to information and to plural value structures, both of which are implicit in democratic political process. On the one hand, the general public would be in a weak position to maintain access to the information on which to exercise its decision-making function, and, on the other, groups within the general public would be in an even weaker position to transmit, receive, or evaluate materials which embody different systems of values. The fact that other groups of citizens might also organize to coerce the communications media in their own behalf should compound rather than soothe the anxiety of the political analyst. Unlike the area of economic organization for

corporate profit or collective bargaining, a democratic government would be unlikely or perhaps even forbidden to regulate
private groups which employ economic coercion as an instrument to influence the ideological content of communications. As a
result the public would be at the mercy of that group which
gained the decisive ascendancy. Again unlike the area of economic organization, the public might never have the opportunity
to regain its free access to the lines of communication.

What are the principles of sound judgment which should govern action by private combinations of citizens and families seeking to influence the communications media? First of all, private
groups, including churches, have the unqualified right to advise
their own members concerning the moral merits and demerits of
books, magazines, or pictures. It is, of course, not only the right
but even the high duty of the church to do so. Economic consequences from the response of members to the admonitions of private, especially religious, spokesmen may well affect specific
communications adversely. But surely no risk of economic loss to
the communications media can diminsh the age-old freedom of
religious teachers to speak out on moral issues. What is incumbent
on them is not to remain silent but to judge wisely. Those who
undertake to advise others on the moral implications of literary
or artistic works must be competent not only to enunciate moral
principles but no less to recognize literary and artistic values.
There is in group censorship no room for the amateur and no substitute for professional competence.

Several organizations advise their members by means of a specific list. In particular, the NODL draws up monthly lists of
paperbacks and magazines found objectionable for youth, and
the Legion of Decency classifies all motion pictures according to
their suitability for children, youth, and the general public. Many
citizens object to such lists of objectionable books or films as a
matter of principle. Yet, to judge the worth of lists one must
evaluate them in terms of their purpose, which is to advise members and the general public on the moral wholesomeness of specific books or films. The average reader or viewer will find it
difficult to arrive at an informed judgment of his own before, and
often even after, he reads the book or sees the film. A list offers
a simple and easy guide to meet this need. So confined, a list of

objectionable material is as proper as any other form of critical judgment communicated by a private group to its members and the public. The value of any particular list, of course, will depend on the soundness of the norms for evaluation, the adequacy of the reviewing procedures, and the competency of the reviewers. But surely no one can object in principle to the propriety of an advisory list available to those who wish to use it for their own guidance.

There is little dispute over the propriety of efforts by religious or private groups to censor books or films for their own members. But there is dispute over attempts by religious or private groups to influence the reading or viewing of nonmembers. At the lowest level the argument revolves around the old liberal saw: "Every individual is free to read or not to read, to see or not to see, anything which he chooses. If some or even most citizens wish not to read a specific book or not to see a specific film, that is their right. But if others do wish to read the book or see the film, why should the others be concerned?" This popular view sounds quite attractive until one reflects that the actions of individuals can in fact affect the common moral climate in which *all* citizens live. We have no difficulty in understanding that the physical or intellectual fitness of individual citizens can affect the welfare of the entire community, yet we often hesitate to admit that the moral actions of individuals can affect the common good of the whole society. The plain truth is that we are our brother's keeper whenever our brother's action adversely and significantly touches us, whether as individuals or as a society. The question is rarely whether citizens should be concerned with the actions of other citizens but rather how they should seek to influence others. Decent literature and decent motion pictures are highly desirable goals for the whole society, and responsible citizens do well to aspire to them. But how are these goals to be realized? What means of influence are proper means?

If an individual or group attempts to persuade other citizens by rational discussion not to buy or not to sell material deemed to be objectionable, this is an indisputably responsible exercise of personal initiative. If an individual or group peacefully protests the purchase or sale of material regarded as indecent, this too is an acceptable means of bringing a particular critical judgment to the attention of the public. The effort to alert public opinion is not reprehensible, whether the effort be general in scope or specifically aimed against particular material deemed to be indecent. All of these methods have rational persuasion as their basis and are therefore fully consistent with responsible citizenship and democratic processes. Of course there are implicit economic consequences on communications if the public is to any extent persuaded not to buy. But the economic consequences fall only as a result of successful persuasion; they are not the means of coercing cooperation.

This brings us to consider the propriety of the method which so strongly aroused editor Fischer's ire: the economic boycott. Is it proper for a religious or private group within a pluralistic society to impose its moral judgment on the entire public through an economic boycott of sellers or theaters which refuse to cooperate voluntarily with a general program or a specific judgment? Such an action would not appear to violate any existing law. The Sherman Act indeed forbids combinations in restraint of trade affecting interstate commerce, but the forbidden combinations are those designed to achieve an economic, not an ideological, monopoly. Whether Congress or the states could constitutionally prohibit economic boycotts for ideological objectives might be the subject of debate. At any rate, from a practical viewpoint, neither Congress nor the states are likely to take any such action. The question of proper self-discipline, therefore, is all the more meaningful in the absence of present or prospective legal restraint.

It could be argued against the doctrinaire that some circumstances might conceivably justify the coercive method of an economic boycott. Few would be so bold as to claim that they could foresee all future contingencies. But even a priori it is hard to understand why an aroused public authority could not liquidate at least the problem of pornography and why an aroused public opinion could not accomplish enough without the coercive threat of an economic boycott. To consider the impropriety of an economic boycott in abstraction from all concrete details, however, is both unreal and unnecessary. The important point is that no concrete situation presented today or in prospect for tomorrow in any part of the United States is sufficient to justify the dangerous implications of a coercive economic boycott. A democratic polity necessarily puts a premium on free access to the media of communication as the basis for the informed exercise of the decision-making function by the popular electorate, and a democratic polity accepts a pluralism of beliefs and values as a corollary to the equal voice of all citizens in the political process. When a private group within the polity imposes its moral judgment by economic coercion on the communications media of the whole public, it is a political threat both to the public's free access to information and to the equal right of citizens to differing beliefs and values. But perhaps the more proximate threat is not so much to strictly political processes as to literary and artistic values. Philistine methods are rarely sensitive to the claims of the literati. The average citizen will be little consoled to learn that he can fight his way to the channels of information and to equal control by organizing along similar lines. Lilliputians do not become free by the unrestrained rovings of more than one giant. Private groups in the field of censorship must not seek to supplant the state's exercise of coercive action; private groups must rather seek to supplement the state's coercive action with voluntary and cooperative efforts at rational presentation and persuasion.

Nor should lists drawn up according to the norms of a private group be used as the basis for public prosecution or as the threat of public prosecution. Such lists represent the critical judgment which spokesmen for a private group suggest for members of the group and propose to others for their voluntary acceptance. Censorship by public law, on the other hand, is narrowly restricted not only in its substantive scope but particularly in its procedural safeguards. This is as it should be, since public censorship has the ultimate of coercive power at its disposal. That the norms of private and of public censorship are different needs but to be considered in order to be acknowledged. Private groups, therefore, must exercise great care over the methods, especially through the mobilization of public opinion, in which they attempt to move public prosecutors to more effective action. Certainly any individual or group is free to notify the prosecutor of likely violations of public law. But no individual or group can make the final judgment whether public law has been violated—this function belongs to judges and juries. No individual or group should suggest to law enforcement officers that they employ a particular list even to threaten a publisher or seller with public prosecution.

Lastly, what of self-regulation by the communications industries themselves? Some profess to see more threat to the freedom of expression in such a system than in any other form of private censorship. Obviously, there does exist the possibility that industrial self-regulation would stifle artistic creativity or restrict worthwhile expression. But, if the past experience of the motion picture and book publishing industries is any guide, self-regulation by the communications media is more likely to be too weak than too strong. The reason is not hard to find. A maverick is always free to produce or publish a work which does not receive the industry's approval. If he is successful, the industry's self-regulatory system is weakened to that extent. The chief value of industry-wide self-regulation, however, does not lie in its coercive power, although this has been considerable at times; it lies rather in the public's access to the industry's own evaluation of its offerings. Provided the norms of review are sound, the reviewing procedures satisfactory, and the reviewers competent, the public will not lose from the self-regulation of the communications media. In fact, the members of every communications industry necessarily exercise some form of self-regulation at least through the effect of their editorial policies.

In the last few years attention has shifted from the purely negative aspect of restraining objectionable material to the positive aspect of creating better opportunities for good literature, dramas, films, and television. Indecent works are as much a testimony to the cultural vacuum of much of American life as to moral decay. Negative efforts at reform have their definite place, but they cannot create the positive stimuli either to a culturally or to a morally vigorous society. Responsible citizens can perform a fine service to American society if they will initiate and support programs to bring good literature, dramas, films, and television to the public. Private, and especially religious, groups may accomplish more by such positive action than they can achieve by merely negative morality.

Catholics, of course, have been among the most active and powerful of private groups fighting against objectionable magazines and films. Their zeal has sometimes prevailed over their good judgment; their concern with the substantive demerits of materials has sometimes blinded them to the exigencies of proper procedure. They must not cease to seek to influence the communications media in the direction of sound values, but they must do so by voluntary and cooperative efforts, by rational presentation and persuasion. They must bring professional competence of the highest order to bear on the problem. Lastly, they must devote themselves not merely to negative action but particularly to positive programs for good literature and films.[57] To do less would be offensive to democratic political processes, a danger to artistic values and, worst of all, a distortion of the Church's own spiritual nature.

NOTES

1. Harold C. Gardiner, S.J., *A Catholic Viewpoint on Censorship* (New York: Hanover House, 1958).

2. *Winters* v. *New York*, 333 U.S. 507 (1948); *Joseph Burstyn, Inc.* v. *Wilson*, 343 U.S. 495 (1952); and *Kingsley International Pictures Corp.* v. *Regents*, 360 U.S. 684 (1959).

3. *Burstyn* v. *Wilson*, 303 N.Y. 242, 258 (1951).

4. *Burstyn* v. *Wilson*, 343 U.S. 495, 505 (1952).

5. *Ibid.*, p. 502.

6. *Ibid.*, pp. 507, 560.

7. *Winters* v. *New York*, 294 N.Y. 545, 550 (1945).

8. *Winters* v. *New York*, 333 U.S. 507, 519, (1948).

9. *Ibid.*, p. 510.

10. *Ibid.*, p. 520.

11. *Ibid.*, p. 523.

12. *Ibid.*, p. 528.

13. *Ibid.*, p. 534.

14. *Ibid.*

15. *Roth* v. *U.S.* and *Alberts* v. *California*, 354 U.S. 476 (1957).

16. *Kingsley International Pictures Corp.* v. *Regents*, 360 U.S. 684 (1959).

17. *Ibid.*, p. 688.

18. *Ibid.*, pp. 688, 689.

19. *Ibid.*, p. 689.

20. *Ibid.*, p. 708.

21. *Ibid.*, p. 701.

22. *Ibid.*, pp. 690, 697.

23. *Ibid.*, p. 698.

24. *Ibid.*, p. 692.

25. William Blackstone, *Commentaries on the Laws of England*, ed. William Lewis (Philadelphia: Rees Welsh and Co., 1897), IV, pp. 151–152.

26. *Times Film Corp.* v. *City of Chicago*, 365 U.S. 43 (1961).

27. The exception was *Kingsley Books, Inc.* v. *Brown*, 354 U.S. 436 (1957).

28. *Roth-Alberts,* pp. 484, 485.
29. *Ibid.,* p. 486.
30. *Ibid.,* p. 487.
31. *Regina* v. *Hicklin,* L.R. 3 Q.B. 360 (1868) and *Roth-Alberts,* p. 489.
32. *Ibid.*
33. *Ibid.,* p. 495.
34. *Ibid.,* p. 496.
35. *Ibid.,* p. 508.
36. *Ibid.,* p. 512.
37. *Butler* v. *Michigan,* 352 U.S. 380, 383 (1957).
38. William Lockhart and Robert McClure, "Censorship of Obscenity: The Developing Constitutional Standards," *Minnesota Law Review,* Vol. XLV (1960), pp. 5–121.
39. *Ibid.,* p. 62.
40. *Times Film Corp.* v. *City of Chicago,* 355 U.S. 35 (1957); *Sunshine Book Co.* v. *Summerfield,* 355 U.S. 372 (1958); and *One, Inc.* v. *Olesen,* 355 U.S. 371 (1958). The first case involved the film *The Game of Love;* the second involved the nudist magazines *Sun* and *Sunshine and Health;* and the third involved *One,* an allegedly homosexual magazine.
41. *Smith* v. *California* 361 U.S. 147 (1959).
42. *Ibid.,* p. 152.
43. *Ibid.,* p. 153.
44. *Ibid.*
45. *Ibid.,* p. 154
46. *Kingsley Books, Inc.* v. *Brown,* 354 U.S. 436 (1957).
47. *Ibid.,* p. 441.
48. *Ibid.,* p. 446.
49. *Ibid.*
50. *Ibid.*
51. *Ibid.,* p. 447.
52. *Ibid.*
53. John Fischer, "The Harm Good People Do," *Harper's Magazine,* October, 1956, pp. 14–20.
54. *Ibid.*
55. Msgr. Thomas J. Fitzgerald, "NODL States Its Case," *America,* June 1, 1957, pp. 280–282.
56. The principles elaborated here owe a considerable debt to Fr. Murray. His admirable essay in the June-July, 1956, issue of *Books on Trial* (reprinted in *We Hold These Truths,* pp. 155–174) is basic reading for any student of private censorship.
57. Catholics have indicated increasing awareness of the need for positive action. See, for example, Most Rev. William A. Scully, "Movies: a Positive Plan," *America,* March 30, 1957, pp. 726–727.

11

The Religions
in America:
Unfinished Business

Americans like to think themselves a showcase of political maturity and religious tolerance. And indeed they have good reason for their satisfaction with the relative harmony which they have achieved out of perhaps the most fragmented religious pluralism to be found anywhere in the world. Americans rightly take pride in the complete liberty of conscience accorded to the faithful of all religious beliefs, even to those whose street preaching or door-to-door canvassing may prove annoying to their fellow citizens. Americans rightly take pride in the openness of their society to the political, economic, and social advancement of all citizens on the basis of individual merit and without regard to religious profession. The election of the first Catholic President, we incline to think, indicates the maturity of our tradition of religious equality.

Yet a slight probe beneath the surface harmony reveals how unfinished is the business of political maturity and religious tolerance. The reactions of the Protestant, Catholic, Jewish, and secular humanist to the chief religio-political issues of the day, elaborated in preceding chapters, illustrate the extent of the danger which today threatens both political union and religious peace. The American showcase is, in fact, something of a spectacle.

The complex problem of religion and education offers an all too clear example of the present situation. Protestants generally defend the place of Bible reading and the Lord's Prayer in the public school. They have always regarded the public school as in some sense their own, and the historical origins of that system make their claim quite understandable. But what of the children of nonbelievers? Here Protestants and Catholics, who also for the most part now support nonsectarian religious practices in the public school, display a rather callous indifference to the sensibilities of the secular humanists. The nonbeliever may be "excused" from these publicly sponsored exercises, but he must petition the privilege not to attend or not to participate. Inconsistently enough, while the Protestant approves a nonsectarian religious orientation to the public school and sectarian instruction on a released or dismissed-time basis, he opposes any public support of church-related schools as a violation of the constitutionally guaranteed separation of church and state.

Catholics, for their part, insist on the primary right of parents in the education of their children when they argue for public support of pupils attending church-related schools. But they remain insensitive and unconcerned with the interests of nonbelievers whose children attend the public schools. Most nonbelievers and Jews cannot be accused of any like inconsistency: they want public support for public schools alone, and they want absolutely no religious orientation or accommodation of those schools. They oppose any public support of children attending church-related schools, any religious orientation of public schools, and even any accommodation of class schedules to permit those pupils to attend religious instruction classes whose parents so wish. Thus they wish the public authority committed exclusively to the cause of secular humanism.

Study of the Sunday laws uncovered another unresolved area of friction. Most Protestants, Catholics, and secular humanists remain indifferent to the plight of the conscientious Sabbatarian whose observance of the laws involves serious economic consequences. In the 1962 session of the New York legislature, for example, outspoken Catholic opposition and covert Protestant complaisance aborted an effort to exempt conscientious Sabbatarian merchants from that state's Sunday sales ban.

In the field of public morals, birth control is at present the chief source of controversy. Non-Catholics seek to end the legislation in Massachusetts and Connecticut which forbids the prescription, sale, and, in the case of Connecticut, the use of contraceptives by married couples. But at the same time many non-Catholics, without respect to the moral sensibilities of Catholics, seek to use public funds to promote the practice of birth control in foreign countries.

Other aspects of public morals provoke similar reactions. Where Catholics are powerful enough, they show a disinclination to accommodate public law to the diversity of moral judgment. In New York, for example, Catholic spokesmen for years have opposed any modification of a divorce law which fosters collusive suits and is circumvented by recourse to the tribunals of other states. Catholics in many areas support and even initiate the "anti-smut" campaigns of public prosecutors without regard for the constitutional subtleties and pluralistic sensibilities involved. Non-Catholics, on the other hand, often urge the relaxation of existing regulations of public morals in a way offensive to Catholics: that morals are not at all a matter of common concern, that Catholic beliefs on marriage and sex are irrational, and so on.

This is not a happy state of affairs, and the misfortune is both religious and political. The religious failure is that few really practice the love of God and man which they profess. Exclusive concern with power and status blurs genuine concern for those of a different religious persuasion. Every intransigence is defended as a "matter of principle," but scant attention is paid to that charity without which we are, in the words of St. Paul, "sounding brass."

While charity or its absence immediately concerns only the world of conscience, its effects overflow into the world of social action. And so, mutual antagonisms among the religions in America have generated a series of political problems to which citizen and statesman alike must devote their energies. It is fatuous, of course, to expect that so deep-seated problems as these can be solved by a few strokes of the pen. But, hopefully, the development of basic principles and their application can make a contribution.

The most important political principle of which Americans of different religious beliefs and ethical convictions should be conscious is the political nature of the religious settlement embodied in the First Amendment. Religious liberty and the equality of all religions before the law are not articles of religious faith but rather articles of political peace. The Constitution does not require citizens to profess that all religions are equal in the eyes of God, but it does require citizens to accept that all religions are equal in the eyes of political authority. Such a settlement was absolutely necessary for even a minimum achievement of political goals in a pluralistic and democratic society.

The shame of the present relations between religion and government is that the central political purpose of the American settlement has been forgotten or ignored. In view of that purpose, I think it safe to say that any interpretation of the settlement is suspect which radically alienates any of the religious communities. This suspicion is not an infallible index, to be sure, because a religious community may desire what is unreasonable. But the appeals of religious minorities should at least raise doubts in the conscience of the reflective citizen.

Some consideration of the constitutional prohibition of a religious establishment is necessary, though far from sufficient. It is unfortunate that attention is often so exclusively focused on the legal aspect of the no-establishment clause, because the result is to obscure the political purpose of the provision, namely, harmony among citizens of different religious beliefs.

It has been assumed throughout this work that in our day religious disbelief is entitled to exactly the same political rights as religious belief. Whatever was the practice in other periods of American history, the creed of secular humanism must be accepted today as a political equal of the other major communities of belief concerning the ultimate meaning of man and his universe. The same consideration which requires the equality of Protestant, Catholic, and Jewish beliefs before the law applies to the nonbeliever. Harmony among all citizens as equal partners in the democratic polity demands no less than this. If the believer finds such a conclusion unpalatable, it is because he confuses the political and the theological orders.

What, then, does the legal equality of all religious beliefs and nonbelief mean? There has been all too much confusion about the meaning of the First Amendment's no-establishment clause in the mind of public and judge alike. The source of confusion lies in the very articulation of the question to be asked. The public and the judge often ask simply whether a particular government action "aids" or "benefits" religion. But to pose the question in this way is to miss the point of the religious establishment clause. The question is rather whether government action *prefers* religious activity. Only public preference for one or all religious beliefs destroys the required legal equality of all religious beliefs and nonbelief. Incidental aid or benefit to religious activity does not necessarily constitute such a public preference. Moreover, if "aid" or "benefit" is made the issue, then the public authority must always in fact prefer nonbelief over religious belief, since this would be the inevitable effect of its action or inaction. The plain truth is that political realism demands only the neutrality, the nonpreference, of the public authority with respect to religious belief or nonbelief. In my view, either the state or the federal government may aid religious institutions performing secular functions or accommodate religious activities in circumstances which preclude any implication of preference for one or all religions.

From this analysis of the First Amendment's no-establishment clause, I have drawn these conclusions about current problems in church-state relations:

1. The public schools may not sponsor any so-called nonsectarian religious exercise or instruction as a program designed for all pupils. This is so whether or not there is provision for "excusing" those pupils whose parents so wish. For the public to sponsor any religious exercise or instruction is to prefer religious belief over nonbelief. This the Constitution forbids.

2. The public schools may adjust their curricular schedules to permit a reasonable amount of religious instruction for those pupils whose parents so request. This should be so whether or not the instruction is held in the public school itself. To accommodate the public school curriculum to the reasonable wishes of parents for the religious instruction of their own children is not to sponsor or prefer religious belief. In fact, the refusal to permit such an accommodation would entail preferring nonbelief over religious belief in the composition of the public school curriculum.

3. Both the federal government and the states may support the reasonable choice of parents to educate their children in church-related schools. Of course, such support would constitute an incidental aid or benefit to religious belief but not a preference of that belief over nonbelief. The public authorities may support whatever education parents choose for their children, whether religiously oriented or not, if that education adequately fulfills educational requirements and violates no public policy.

4. Sunday laws claim to have the secular purpose of securing a common day of rest for all citizens. For that reason, perhaps, it may be difficult to say that they violate the letter of the Constitution. At least the Supreme Court refused to conclude that the purpose of the laws was religious, that is, to prefer the beliefs of orthodox Christians over those of Sabbatarians. But exemptions for self-employed merchants who observe Saturday as their day of rest would not be likely to interfere radically with the common rest nor confer a very distinct economic advantage on the Sabbatarian. Ten states have judged this to be the case, and the remaining states can at least investigate the feasibility of such exemptions.

The problem of morals and public law is much more complicated and much less capable of summary conclusions. The public authority may be able to profess neutrality with respect to religious belief or disbelief, but no similar total abstinence in matters of public morals is possible. Moral action can affect the community and so be a cause of concern. Citizens cannot isolate themselves from the public climate which results from the moral character of the individual actions, any more than they can escape the public effects of individual actions in economic affairs. All citizens dwell in one and the same society.

Yet legislation which seeks to advance the welfare of the community in one respect often adversely affects the community in another. This is especially true in the case of legislation enforcing public morals. The task of political wisdom is to weigh the magnitude of the danger to the moral good of the whole community from individual actions against the dangers inherent in the exercise of the coercive power of the state. In particular, the ethical pluralism of the American polity must be carefully considered in any question of the enforcement of public morals.

With respect to the birth control legislation of Massachusetts and Connecticut, I have previously indicated my opinion that Catholics, who comprise a majority or near-majority of the population of those states and are responsible for the continued existence of the legislation, should support the legal right of married couples to the prescription, sale, and use of contraceptives. They can readily make clear that they advocate modification of the contraceptive legislation of their states on strictly political and legal grounds which in no way affect their theological and moral opposition to the practice of artificial birth control. When so many conscientious non-Catholics believe the practice morally licit, the present legislation, without any hope of enforcement, unjustifiably increases hostility among citizens of different religious beliefs and moral codes. Catholics should restrict their legislative goals to those which command the general approval of the community, such as the prohibition of the sale of contraceptives from slot machines or to unmarried minors.

Domestic regulation of contraception, however, is a public problem of relatively limited practical significance. The problem of policy which today more actively agitates the public is whether the United States and the United Nations should sponsor or support programs of artificial birth control abroad in an effort to control the "population explosion." There is no need to deny the dimensions of the population problem and the urgent need for action to deal with it. But in a pluralistic society, public funds should not be employed to sponsor or support programs which are morally offensive to one or more religious groups, if this is at all compatible with the goals of organized society.

Therefore, as Catholics display a gross lack of political conscious-ness when they help to perpetuate legislation which prohibits the practice of artificial birth control at home, so non-Catholics dis-play an equal lack of political consciousness when they press for the implementation of artificial birth control abroad through the use of public funds. Catholics and non-Catholics alike would do better to work together with all deliberate speed and dedication to develop world resources and to control world population by means morally acceptable to all.

Censorship of the communications media constitutes the issue of public morality which, after that of birth control, has most threatened to disrupt relations between citizens of different ethi-cal codes. The zeal of good people against objectionable books, magazines, and films has often prevailed over their good judg-ment; their concern with the substantive demerits of materials has often blinded them to the demands of political process. They may and should seek to influence the communications media in the direction of sound values by voluntary cooperation and ra-tional persuasion, but above all they must respect the pluralistic character of American democracy.

The chapters of this book have touched on a large number of sensitive issues. No doubt opinions will differ concerning some of the suggestions advanced. But of this I am certain, that the quickening spirit of religious charity and the painstaking exercise of political reason will show Americans a way to make a still more resplendent showcase of their religious equality and polit-ical maturity, if they but have the will.

Table of Cases

Bold-faced numbers indicate places in the text where cases are treated more systematically.

283

Index